CURRENT ECONOMIC ISSUES: PROGRESSIVE PERSPECTIVES FROM *DOLLARS & SENSE*

Eighth edition

Edited by Amy Gluckman, Amy Offner, Alejandro Reuss,
Thad Williamson, and the *Dollars & Sense* Collective

ISBN: 1-878585-43-6

Published by:
Dollars & Sense
Economic Affairs Bureau, Inc.
740 Cambridge Street
Cambridge, MA 02141
Phone: (617) 876-2434
Fax: (617) 876-0008
E-mail: dollars@dollarsandsense.org
Web: www.dollarsandsense.org

Current Economic Issues is edited by the *Dollars & Sense* Collective, which also publishes *Dollars & Sense* magazine and the classroom books *Real World Macro, Real World Micro, Real World Globalization, Real World Banking, The Environment in Crisis, Introduction to Political Economy,* and *Unlevel Playing Fields: Understanding Wage Inequality and Discrimination.*

The 2003 Collective:
Ben Boothby, Marc Breslow, Beth Burgess, Chuck Collins, Ellen Frank, Amy Gluckman, Erkut Gomulu, Maryalice Guilford, Darius Mehri, John Miller, Amy Offner, Laura Orlando, Alejandro Reuss, Adria Scharf, Chris Sturr, Chris Tilly, Rodney Ward, Adam Weiss, Thad Williamson, Jeanne Winner.

Cover Design: Nick Thorkelson
Cover Art: Mauricio Alberto Cordero
Production: Alyssa Hassan

Manufactured by Transcontinental Printing
Printed in Canada

TABLE OF CONTENTS

Chapter 10: Positive Directions

Chapter I

THE "NEW ECONOMY" AND THE STOCK BUBBLE

INTRODUCTION

Today, in the midst of economic stagnation, attacks on workers' rights, budget deficits, and rising inequality, it is hard to believe that a few years ago, the business press was announcing a permanent golden age for the U.S. economy. Economists and CEOs had found a lasting solution to economic problems: a system that guaranteed rising productivity, self-perpetuating growth, breathtaking innovations, and six-figure fortunes for ordinary people. What's more, they promised that the system could deliver without any government regulation.

The name for that system? The "New Economy."

The phrase "New Economy" reflected the idea that emerging technologies and information-related industries had fundamentally changed the U.S. economy. In the 1990s, the Internet gave individuals, organizations, and businesses new possibilities for communication—and if you read publications like *Business Week,* it seemed that everyone was getting involved in the "cutting-edge" world of software development and Internet start-ups. Optimistic economic gurus foresaw continually-rising demand for new-tech products, and concluded that these products would fuel long-term economic growth and make the business cycle obsolete.

It's harder today to find economists and business cheerleaders willing to wax so enthusiastically about the New Economy. The stubborn facts speak for themselves. As Phineas Baxandall shows in this chapter, the productivity gains of the late 1990s were actually rather tame compared with those of previous economic expansions, especially the "old economy" 1960s ("Is the 'New Economy' More Productive?"). What *was* exceptional about the 1990s was its overheated stock market, whose ephemeral highs were, according to Baxandall, the basis of the entire New Economy myth ("High-Tech Stocks and 'New Economy' Hype). And how much did the stock bubble help most Americans? Not much, according to Thatcher Collins: while more Americans do own at least some stock now than in previous decades, the underlying inequalities of stock holding remain ("Mind the Gap").

Perhaps the most dangerous part of the New Economy was not its failure as a model, but its underlying ideology: the notion that high-tech advances make self-regulating markets possible, desirable, and necessary. For New Economy boosters, markets worked miracles, and regulation in the public interest was purely destructive. Baxandall debunks several core myths of New Economy thinking, from the supposed impossibility of regulating information technology to the purported necessity of intellectual property rights ("Does the 'New Economy' Tilt to the Right?").

DOES THE "NEW ECONOMY" TILT TO THE RIGHT?
By Phineas Baxandall
March/April 2002

Back in the 1950s, the Soviet Union proclaimed that computerization heralded the triumph of centralized economic planning over decentralized markets. Computers would allow planners to process unprecedented amounts of information and accurately forecast and fine-tune the economy. Success with computerization at individual plants and regional ministries only made Soviet officials more confident of its potential for the economy as a whole. Across the sea, U.S. officials fretted that the Soviets were right, that the Soviet economy was catching up to the West, and that computerization would show the world that markets were obsolete.

The Soviet vision of a computer-planned future may seem silly today, but it puts in perspective the recent free-market hype about the so-called "New Economy." Free-marketeers, no less that Soviet bureaucrats, tend to project their own fondest wishes onto technology itself. "Governments of the Industrial World, you weary giants of flesh and steel," cyberlibertarian John Perry Barlow demands, "on behalf of the future, I ask you of the past to leave us alone." The main effect of the "New Economy" has been to convince people that information technology and computer networks somehow make government regulation obsolete—more or less the Soviet dream in reverse.

Today, the bloom is off the rose of the "New Economy." With high-tech stock prices plummeting after March 2000 (the NASDAQ index lost over half its value within a year), few people still believe that a computer and an online stock account guarantee overnight riches. Dot-com millionaires no longer represent the glorious future, and chastened "New Economy" boosters have had to accept that the business cycle is not just an iron-age relic. Nonetheless, even in today's recession, we still hear that government regulation is an "Old Economy" dinosaur.

Three largely unexamined myths perpetuate this nonsense. First, the belief that information inherently resists regulation. Second, that the networked economy favors spontaneous markets over slow-footed government bureaucracies. And third, that new technologies have globalized the economy beyond the influence of national governments. There is a grain of truth in each, but none of it leads to the conclusion that public regulation is either impossible or undesirable.

Myth #1: Information must be governed by "free markets" because "information must be free."

Free-market enthusiasts have missed the most novel thing about information goods as a commodity—that after the research and development is done, the cost of producing each unit is very low. Think of software giants. It costs just a few cents to burn each copy of WindowsXP or Excel onto a CD. For digitalized property such as databases, electronic music files (such as the "MP3s" exchanged on Napster), or password-protected information, there is virtually no cost for an additional copy. In economics lingo, the "marginal cost" of these goods is zero or close to zero.

Mainstream "neoclassical" economics argues that the most efficient price for a product is equal to its marginal cost. If the price is lower, people who do not value the product as much as its cost will buy it. If the prices is higher, people who value the product more than its cost will forego it. Either way, there will be a "net welfare loss" to society. The neoclassical argument that competitive markets are efficient depends on the view that they push prices to this efficient level. But "zero marginal cost" goods turn these arguments on their head. In the words of Berkeley economist Brad DeLong, the "assumptions ... of the *invisible hand* fray when transported into tomorrow's information economy."

Take the analogy of paying for a bridge. The bridge is expensive to build, but once it is constructed there is virtually no additional cost for an additional individual to use it. If people are charged more than this miniscule cost, there will be a net welfare loss (since some people who would benefit from using the bridge will be prevented from using it by the artificial cost of the toll). Even mainstream economists are forced to conclude that a private toll is a less efficient way to pay for a bridge than a general tax. The same is true for information goods like digital music files. Once you pay the members of the band and the sound engineers, for example, pretty much all the costs of producing a Metallica song are accounted for, whether you create one digital sound file or millions. Therefore, charging people to download the file would cause a net welfare loss. "Even though economic theory is severely biased toward markets," concludes economist Michael Perelman, "according to the criteria of economics, information should not be treated as private property."

Following this logic, the Canadian government levies a small tax on recording media, such as blank CDs and tapes, and uses the revenue to fund Canadian artists who lose sales as a result of people recording their work for free. Germany and other European countries have explored attaching a fee to the sale of computers and other devices that can be used to copy recorded music. The revenue from this fee would then be distributed to recording companies to compensate them for royalties lost due to unauthorized copying of their copyrighted music. As economist Dean Baker of the Economic Policy Institute argues, this approach has great advantages over prosecuting information "pirates" or adding elaborate mechanisms to disrupt copying: "While there are problems with the system devised by Germany, it should lead to vast economic gains compared to the systems being developed in the United States. The inefficiency associated with the traditional copyright is enormous in the Internet age."

The Internet itself did not result from "free markets" but centralized planning. In the early years of the Cold War, the U.S. Defense Department sought to establish communications networks that might survive a nuclear war. At the time, only the military and large universities had powerful computers, which researchers across the country wanted to use. Networking prevented them from sitting idle. In order to enable different computers to talk to each other, the Defense Department funded the development of communications standards called TCP/IP, adopting them in 1980.

The Defense Department then released the standards for free to the general public. Nobody has to pay to use these technical protocols to send email or post or view web pages. The U.S. government even pushed for the widespread adoption of the freely available TCP/IP standards, instead of alternate versions developed by private European companies that refused to share their inventions. The Web has grown so quickly and become such a rich and varied source of information largely because these open standards make it accessible to anyone with a computer and a modem.

Even outside of government, some of the fastest-growing parts of the "New Economy" have flourished by making technologies freely available. The most important email transport software (Sendmail), the most important internet server software (Apache), the most widely used programming language on the Web (Perl), the domain-name service for the entire Internet (BIND), and the fastest-growing computer operating system (Linux) are all examples of public domain (or "open-source") software.

Linux is the best known of these "open-source" products. Linus Torvalds, a Finnish computer-science student, invented the new computer operating system in 1991, based on the existing strengths of the UNIX system. But instead of applying for a patent, he posted the code on the Internet for other programmers to add to and improve. Many programmers were interested in the Linux project because UNIX had just been taken over by private firms like IBM. These companies kept their underlying code secret and designed their programs to lock users into their products. Programmers were also worried about the growing dominance of Microsoft's clumsy operating systems. By 1998, over 10,000 software developers from 31 different countries had contributed improvements or helped develop new versions of Linux. By the year 2000, the program boasted about 16 million users and a quarter of the market share. Major high-tech firms, like Intel, Oracle, Dell,

Hewlett-Packard, IBM, and Compaq, have all made major commitments to use Linux or cater to Linux users.

A conventional argument for private ownership is that owners have greater incentive to produce things. People are more willing to cultivate a garden on a piece of ground they can fence off, more willing to improve a house when they own it, and more willing to work hard in a business if they share in the profits. But intellectual products can be shared with others without diminishing their value. In fact, computer programs and other information technology are often *more* valuable when many other people also have them. Many users, for example, do not buy Microsoft Word because they think it is the best word-processing program, but because they know others use the program and will be able to read their files. Likewise, Linux and similar "open-source" projects work so well because they have large numbers of users who identify glitches and devise improvements. They can expect that future versions of the operating system will include not only their contributions but also those of thousands of other contributors. Online communities of programmers voluntarily contribute their efforts to building better software because the product remains in the public domain.

Allowing others to reproduce a computer program does not take anything away from the owner. It merely refuses to help the owner get rich from artificially enforced scarcity. As *Wired* magazine puts it, "The central economic distinction between information and physical property is that information can be transferred without leaving the possession of the original owner. If I sell you my horse, I can't ride him after that. If I sell you what I know, we both know it." This feature of information goods might make redistribution from property owners to the public more politically appealing in the "New Economy" than in the "Old Economy." Seizing somebody's land or factory to help the poor deprives the old owners of what was theirs. Not so with computer software or digital audio files.

Myth #2: The "networked" economy favors spontaneous and flexible markets over slow-footed regulators.

To many free-marketeers, the Internet is like heaven on earth. It seems to exhibit all the ideal qualities of markets: decentralized, instantaneous, unregulated. The wild growth of online trading (at sites like E*Trade and Ameritrade) and auction sites (like eBay) seems to prove some kind of affinity between "free markets" and the digital age. A recent article in the *Wall Street Journal* urges us to "Think of the Internet as an economic-freedom metaphor for our time. The Internet empowers ordinary people and disempowers government."

While it is true that the 1990s saw a rollback in government regulation *at the same time* as a rapid growth of information technology, the new technology did not *cause* the tilt towards "free-market" capitalism. Businesses have certainly implemented new technologies in ways that make certain kinds of regulation more difficult. And politicians have often used the "New Economy" as a pretense for opposing social programs or regulatory policies. But these are ultimately *political* issues. New information technologies did not require the deregulation associated with the "New Economy," and a changing political tide could reverse the ways those technologies have been implemented.

As with all markets, the results of electronic production and commerce depend on what rules govern businesses: what businesses can own, what privileges and responsibilities come with ownership, what kinds of contracts are legally binding, how they will be taxed, etc. This institutional "architecture" of markets is especially important in information technologies.

Unlike traditional markets, whose rules have evolved over hundreds of years, the online architecture is new enough that we can see how it results from specific policies of governments and corporations. Such thinking challenges the notion that market outcomes are "spontaneous" at all.

People in power can use architecture to control the behavior of others, designing environments to encourage certain kinds of actions while discouraging others. If a local government wants to discourage motorists from driving fast down a street, one way is to legislate a speed limit and have police chase down cars that drive too fast. But another way is through the architecture of a speed bump, which changes behavior more automatically, without obvious laws or games of cat and mouse. Architecture can also be used to change behavior in more insidious ways. In the wake of late-1960s campus protests, for example, universities redesigned campuses with fewer open common areas, in order to discourage student demonstrations.

Just as the architecture of buildings manipulates the laws of physics to human ends, so does the architecture of cyberspace constrain online interactions to serve the ends of those who design or control it. America Online (AOL), for example, limits the number of people who can join one of its chat rooms to 23. The AOL rule can't even be broken in protest because the prohibition is enforced automatically by the software code itself. Attempts to be the 24th participant in the conversation are just met with an error message.

As Internet traffic moves increasingly from phone lines into the control of cable-TV companies, these companies will try to exert even greater control over the traffic they carry. Already some cable companies have tried to prevent Internet users from using "streaming video," which competes with the companies' own pay-per-view channels. Internet companies like Yahoo, which provide "portals" for reaching other websites, already steer people towards businesses that pay to have "banner" ads linking to their sites or to get top billing when people use a search engine. The logical next step is for media conglomerates to use their cable companies to make it faster and easier to reach their product content, to view trailers for their movies, and perhaps to charge users extra for any time spent out of their universe of "infotainment." The trend gives more power to large media conglomerates. The majority of Internet traffic has already been gobbled up by corporations like AOL Time Warner (which owns CNN.com) and Disney (which owns ESPN.com).

Stanford law professor Lawrence Lessig points out, however, that "the changes that make [Internet] commerce possible are also changes that will make regulation easy." For instance, business continues to struggle with how to authenticate who is logging on, and if they really are who they say. E-business has long favored a system of digital certificates that could authenticate a user's identity when surfing the web. Such a system could pose serious dangers—to reduce users' privacy or even threaten their civil liberties. But it could also mean greater abilities to implement public regulations. For example, states do not currently charge state sales tax on purchases made over the internet. Digital certificates could allow states (or even cities) to charge taxes for online purchases to the certificate holder.

Myth #3: As a result of the information revolution, the global economy can no longer be influenced by government.

New information technologies are often seen as having made governments impotent to influence anything on the Net, since web sites can relocate outside the legal jurisdiction of governments that wish to regulate them. The state of Missouri can make it illegal to host a gambling or pornography site from a computer within the state, but it can't stop people from logging onto such a site launched from another state or country. The Amazon.com site based in Germany may comply with that country's laws by refusing to carry Nazi literature, but cyber-Nazis in Germany can order Hitler's *Mein Kampf* from Amazon.com sites hosted in the United States or other countries.

But electronic finance is different. When a bank wires money, it relies on a centralized infrastructure guaranteed by governments to make sure that money is subtracted from one account and added to another. A system of mutual recognition and settlement between powerful institutions like central banks confirms that the person transferring the money actually has those funds and is not simultaneously promising them to banks all over the world. Globalized money will, for this reason, never fully conform to the libertarian fantasy. The same infrastructure that makes it possible to send money electronically across borders also makes it technically possible to restrict and tax these transfers.

Governments have done just that for over a century. It has been possible to wire funds more or less instantaneously since the invention of the telegraph. Even today, most capital transfers are communicated through faxes or telex machines and authenticated with pen-and-ink signatures. Today's system of capital transfers, however, has become centralized through national central banks. This system already assigns a unique identifying number to each capital transfer. Far from making regulation unfeasible, the more these finance systems are digital and networked, the more viable regulation will become.

A system of capital controls would make it possible to stop international money laundering, which the IMF estimates drains away 2–5% of the world's income, and to squelch corruption—especially in poorer countries where warlords or kleptocrats steal essential investment funds. A tiny transaction fee of the kind charged by the Securities and Exchange Commission (SEC) in the United States could discourage market volatility caused by trigger-happy investors seeking tiny profit margins on huge currency transactions. More ambitiously, a levy of one penny on every million dollars in international financial transfers would not discourage any productive investment, but would raise more money than the UN estimates is required to provide for basic health, nutrition, education, and water sanitation to the 1.3 billion people on the planet who live without.

Creating an international architecture of capital controls would not be easy. The big U.S. banks might be particularly resistant to capital controls. U.S. banks receive large quantities of international money partially due to the United States' weak laws on disclosure and taxation of foreign funds. Foreign investors, unlike U.S. citizens or residents, pay no tax on interest or capital gains and do not have to disclose the sources of their earnings to the IRS.

Just as the Great Depression made the federal government establish the agencies that regulate domestic finance (the SEC, the Federal Deposit Insurance Corporation, etc.), the September 11 destruction has brought more attention to the need for regulation of international finance. Some commentators have called for greater international scrutiny of secretive Saudi banks, the likely conduits of terrorist funds. Legislation signed into law in October 2001 bars U.S. banks, which often do business with overseas "paper" corporations, from dealing with a foreign bank unless the latter has a physical existence somewhere with at least one employee. The Treasury Department can now require banks to monitor accounts formally held by overseas banks, especially to determine who is the real owner of the account.

So far, it is not clear that these few, halting steps will lead to real change, but new wisdom has a way of gaining momentum as new practices become more common. Once a capital control system got under way, banks might find it to be in their interests to comply with regulations on international transactions, or face exclusion from the centralized payment systems that make this lucrative business possible. Who knows? They might even reassure their stockholders that, after all, information technology makes it inevitable.

Whatever the future of the Internet may bring, the way markets will operate in cyberspace will not result from some inexorable logic of technology itself. The logic of the Net will depend on the architecture built there—and who has the power to build it.

Thanks to Alexandra Samuelson for her useful input and suggestions on this article.

IS THE "NEW ECONOMY" MORE PRODUCTIVE? SORTING FACT FROM FICTION
By Phineas Baxandall
May/June 2002

One of the great glories of the so-called "New Economy" was supposed to be that information-age advances in productivity were making possible a soaring stock market and a permanent economic boom. Starting in the mid-1990s, the official measure of national productivity—calculated as Gross Domestic Product (GDP), or total income, divided by the number of hours worked—finally gave credence to those, like Federal Reserve Chair Alan Greenspan, who crowed that rising output per worker was changing the very nature of the economy. In late 1995, a *BusinessWeek* cover proclaimed, "Productivity to the Rescue." And when preliminary estimates showed that productivity had shot up a blazing 3.4% in 1999 and 2000, Greenspan spoke of "not just a cyclical phenomenon or a statistical aberration ... [but] a more deep-seated, still developing shift in our economic landscape," with the potential for even more gains in the future as information technology continued to spread.

A lot is at stake in these numbers. Productivity growth indicates how fast the economic pie is enlarging, and a few tenths of a percentage point over a period of years can have an enormous impact on things like budget deficits, corporate revenue projections, Social Security forecasts, and interest rates. If the same inputs will produce a lot more than they used to, all sorts of economic fantasies become possible. Thanks to the glowing productivity picture, stockbrokers were able to tell their clients that the unbelievable 86% increase in NASDAQ stocks in 1999 was somehow based on sound economic foundations. (See Phineas Baxandall, "High-Tech Stocks and 'New Economy' Hype," p. 11.) Similarly, President Bush used a sunny best-case scenario, which included very optimistic productivity forecasts, as a way to convince legislators to support his massive tax cut for the wealthy.

But the numbers weren't as solid as they seemed. When more complete data became available, the "brave new world" productivity figures for 1999 and 2000 got revised downward from 3.4% to 2.6%. They still look good compared to the 1980s, when productivity rose at a rate of about 2.2% each year—but they're well below the 2.9% average that held between 1947 and 1973. And besides, the United States uses controversial techniques that artificially boost productivity figures, such as including productivity bonuses for new and improved products that aren't reflected in the prices of goods. Studies by European statistical offices suggest that, if European countries tried these methods, they could show a great increase in their own supposedly slower productivity growth.

Overall, the 1990s New Economy boom wasn't anything so special if you weren't deep into stocks. Annual GDP growth averaged 3.1% in the last decade, only slightly higher than the 2.9% average for the 1980s cycle—and below the 3.3% average for the 1970s and the 4.4% average for the 1960s. Wages for the average worker increased by less than 0.5% per year over the 1990s. Much of the alleged gain in productivity actually may have come at workers' expense, because new technology like laptops and cell phones have, if nothing else, made people work more off the job. Official productivity numbers only count the hours workers report on company time sheets, not the time information workers spend on their laptops on the train or after the kids go to bed.

And there's another reason to be skeptical about the "productivity revolution": Just three broad sectors—finance, real estate, and insurance; wholesale and retail trade; and business services—account for about 80% of all computers used in industry. According to the New Economy productivity spin, the not-actually-so-impressive productivity rate will accelerate as information technology spreads to the rest of the economy. But as economist Robert Gordon has shown, productivity growth has been lagging in precisely the industries that form the information-technology vanguard. Gordon goes so far as to say that it's "likely that the greatest benefits of computers lie a decade or more in the past, not in the future."

Few progressive economists have called out to tell the truth about the emperor's new clothes—perhaps because the Fed's new religion has tamed its fears of inflation, thus keeping it from its usual practice of cutting the money supply and thereby throwing people out of work out of fear of inflation. Gordon is a welcome exception. He points out that, although Internet and e-commerce will keep growing, on-line sales are mainly replacing off-line sales that would have occurred anyway. And while computer speed and memory may continue to grow exponentially, individuals' limited supply of time will prevent productivity and output from matching these gains. As Gordon reminds us, although computers have come a long way, we can't type, think, read, or even talk much faster than we could two decades ago.

Resources: Robert J. Gordon, "Does the 'New Economy' Measure up to the Great Inventions of the Past?" *Journal of Economic Perspectives* (Fall 2000); Jack Triplett, "Economic Statistics, the New Economy, and the Productivity Slowdown," *Business Economics* (April 1999); "Did Greenspan Push High-Tech Optimism On Growth Too Far?" *Wall Street Journal*, 28 December 2001; "Notions of New Economy Hinge on Pace of Productivity Growth," *New York Times*, 3 September 2001; John Cassidy, "The Productivity Miracle," *The New Yorker* (November 2000).

HIGH-TECH STOCKS AND "NEW ECONOMY" HYPE
By Phineas Baxandall
May/June 2002

Some day, we'll look back on the "New Economy" much as we do the "New Coke" marketing bonanza or Microsoft's latest Windows upgrade.

Since the mid-1990s, we heard a lot of noise about how the Internet was sending the business cycle into a permanent upswing to the stars. But now we know it didn't happen, nor did computer technology give us the productivity turbo-boost that the "New Economy" gurus claimed. The New Economy, it seems, was little more than the irrational exuberance that fed (and was stoked by) an overvalued stock market.

I conducted a search on Lexis-Nexis (the periodicals database) for articles in 50 "major newspapers" read in the United States, starting in December 1990, to see how many mentioned the "New Economy" each month. Then, I compared the findings with the NASDAQ stock index. As you can see, the number of articles referring to the "New Economy" closely mirrored the ups and downs of the technology-startup heavy NASDAQ index.

Why all the hype? Because investors, politicians, and pundits wanted to believe that the soaring price of technology stocks wasn't just an old-fashioned speculative bubble. The media played along, selling us a "positive thinking" message that suggested we could privatize Social Security, slash taxes for the rich without running up deficits, and even afford that diamond necklace advertised in the glossy Sunday magazine.

As manufacturers of sugary breakfast cereal have known for a long time, the label "New and Improved!" gets boxes moving off the shelves.

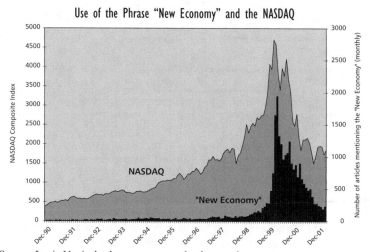

Use of the Phrase "New Economy" and the NASDAQ

Source: Lexis-Nexis database; <www.marketdata.nasdaq.com>.

MIND THE GAP

By Thatcher Collins

November/December 2002

Two and a half years ago, a House of Representatives study touted increasing stock ownership as "cultivating a deeper appreciation and understanding of private enterprise," spreading "a better understanding of financial matters," and "erod[ing] class conflict." Now that the stock market bubble has burst, the report seems just a bit dated. Enron workers may have gained a "better understanding of financial matters" the hard way, though they probably haven't formed a "deeper appreciation of ... private enterprise." But did the 1990s boom really "democratize" stock ownership and private wealth, even before the crash?

The most recent major survey by the Federal Reserve Board (2000) study shows that the percentage of people in the United States who owned at least some stock rose from 31.6% to 48.8% between 1989 and 1998. Stock ownership increased across the board, among not only low-to-moderate income people, but also among the rich. Notice the near-parallel lines in Graph 1. These lines show that the differences in rates of stock ownership between different income groups hardly changed at all.

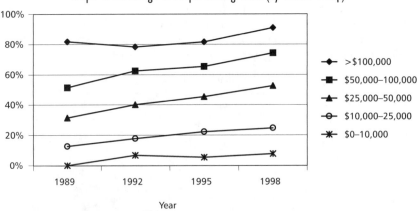

Graph 1: Percentage of People Owning Stock (By Income Group)

Legend:
- ◆ >$100,000
- ■ $50,000–100,000
- ▲ $25,000–50,000
- ⊖ $10,000–25,000
- ✳ $0–10,000

Source: Arthur B. Kennickell, Martha Starr-McCluer, and Brian J. Surette, "Recent Changes in U.S. Family Finances: Results from the 1998 Survey of Consumer Finances," *Federal Reserve Bulletin*, vol. 86 (January 2000), Table 6. Direct and indirect stock ownership, by selected characteristics of families.

Voting in a democracy may be "one person, one vote," but voting in a corporation is "one share, one vote." So power and influence over those companies goes mainly to those with the largest stock holdings. Of course, people in the higher-income brackets are not only more likely to own stock, but also own larger quantities of stock than their lower-income counterparts. According to the same Fed study cited above, among those with incomes lower than $10,000 who owned stock, average total holdings were only $4,000, even at the height of the stock boom in the late 1990s. Meanwhile, average holdings were $150,000 for stock owners with incomes above $100,000. The average value of stock holdings for the low-income group hardly changed in the years between 1989 and 1998, while the average holdings of the stock owners with incomes between $25,000 and $50,000 roughly doubled in value, and those of people with incomes above $50,000 roughly tripled (see Graph 2). So upper-income groups have actually increased their wealth (and power) relative to the groups below them. This is actually a step backward—and hardly likely to "erode class conflict."

Graph 2: Average Holdings Among Those Owning Stock (By Income Group)

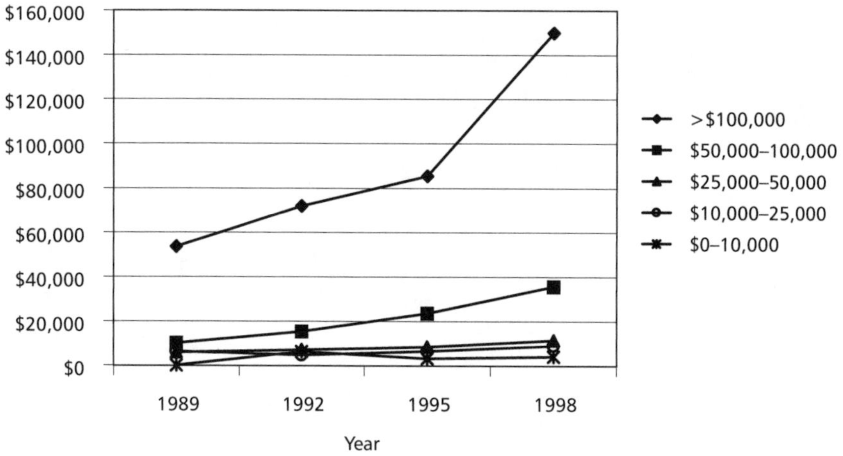

Source: Arthur B. Kennickell, Martha Starr-McCluer, and Brian J. Surette, "Recent Changes in U.S. Family Finances: Results from the 1998 Survey of Consumer Finances," *Federal Reserve Bulletin*, vol. 86 (January 2000), Table 6. Direct and indirect stock ownership, by selected characteristics of families.

Chapter 2

THE BUBBLE BURSTS AND THE SCANDALS BREAK

INTRODUCTION

During the late 1990s, the business press insisted that everyone could get rich. With stock prices skyrocketing and the promise of a "New Economy" that would deliver unending economic growth, millions of Americans scrambled to get in on the action by putting their savings in the stock market. Corporations, for their part, rushed to transform their retirement plans, replacing pensions that provided guaranteed levels of income with 401(k) plans that tied retirement income to the ups and downs of the stock market.

While some investors made out like bandits during the boom—and many corporate executives took home huge bonuses tied to company share prices—most Americans didn't do so well. For small investors, workers with 401(k) pension plans, and many nonprofit institutions, the promise of ever-increasing stock prices proved to be fool's gold.

In this chapter, Ellen Frank explains that falling stock prices were not a matter of bad luck, but of inevitable economic reality. Stock market prices cannot outpace actual economic growth over the long term—except to the degree that corporations pocket larger profits at the expense of workers' wages. This was just what corporations did during the 1990s, and they used the unsustainable stock prices they achieved to promote 401(k) accounts packed with company stock. Frank shows what a swindle corporations pulled off, and reminds us just how risky retirement plans based on stock market prices are ("The Great Stock Illusion").

If stock market prices are, in the long run, linked to the health of the real economy, how is the real economy doing? Not too well in the first half of the Bush administration, reports John Miller. The recent economic downturn took place just as workers were finally starting to see wage gains for the first time in a quarter century. Miller warns that both workers and failed investors face a period of belt-tightening—and that even an economic recovery will not guarantee higher demand for workers or falling unemployment. Today, with the recession officially over, Miller's warning is being borne out by a "jobless recovery" in which the unemployment rate hovers around 6% ("Recession for the Holidays").

When the stock bubble began to burst in 2000, so too did the fortunes of many corporations. Workers at these companies did not just lose pension fund value: many also lost their jobs. Nomi Prins describes how telecom workers have had to fight for severance pay at WorldCom—and how the meltdown in corporate telecommunications has inspired a new wave of union activism in the industry, bringing together organized labor and retirees' groups ("Whose Jobs? Our Jobs!").

Of course, in the telecom industry and elsewhere, corporate executives' out-and-out looting of investors has garnered plenty of news coverage. But the mainstream media has tended to treat cases like Enron and WorldCom as shocking anomalies. Alejandro Reuss reminds us that robbery is business as usual at successful corporations such as Wal-Mart—it's just that the victims are usually workers, not investors. Reuss closes the chapter by challenging readers to ask why workers getting cheated out of millions of dollars in wages is not considered as newsworthy as recent cases in which investors lost out ("It All Depends on Who You Rob").

THE GREAT STOCK ILLUSION
By Ellen Frank
November/December 2002

During the 1980s and 1990s, the Dow Jones and Standard & Poor's indices of stock prices soared ten-fold. The NASDAQ index had, by the year 2000, skyrocketed to 25 times its 1980 level. Before the bubble burst, bullish expectations reached a feverish crescendo. Three separate books—*Dow 36,000, Dow 40,000* and *Dow 100,000*—appeared in 1999 forecasting further boundless growth in stock prices. Bullish Wall Street gurus like Goldman's Abby Cohen and Salomon's Jack Grubman were quoted everywhere, insisting that prices could go nowhere but up.

But as early as 1996, skeptics were warning that it couldn't last. Fed chair Alan Greenspan fretted aloud about "irrational exuberance." Yale finance professor Robert Shiller, in his 2001 book titled *Irrational Exuberance*, insisted that U.S. equities prices were being driven up by wishful thinking and self-fulfilling market sentiment, nourished by a culture that championed wealth and lionized the wealthy. Dean Baker and Marc Weisbrot of the Washington-based Center for Economic and Policy Research contended in 1999 that the U.S. stock market looked like a classic speculative bubble—as evidence they cited the rapidly diverging relationship between stock prices and corporate earnings and reckoned that, to justify the prices at which stocks were selling, profits would have to grow at rates that were frankly impossible.

In 1999 alone, the market value of U.S. equities swelled by an astounding $4 trillion. During that same year, U.S. output, on which stocks represent a claim, rose by a mere $500 billion. What would have happened if stockholders in 1999 had all tried to sell their stock and convert their $4 trillion into actual goods and services? The answer is that most would have failed. In a scramble to turn $4 trillion of paper gains into $500 billion worth of real goods and services, the paper wealth was bound to dissolve, because it never existed, save as a kind of mass delusion.

The Illusion of Wealth Creation

Throughout the 1990s, each new record set by the Dow or NASDAQ elicited grateful cheers for CEOs who were hailed for "creating wealth." American workers, whose retirement savings were largely invested in stocks, were encouraged to buy more stock—even to bet their Social Security funds in the market—and assured that stocks always paid off "in the long run," that a "buy-and-hold" strategy couldn't lose. Neither the financial media nor America's politicians bothered to warn the public about the gaping disparity between the inflated claims on economic output that stocks represented and the actual production of the economy. But by the end of the decade, insiders saw the writing on the wall. They rushed to the exits, trying to realize stock gains before the contradictions inherent in the market overwhelmed them. Prices tumbled, wiping out trillions in illusory money.

The case of Enron Corp. is the most notorious, but it is unfortunately not unique. When Enron filed for bankruptcy protection in November of 2001 its stock, which had traded as high as $90 per share a year before, plummeted to less than $1. *New York Times* reporter Jeffrey Seglin writes that the elevators in Enron's Houston headquarters sported TV sets tuned to CNBC, constantly tracking the firm's stock price and acclaiming the bull market generally. As Enron stock climbed in the late 1990s, these daily market updates made employees—whose retirement accounts were largely invested in company shares—feel quite wealthy, though most Enron workers were not in fact free to sell these shares. Enron's contributions of company stock to employee retirement accounts didn't vest until workers reached age 50. For years, Enron had hawked its stock to employees, to pension fund managers, and to the world as a surefire investment. Many employees used their own 401(k) funds, over and above the firm's matching contributions, to purchase additional shares. But as the firm disintegrated amid accusations of accounting fraud, plan managers froze employee accounts, so that workers were unable to unload even the stock they owned outright. With employee accounts frozen, Enron executives and board members are estimated to have dumped their own stock and options, netting $1.2 billion cash—almost exactly the amount employees lost from retirement accounts.

Soon after Enron's collapse, telecommunications giant Global Crossing imploded amid accusations of accounting irregularities. Global Crossing's stock, which had traded at nearly $100 per share, became virtually worthless, but not before CEO Gary Winnick exercised his own options and walked away with $734 million. Qwest Communications director Phil Anschutz cashed in $1.6 billion in the two years before the firm stumbled under a crushing debt load; the stock subsequently lost 96% of its value. The three top officers of telecom equipment maker JDS Uniphase collectively raked in $1.1 billion between 1999 and 2001. The stock is now trading at $2 per share. An investigation by the *Wall Street Journal* and Thompson Financial analysts estimates that top telecommunications executives captured a staggering $14.2 billion in stock gains between 1997 and 2001. The industry is now reeling, with 60 firms bankrupt and 500,000 jobs lost. The *Journal* reports that, as of August 2002, insiders at 38 telecom companies had walked away with gains greater than the current market value of their firms. "All told, it is one of the greatest transfers of wealth from investors—big and small—in American history," reporter Dennis Berman writes. "Telecom executives ... made hundreds of millions of dollars, while many investors took huge, unprecedented losses."

Executives in the energy and telecom sectors were not the only ones to rake in impressive gains. Michael Eisner of Disney Corp. set an early record for CEO pay in 1998, netting $575 million, most in option sales. Disney stock has since fallen by two-thirds. Lawrence Ellison, CEO of Oracle Corp., made $706 million when he sold 29 million shares of Oracle stock in January 2001. Ellison's sales flooded the market for Oracle shares and contributed, along with reports of declining profits, to the stock's losing two-thirds of its value over the next few months. Between 1999 and 2001, Dennis Kozlowski of Tyco International sold $258 million of Tyco stock back to the company, on top of a salary and other compensation valued near $30 million. Kozlowski defended this windfall with the claim that his leadership had "created $37 billion in shareholder wealth." By the time Kozlowski quit Tyco under indictment for sales tax fraud in 2002, $80 billion of Tyco's shareholder wealth had evaporated.

Analyzing companies whose stock had fallen by at least 75%, *Fortune* magazine discovered that "executives and directors of the 1035 companies that met our criteria took out, by our estimate, roughly $66 billion."

The Illusion of Retirement Security

During the bull market, hundreds of U.S. corporations were also stuffing employee savings accounts with corporate equity, creating a class of captive and friendly shareholders who were in many cases enjoined from selling the stock. Studies by the Employee Benefit Research Council found that, while federal law restricts holdings of company stock to 10% of assets in regulated, defined-benefit pension plans, 401(k)-type plans hold an average 19% of assets in company stock. This fraction rises to 32% when companies match employee contributions with stock and to 53% where companies have influence over plan investments. Pfizer Corporation, by all accounts the worst offender, ties up 81% of employee 401(k)s in company stock, but Coca-Cola runs a close second with 76% of plan assets in stock. Before the firm went bankrupt, WorldCom employees had 40% of their 401(k)s in the firm's shares. Such stock contributions cost firms virtually nothing in the short run and, since employees usually aren't permitted to sell the stock for years, companies needn't worry about diluting the value of equity held by important shareholders—or by their executive option-holders. Commenting on recent business lobbying efforts to gut legislation that would restrict stock contributions to retirement plans, Marc Machiz, formerly of the Labor Department's retirement division, told the *Wall Street Journal*, "business loves having people in employer stock and lobbied very hard to kill this stuff."

Until recently, most employees were untroubled by these trends. The market after all was setting new records daily. Quarterly 401(k) statements recorded fantastic returns year after year. Financial advisers assured the public that stocks were and always would be good investments. But corporate insiders proved far less willing to bank on illusory stock wealth when securing their own retirements.

Pearl Meyer and Partners, an executive compensation research firm, estimates that corporate executives eschew 401(k) plans for themselves and instead negotiate sizable cash pensions—the average senior executive is covered by a defined-benefit plan promising 60% of salary after 30 years of service. Under pressure from the board, CEO Richard McGinn quit Lucent at age 52 with $12 million in severance and a cash pension paying $870,000 annually. Lucent's employees, on the other hand, receive a 401(k) plan with 17% of its assets invested in Lucent stock. The stock plunged from $77 to $10 after McGinn's departure. Today it trades at around $1.00. Forty-two thousand Lucent workers lost their jobs as the firm sank.

When Louis Gerstner left IBM in 2002, after receiving $14 million in pay and an estimated $400 million in stock options, he negotiated a retirement package that promises "to cover car, office and club membership expenses for 10 years." IBM's employees, in contrast, have been agitating since 1999 over the firm's decision to replace its defined benefit pension with a 401(k)-type pension plan that, employee representatives estimate, will reduce pensions by one-third to one-half and save the firm $200 million annually. Economist Paul Krugman reports in the *New York Times* that Halliburton Corp. eliminated its employee pensions; first, though, the company "took an $8.5 million charge against earnings to reflect the cost of its parting gift" to CEO Dick Cheney. *Business Week*, surveying the impact of 401(k)s on employee retirement security, concludes that "CEOs deftly phased out rich defined-benefit plans and moved workers into you're-on-your-own 401(k)s, shredding a major safety net even as they locked in lifetime benefits for themselves."

Since 401(k)s were introduced in the early 1980s their use has grown explosively, and they have largely supplanted traditional defined-benefit pensions. In 2002, three of every four dollars contributed to retirement accounts went into 401(k)s. It is thanks to 401(k)s and other retirement savings plans that middle-income Americans became stock-owners in the 1980s and 1990s. It is probably also thanks to 401(k)s, and the huge demand for stocks they generated, that stock prices rose continuously in the 1990s. And it will almost certainly be thanks to 401(k)s that the problems inherent in using the stock market as a vehicle to distribute income will become glaringly apparent once the baby-boom generation begins to retire and liquidate its stock.

If stocks begin again to rise at historical averages—something financial advisors routinely project and prospective retirees are counting on—the discrepancy between what the stock market promises and what the economy delivers will widen dramatically. Something will have to give. Stocks cannot rise faster than the economy grows, not if people are actually to live off the proceeds.

Or rather, stock prices can't rise that fast unless corporate profits—on which stocks represent a legal claim—also surpass GDP gains. But if corporate earnings outpace economic growth, wages will have to stagnate or decline.

Pension economist Douglas Orr believes it is no accident that 401(k)s proliferated in a period of declining earnings and intense economic insecurity for most U.S. wage-earners. From 1980 until the latter half of the 1990s, the position of the typical American employee deteriorated noticeably. Wages fell, unemployment rose, benefits were slashed, stress levels and work hours climbed as U.S. firms "downsized" and "restructured" to cut costs and satiate investor hunger for higher profits. Firms like General Electric cut tens of thousands of jobs and made remaining jobs far less secure in order to generate earnings growth averaging 15% each year. Welch's ruthless union-busting and cost-cutting earned him the nickname "Neutron Jack" among rank-and-file employees. GE's attitude towards its employees was summed up by union negotiator Steve Tormey: "No matter how many records are broken in productivity or profits, it's always 'what have you done for me lately?' The workers are considered lemons and they are squeezed dry." Welch was championed as a hero on Wall Street, his management techniques widely emulated by firms across the nation. During his tenure, GE's stock price soared as the firm slashed employment by nearly 50%.

The Institute for Policy Studies, in a recent study, found that rising stock prices and soaring CEO pay packages are commonly associated with layoffs. CEOs of firms that "announced layoffs of 1000 or more workers in 2000 earned about 80 percent more, on average, than the executives of the 365 firms surveyed by *Business Week*."

Throughout the 1980s and 1990s, workers whose jobs were disappearing and wages collapsing consoled themselves by watching the paper value of their 401(k)s swell. With labor weak and labor incomes falling, wage and salary earners chose to cast their lot with capital. In betting on the stock market, though, workers are in reality betting that wage incomes will stagnate and trying to offset this by grabbing a slice from the profit pie. This has already proved a losing strategy for most.

Even at the peak of the 1990s bull market, the net wealth—assets minus debts—of the typical household fell from $55,000 to $50,000, as families borrowed heavily to protect their living standards in the face of stagnant wages. Until or unless the nation's capital stock is equitably distributed, there will always be a clash of interests between owners of capital and their employees. If stocks and profits are routinely besting the economy, then either wage-earners are lagging behind or somebody is cooking the books.

Yet surveys show that Americans like 401(k)s. In part, this is because savings accounts are portable, an important consideration in a world where workers can expect to change jobs several times over their working lives. But partly it is because savings plans provide the illusion of self-sufficiency and independence. When retirees spend down their savings, it feels as if they are "paying their own way." They do not feel like dependents, consuming the fruits of other people's labor. Yet they are. It is the nature of retirement that retirees opt out of production and rely on the young to keep the economy rolling. Pensions are always a claim on the real economy—they represent a transfer of goods and services from working adults to non-working retirees, who no longer contribute to economic output. The shift from defined-benefit pensions to 401(k)s and other savings plans in no way changes the fact that pensions transfer resources, but it does change the rules that will govern how those transfers take place—who pays and who benefits.

Private defined-benefit pensions impose a direct claim on corporate profits. In promising a fixed payment over a number of years, corporations commit to transfer a portion of future earnings to retirees. Under these plans, employers promise an annual lifetime benefit at retirement, the amount determined by an employee's prior earnings and years of service in the company. How the benefit will be paid, where the funds will come from, whether there are enough funds to last through a worker's life—this is the company's concern. Longevity risk—the risk that a worker will outlive the money put aside for her retirement—falls on the employer. Retirees benefit, but at a cost to shareholders. Similarly, public pension programs, whether through Social Security or through the civil service, entail a promise to retirees at the expense of the taxpaying public.

Today, the vast majority of workers, if they have pension coverage at all, participate in "defined contribution" plans, in which they and their employer contribute a fixed monthly sum and invest the proceeds with a money management firm. At retirement, the employee owns whatever funds have accrued in the account and must make the money last until she dies. Defined-contribution plans are a claim on nothing. Workers are given a shot at capturing some of the cash floating around Wall Street, but no promise that they will succeed. 401(k)s will add a huge element of chance to the American retirement experience. Some will sell high, some will not. Some will realize gains. Some will not.

Pearl Meyer and Partners estimate that outstanding, unexercised executive stock options and employee stock incentives today amount to some $2 trillion. Any effort to cash in this amount, in addition to the stock held in retirement accounts, would have a dramatic impact on stock prices. American workers and retirees, in assessing their chances for coming out ahead in the competition to liquidate stock, might ponder this question: If, as employees in private negotiations with their corporate employers, they have been unable to protect their incomes or jobs or health or retirement benefits, how likely is it that they will instead be able to wrest gains from Wall Street where corporate insiders are firmly in control of information and access to deals?

RECESSION FOR THE HOLIDAYS
John Miller
January/February 2002

Talk about a lump of coal in your stocking. Late in November, just as the holiday season was taking hold, the National Bureau of Economic Research (NBER)—the nation's official arbiter of the business cycle—declared the economic slowdown that began in March 2001 to be a recession.

In some ways, the NBER declaration was hardly big news. Even before last March, many had already fallen on hard times. During the fall of 2000, economic growth—which had averaged a brisk 5% over the previous year—suddenly slowed to just over 1%. Manufacturing slumped, dot-coms shut their doors, and the stock-market boom fizzled.

In other ways, though, the announcement was surprising. By declaring that the recession began back in March, the NBER confirmed that the economy was well into a downturn before September 11. The economic fallout from the September 11 attacks did cause a faster and deeper drop-off in economic activity, and did help to convince the NBER that the downturn would neither reverse itself quickly nor be so mild as to not qualify as an actual recession. But now it's official: It didn't cause the recession.

In addition, by dating the onset of the recession back to March, the NBER ignored the economist's shorthand definition of a recession: two consecutive quarters of decline in Gross Domestic Product (the broadest single measure of economic output) adjusted for inflation, or real GDP. Real GDP fell in the third quarter of last year and undoubtedly contracted again in the last three months of 2001, but the NBER found a significant decline in economic activity well before then. Both industrial production and real (adjusted for inflation) sales in the manufacturing, wholesale, and retail sectors peaked early in the fall of 2000, and have fallen steadily since then. Once overall employment began to drop after March 2001, as job losses in manufacturing started to outweigh job gains in other sectors of the economy, the downturn was underway.

The official declaration also closed the book on the longest economic expansion in U.S. history, which began in March 1991 and lasted for 120 months. The much-heralded 1990s boom had inspired paeans to the "New Economy" and anointed Federal Reserve Chair Alan Greenspan as "Wizard Deluxe" of economic policy making. Nowadays, we don't hear much about either. The collapse of NASDAQ (the high-tech stock index) and the disappearance of gaggles of dot-com venture capitalists have raised doubts about whether the "New Economy" was authentic. Nor did the bursting of the stock market bubble do much for Greenspan's reputation. Greenspan did issue a 1997 warning about the market's "irrational exuberance." But in an act of colossal neglect, he took no direct action to deflate the bubble; for example, he could have raised the margin requirement (or down payment) for purchasing stock on credit. The current economic contraction, brought on in part by Greenspan's repeated interest rate hikes in the second half of 1999 and the first half of 2000—and so far immune to his now-furious cutting of interest rates—has further exposed the man behind the Fed's curtain.

How long will the recession last? That's hard to say. Since World War II, U.S. recessions have averaged 11 months. As you read this, the economy will already have logged about ten months of contraction. Most financial analysts believe recovery will begin in the first half of 2002. The November 2001 turnaround in the stock market made up the ground lost since September 11, and stronger-than-predicted consumer spending at the start of the holiday season gave cause for optimism too. In fact, a few economic forecasters are already yammering about a shallow recession, no worse than that of 1990-91, soon to be followed by the return of rapid economic growth.

But there are good reasons to believe that this downturn will be neither short nor shallow. Each positive piece of economic news last fall was matched by equally bad economic tidings. Consumer confidence plummeted to an eight-year low as job losses mounted; consumer debt exceeded the levels reached in 1990-91; stock market indicators remained below March 2001 levels; and stocks continued to be overvalued by historical standards, suggesting that a stock market rally is unlikely to be sustained.

There are other indications that this recession will be no better—and could be worse—than the usual postwar fare. First, for the first time since 1974, a recession in the United States has coincided with economic downturns in Europe, Japan, and much of the developing world. Simultaneous slowdowns across the globe will feed on each other, making for a prolonged downturn. For example, the worldwide 1974-75 recession dragged on in the United States for 16 months. Second, unlike every other postwar recession, the current downturn is business-led, not consumer-driven. The bursting of the stock-market bubble, the collapse of the dot.coms, and the decline of the manufacturing sector all contributed to the recession. By September 2000, industrial production had already fallen off by 6%, surpassing the average decline of 4.6% for earlier postwar recessions. The drop in consumer spending, made worse by September 11, came later.

Beyond that, the Fed will be hard put to counteract the downturn. With lingering excess productive capacity across the economy, devastated conditions in manufacturing, and a high-tech sector in disarray, businesses will be reluctant to make new investments even if the Fed cuts interest rates further. Lakshman Achuthan, managing director at the Economic Cycle Research Institute (the New York City-based group that, back in March, said a recession was "no longer avoidable"), points out that the last time business led the way downward was during the Great Depression.

This is not to suggest that a depression is in our immediate future. But, whether an official recovery comes early or later, the economy will continue to sputter. Even the business press is worried that the post-bubble economy will slip into a period of prolonged stagnation. In early November, one *Wall Street Journal* headline dared to ask, "Is the U.S. Economy At Risk of Emulating Japan's Long Swoon?"

Whether the economy expands or contracts, this much is clear: Working people will be tightening their economic belts for the foreseeable future. Workers did not begin to make significant gains during the 1990s boom until labor markets tightened—well into the second half of the expansion. And even when the current flagging economy begins to recover, unemployment rates will keep climbing— because employers will do little hiring until economic gains are solidified, and the hardest-hit sectors will continue to lay off workers. Should the economic stimulus package currently before Congress be passed into law, it will do more to relieve large corporations of their tax burden than to provide relief for those thrown out of work by the recession.

WHOSE JOBS? OUR JOBS!
WORKERS AND THE TELECOMMUNICATIONS MELTDOWN
By Nomi Prins
March/April 2003

At some point, you become numb to the stories of greedy execs who scammed billions of dollars from their shareholders and workers. The $95 million Bel Aire mansions. The $15,000 umbrella stands. The tax-deductible private jets. Even more maddening, many executives walked away from their fraud-infested firms with multi-million dollar exit perks.

There were no such golden parachutes for the over half a million laid-off telecom workers. They lost out three times. First, the value of their stock-filled retirement plans plummeted. Then, their jobs were cut. Finally, many did not receive the severance pay and benefits to which they were legally entitled.

But one important part of the telecom tale has yet to be told: the story of unions' role in securing jobs and severance pay in the face of the sector-wide meltdown. Unionized workers have survived the crisis with fewer scrapes than their nonunion peers. Unionized companies have had fewer scandals, and have been less prone to cut costs by simply axing their workforce. Even employees laid-off from nonunion telecom companies have turned to the AFL-CIO for help, and for good reason.

Telecom Meltdown

Since January 2001, the telecom industry produced 11 of the top 25 U.S. corporate bankruptcies, six of which are under Securities and Exchange Commission (SEC) investigation. Additionally, over 27% (or 540,000) of the country's 2 million layoffs came from this one sector.

Topping the charts is WorldCom. The world's largest Internet provider and country's number two long-distance phone company, WorldCom went belly-up in July 2002. The company cut 5,100 employees from its 79,000-person payroll in June 2001. By the time it announced additional cuts of 17,000 workers in July, it was heading to bankruptcy court. WorldCom axed workers from all levels of the company—rank and file through vice president—and from sites spanning St. Louis, Tulsa, Clinton, Colorado Springs and Atlanta. The wireless divisions were particularly hard hit, and the brutal drain continues.

As one terminated "WorldCommer," the head of a family of four, put it, "I gave eight years of honest, hard work to WorldCom and MCI. When they showed me the door, they didn't even say thank you." Furthermore, termination at WorldCom was subject to favoritism. Sources say it seemed arbitrarily geared toward those who did not have the best relationships with their superiors. And, according to Kate Lee, a 14-year WorldCom veteran, "it seemed to be disproportionately targeted at the health disadvantaged, those with medical disabilities."

Employees in the heavily unionized Bells have also seen their share of pain, with 70,000 layoffs out of a 651,000-person peak workforce. Although some of the layoffs are considered voluntary departures, "to us, they are all workforce reductions," says Malinda Brent, spokesperson for the International Brotherhood of Electrical Workers (IBEW). "Those workers are still out of a job." Unforturnately, the pain continues. Verizon, the nation's largest telecom, recently announced plans for thousands of additional job cuts. Industry-wide, about 40,000 Communications Workers of America (CWA) jobs have been eliminated.

Still, union workers have fared better than nonunionized employees in terms of their layoff conditions. "Of those cuts, less than 10,000 people were involuntarily thrown out of their jobs," says Morton Bahr, President of the 740,000 member CWA. "That's because of all the protection innovations we came up with, like avoiding involuntary departures by negotiating early retirement benefits and substantially increased severance pay. With a union contract, at least there's a seat at the negotiation table and alternatives can be considered."

Union representation has protected many from arbitrary termination driven by favoritism. "That's the kind of thing that wouldn't happen with a strong union," says Bahr. "When there's no union contract, they lay off who they want when they want."

Those union workers who do get pink slips receive substantially better severance pay than similar workers at nonunion firms. Partly this is because union salaries are higher to begin with, especially for lower skilled jobs. Suman Ray, senior analyst at CWA, explains, "Typically, the union-non-union salary discrepancy can be as much as 25%. The difference narrows with skill level, but nonetheless remains." In certain cases the CWA has negotiated severance amounts that exceed the number of years worked. For example, at SBC Communications, laid-off senior employees' severance pay was computed based on employee tenure-plus-6 years, resulting in an additional $500 a month, thanks to CWA efforts.

Not only are union workers paid more severance; they actually receive the severance pay they were promised—that is, they get the amount they expect to get. This is in stark contrast to the experience of laid-off employees in the nonunion Internet sector, where firms (including WorldCom and Global Crossing) chose not to honor their severance contracts.

The CWA also fights to protect its members' pension dollars (or tries to), taking employers to court when necessary. When nonunion Global Crossing acquired the unionized Frontier Communications in late 1999, it also acquired almost $600 million of Frontier worker pension assets. Global Crossing then sold part of Frontier to Citizens Communications two years later, but kept the pension assets of the Frontier employees—a blatant maneuver to pump up its own balance sheet.

CWA head Bahr confronted Global Crossing chairman Gary Winnick, saying, "Those assets should be with the workers, not with you. Pension assets belong to the current and future retirees." The CWA ultimately took Global Crossing to court. But the corporation deliberately dragged its feet. First, bankruptcy filing became a convenient excuse. Another speed bump arose when creditors and new owners agreed to purchase the restructured Global Crossing. The CWA continues its fight. It is a battle that Bahr and the union are committed to win.

Struggle for Severance Pay at WorldCom

WorldCom's massive job cuts cost employees more than their jobs; the company also withheld severance pay. Under U.S. bankruptcy code, when a corporation files for chapter 11, any severance pay due to the employees terminated pre-filing can be capped at $4,650. The figure represents an inflation-adjusted payment that started as $1,600 in 1979 when Congress passed the original code. Where did that number come from? "Well," explained one New York City corporate bankruptcy lawyer involved in the case, "the legislators at the time pulled it out of their ears."

WorldCom lawyers asked the bankruptcy court to allow it to pay just the severance cap amount, even though many terminated workers were owed far more—and had employment and severance contracts to prove it. As it turned out, WorldCom did not even make these small payments in a timely manner.

For Dawn Harden, ex-financial systems analyst from Atlanta and single mother of three, this was hard to swallow. "I went from $50,000 to food stamps. They have the money. Why haven't they paid me my money and benefits like they promised?"

That's a question that Kate Lee, now chairwoman of the ex-WorldCom Employees Assistance Fund, took to heart, to the bankruptcy courts, and to Congress. The assistance fund was created by Lee and three other casualties of the

June WorldCom layoffs. It was modeled on a relief fund that a former Enron employee set up to provide laid-off Enron employees with financial assistance. In its first few months, the fund raised over $190,000. Contributions flowed from the Democratic Congressional Campaign Committee, various senators, and sympathetic members of the public. Not a single WorldCom executive chose to make a contribution.

In early July 2002, WorldCom owed 4,000 severed employees $36 million. The AFL-CIO quickly mobilized to help Lee and other laid-off WorldCom workers retrieve due severance pay. Several levels of the AFL-CIO were involved in the legal effort, from lawyers to union activists to John Sweeney, the President of the AFL-CIO. Damon Silvers, associate general counsel for the AFL-CIO explained, "We had just come off a bankruptcy court coup against Enron, getting $35 million in severance for 4,500 laid-off employees. We had built up the expertise in the courts and knew how to exert pressure to retrieve severance and other benefits. Then, bang. WorldCom happened. We knew what we had to do and went out and did it."

In addition to the legal assistance, AFL-CIO activists set up laid-off worker information websites. They leafleted WorldCom jobsites and call centers. John Sweeney committed the AFL-CIO's support to the WorldCom workers during a Wall Street rally to raise awareness about corporate governance. Hundreds of formerly non-active workers were catalyzed to fight. "There's no way we could have gotten as far as we did without the help of the AFL-CIO," said Lee.

In October, WorldCom went to bankruptcy court, supposedly on behalf of its workers, to request the ability to pay severance benefits. WorldCom appeared not out of the goodness of its corporate heart but in response to the concerted pressure exerted by the AFL-CIO, its network of lawyers, and the former WorldCom employees.

When the court agreed to permit the company to pay severance, the WorldCom public relations machine spread the news of its generosity. Company attorney Marcia Goldstein testified that the payments would allow WorldCom to "restore the confidence of its employees, whose cooperation and continued loyalty are essential." Yet behind the scenes, WorldCom chose not to pay that severance in the lump sums its employees requested, opting instead for biweekly payments.

"You know, it's like a rounding error to them," says Lee of the $36 million, "And yet, do you think, just maybe they could do the right thing, after all the negative publicity, just once do the right thing by their workers?" Indeed, many who had counted on that money were well behind in mortgage and medical payments, some facing home foreclosures and car repossessions.

Moreover, some ex-WorldCom employees also found the company had adjusted their severance payments down by inserting unexplained numbers of vacation days. When one ex-employee called WorldCom's severance dispute hotline to find out why the amount of vacation he had taken had doubled, he was told, "I don't know. I'm not sure. Perhaps. Maybe. I don't have information on that." Other ex-employees have complained of similar treatment.

Some sources claim that internal departments including Human Resources, Finance, and the post-bankruptcy Restructuring Department were given financial incentives to retain as much cash as possible. Such incentives are just one insidious way that post-chapter 11 corporations placate bank creditors at the expense of workers.

Not only did WorldCom shirk severance responsibilities. Its severance packages were not all created equally. While groups like Lee's battled for severance and health care benefits, a subgroup of 19 employees, all Vice Presidents, were treated suspiciously well. All 19 had links to the international customer base, particularly the billing of goliath multinationals like BP, McDonalds, and MasterCard.

Monica Didier, who resigned from her position as a Director of Executive Product Program Management at WorldCom in June, regularly attended internal meetings run by Scott Sullivan, WorldCom's indicted ex-CFO. "As the company stock sank, even before the accounting allegations were exposed," she recalled, "Scott was under pressure to put together a set of acceptable company numbers to keep the analysts, press and shareholders at bay."

He said that growth would come from the international customer base. Indeed, the only two positive growth areas in the 2001 annual report (prior to being hit by the infamous $9 billion earnings "misclassification") were the Internet and International departments, whose earnings have not yet been restated. Could they be next?

While no wrongdoing has been established, the 19 did receive full severance with no payment disruptions and superior health care packages. Says Didier, "All other severance agreements had health care coverage lasting until December, but these people got coverage until spring (2003)."

Groups including Lee's organization and the AFL-CIO continue to fight for bankruptcy code revisions that would give higher priority to employees and provide a specific seat for an employees' committee in bankruptcy court. Creditor committees, mostly representing Wall Street banks, simply do not take into account employee interests in their efforts to recoup assets. Current federal law effectively sacrifices employees first when companies go under. Without changes to ensure appropriate employee representation at the bankruptcy court table, workers will continue to pay a high price for corporate fraud-induced bankruptcy.

Effects of the Telecom Bust on Retirement Funds

After the Telecommunications Act of 1996, new entrant Internet firms went on a shopping spree using inflated stock as currency. Qwest bought USWest (formerly Bell) with $36 billion of stock; Global Crossing bought Frontier Communications (a local phone company) with $10 billion of stock; and WorldCom bought MCI (a long-distance company) with $37 billion of stock. As a result, workers in these companies saw the old company stock in their savings plans converted to highly inflated new company stock.

In the telecommunications sector, 70% of union workers have defined benefit pensions that provide a guaranteed level of retirement income. In comparison, just 16% of nonunion telecom workers have defined benefit plans. Most nonunion workers rely on 401(k) and other defined contribution plans with no retirement income guarantee. Such plans may be legally filled with employer stock.

At unionized USWest and Frontier Communications, workers had 401(k) plans in addition to their defined benefit pensions. Their 401(k)s were injected with Qwest and Global Crossing stock respectively. At nonunion MCI, employees relied on 401(k)s as their primary retirement plan. These were filled with WorldCom stock—as much as 55% of total 401(k) assets in 1999 and 32% in 2000.

Employees report they were under pressure to buy and hold stock even as executives were selling. Even as their retirement money dwindled, companies pumped them with rhetoric about future riches and the need for patience, all while executives were cashing out. WorldCom workers lost between $600 million and $1.8 billion from their 401(k) savings plans, according to the Employee Benefits Research Institute (EBRI). Global Crossing workers lost around $275 million in 401(k) plans filled with Global Crossing stock. These retirement plans had 5-year lock-out periods prohibiting stock sales.

Under the bright lights of a congressional hearing last October, Winnick offered to give up $25 million of "his own money" to help those employees who had lost theirs. That is a mere fraction of the $735 million that he pocketed from stock and option sales. (He didn't have a lock-out period.) So far, there has been no distribution of that promised money, nor any agreement on the terms of distribution. Winnick quietly resigned as chairman on New Year's eve.

Recent union interventions have not gone unnoticed by nonunion ex-"WorldCommers." Said one former employee from New York, "I never thought much of unions before this happened, thought they were a relic of a past time—you know, children working too long, factory workers, low wages and the like. I've had a change of heart. The rank and file need someone who is on their side, against companies who treat us like disposable assets."

But despite a very troubled industry, union organizing does not become simpler overnight. According to Ray, "The rules of the game are heavily stacked by the corporations. Just because some employees are more sympathetic does not always make it easier. That change in opinion, while encouraging, does not immediately translate into huge organizing increases." Still, there is hope that the current executives-come-first environment will foster more union support. Meanwhile, CWA organizing efforts march forward, particularly in the cable industry where Adelphia's massive corruption has been met with intensified union activity.

Others in the Fight

A new voice in the fight for employee rights is coming from the retirement community.

Bill Jones, a former middle manager at Bell Atlantic Telephone, formed a retiree group with a colleague in late 1995. Under old company policy, pension benefits were supposed to increase every two years with inflation. Instead, they discovered, though pension fund surpluses at "Bell Tel" were increasing, as was executive compensation, payouts were not.

Fast forward seven years and Bell Tel has become part of what is now Verizon. The Bell Tel Retiree organization has grown from a two-person operation to 165,000 members. Membership has increased by 25% over just the past year. Today, the group is mixed, with 40% former union members and 60% former managers. Jones argues, "once you become a retiree, that's your label—doesn't matter if you were management or union."

Many other retiree organizations were also formed in the mid-1990s, including many established by employees who had worked at pre-divestiture AT&T and later at the various Bells—employees who remembered times when workers' security and benefits meant something. As Nelson Phelps, founder of the growing Association of USWest Retirees (AUSWR) put it, "We realized that corporations couldn't be trusted and no one was going to protect our rights, but us."

Together, the retiree organizations formed the National Retiree Legislative Network (NRLN) which represents almost two million retirees. The NRLN is fighting for legislation to ensure federally guaranteed maintenance of health care benefits, much like the 1974 Employee Retirement Income Security Act guaranteed defined benefit pensions through the pension benefit guarantee corporation (PBGC). They are also fighting for stricter corporate governance measures.

Jones and other NLRN shareholder activists argue for:

- Truly independent boards. Boards should have limited or no representation from management ranks. This is key to establishing checks and balances within corporations. (Some members of the retiree and union movements advocate employee or union leader representation on boards as well.)

- Removal of pension asset performance projections from company income statements. This is essential to giving shareholders and employees a more accurate view of a firm's performance.

- Broad shareholder review of golden parachute packages. All shareholders, and not just members of the firm's compensation committee (who have a vested interest in treating their ex-bosses fairly) should have the right to inspect—and reevaluate—the excessive exit perks handed to corporate executives. Redistributing CEOs' multi-million dollar parting gifts to current and former telecom workers would be a good first step toward fairer treatment of the sector's workforce.

Corporate practices are difficult to change, however. This was a lesson members of the AUSWR learned when they presented two proposals limiting executive benefits at Qwest's annual shareholder's meeting last June. The first was a golden parachute proposal that would subject executive packages to a general shareholder vote. The second was a proposal to eliminate executives' ability to garner bonuses based on the firm's pension fund performance—a widely used corporate tactic. Though shareholders rejected both proposals, the pension incentive proposal received 39% approval (more than double the prior year). The golden parachute proposal earned 17% approval.

Bell Tel Retirees fared slightly better when they presented similar proposals at Verizon's annual meeting last April. That's because they were not hampered by one large shareholder. At Qwest, billionaire former chairman Phillip Anschutz owns 18% of company stock and holds the associated voting rights.

Facing the Future

Rather than learning from past mistakes, the Federal Communications Commission (FCC) approved yet another mega-merger between AT&T Broadband and Comcast in an all-stock deal on November 13, 2002. AT&T Comcast retained $26 billion of debt left over from AT&T's previous four mergers and got 30% of the U.S. cable market. The Wall Street advisors for the deal bagged $221 million in fees, while 1,700 employees got axed.

Global Crossing will emerge from bankruptcy protection sometime this year. Other telecoms have already resurfaced. With their debts erased, they will once again be able to pile on loans. And again, banks will rush in to help them, in return for fees, despite their horrendous track records. Also troubling: despite high debt, Bells like SBC Communications are going shopping. SBC recently announced its intent to buy unregulated DirecTV as part of an expansion into cable. Unfortunately, without major regulatory changes, the cycle of debt, earnings peppered with creative accounting, and layoffs is destined to continue.

WorldCom will likely be resurrected in some form later this year, possibly under the old MCI moniker, or cut up into parts and sold off to a Bell. Astonishingly, the SEC (whose primary mission is to protect investors) granted WorldCom a permanent injunction (a pardon) on November 26, 2002, for its $9 billion in misstated earnings, a move that received no front-page coverage.

Equally remarkable is that WorldCom named Hewlett Packard's Michael Capellas to all three of the top spots at the firm: president, CEO, and chairman of the board, with an $18 million sign-on package. Even though so many of WorldCom's problems stemmed from its lack of an independent board, and the unchecked authority of former President and CEO Bernie Ebbers and his cronies, WorldCom failed to divide the power of its top three positions. There is no possibility of board independence when the chairman happens to be the CEO.

Fortunately, counteracting this corporate maneuvering, there is evidence of a growing and increasingly united struggle. Whether it is unions fighting for workers' rights, collective action campaigns, ex-employees advocating changes to bankruptcy codes, or retirees promoting health benefit guarantees, working people are coming together to help each other. Together, laid-off telecom workers, retiree groups, and the AFL-CIO represent 17 million people. That's a lot of votes. It's crucial that these groups continue to mobilize to strengthen a corporate corruption-resistance movement. It's a long haul littered with opposition from the same corporations and legislators that combined forces to create the current mess, but the battle is building up steam.

IT ALL DEPENDS ON WHO YOU ROB
By Alejandro Reuss
November/December 2002

Considering all the stories of corporate treachery that have made headlines over the last year, you would think that accusations of massive and systematic theft at the United States' largest corporation would inspire exposés, set off investigations, perhaps even lead to arrests. So why aren't the mainstream media and the government up in arms about the "Wal-Mart scandal"?

Lawsuits filed by current and former Wal-Mart workers in 28 states have accused the company of forcing them to work "off the clock" for no pay—robbing them of wages to which they are entitled by law and by right. The recent suits—which allege that Wal-Mart supervisors make employees work, sometimes for hours, before clocking in, work through scheduled breaks, and continue working after punching out at night—are by no means small potatoes. In 2000, the company settled a class-action suit, covering nearly 70,000 Colorado workers who had been forced to work off the clock, for $50 million. A current suit, covering 200,000 Texas workers, alleges that Wal-Mart robbed them of over $150 million in wages by forcing them to work, unpaid, through their breaks.

So why haven't cops hauled Wal-Mart executives away in handcuffs? Why haven't the accusations of massive theft warranted the "scandal" treatment the press and politicians have given Enron, Halliburton, Adelphia, Tyco, WorldCom, etc.? At Enron and companies like it, the discovery of fraudulent corporate profit reports (which had inflated stock prices long enough for the executives to cash in) set off stock-price meltdowns. Stock holders were among the prominent "victims," and each new revelation made for a juicy "corrupt executives vs. deceived investors" morality play. The Wal-Mart lawsuits, which tell a story of everyday (though criminal) exploitation, just do not fit the script.

Carried away by the "irrational exuberance" of the late 1990s, the capitalist media virtually declared that a booming economy was synonymous with a booming stock market. As often as they crowed that nearly half of all U.S. households now owned stock, they apparently missed the converse—that more than half owned no stock at all. The triumphal story of the stock boom ignored this "silent majority." So do media scandals that focus on imploding stocks and investors left holding worthless paper.

As economist James K. Galbraith wrote in the *Texas Observer*, it was "not only small fry [investors], but modest millionaires in some cases, who lost their 401(k)s" in the Enron meltdown. "And there is nothing a hardworking middle manager fears more, than to end up on Social Security like ordinary folk." The power of companies over even relatively privileged employees—many of whom were barred from selling their stock holdings while company executives cashed in—is clear in the Enron scandal and others like it. By focusing on the "modest millionaires," however, the scandal coverage implicitly tells the "ordinary folk" that it's not such a big deal when they get robbed.

The "profits" at Enron may have been phony, but Wal-Mart's are very real—over $6 billion last year. The *New York Times* reports how the company has built its empire: "Many analysts say Wal-Mart's push to minimize costs is the fiercest in the industry, and holding down labor costs—including fighting off unionization at its stores—is at the heart of Wal-Mart's effort to be the nation's low-cost retailer." Low wages, meager benefits, and union busting for Wal-Mart's U.S. employees, not to mention sweatshop work and poverty pay for the Third World workers that produce the company's wares—all boost company profits and "shareholder value."

Every once in a while investors fall victim to fraud. But they are among the main beneficiaries of this daily exploitation. According to the official U.S. government National Income and Product Accounts, income from capital—including rent, dividends, interest, and realized capital gains—accounts for about one fifth of the U.S. money economy. Nearly half of that goes to the richest 1% of the U.S. population. Over seven tenths, well over $1 trillion in annual income, enrich the top 10%—just for owning property.

Fast Company founding editor Alan M. Weber writes, "Most CEOs aren't crooks—but they are incredibly competitive, financially motivated individuals ... that's exactly what investors pay CEOs to be. So the real remedy is not to arrest them and send them to jail. It's to reward them for creating wealth for the company and for the shareholders...." That, of course, is just what Wal-Mart executives have done. And if they have "created" that wealth by plundering workers, where's the scandal? That's just capitalism as usual.

Chapter 3

LABOR REVIVES—AND FACES NEW ATTACKS

INTRODUCTION

Within the U.S. labor movement, George W. Bush has become known as the most anti-union president in the country's history. In less than four years, he has stripped 60,000 airport screeners of their right to join a union, released plans to outsource 850,000 unionized federal jobs, and secured the right to unilaterally cancel the collective bargaining rights of 170,000 workers in the new Department of Homeland Security. Bush has tried to justify each of these moves with appeals to "national security," arguing that "inflexible" union protections are too unwieldy for the post-9/11 world. "It's important during times of war that we be flexible to meet our needs," he explained in 2002. Union contracts—full of scheduled raises, guaranteed sick days, and assured job protections—are, in Bush's words, "bureaucratic rules and obstacles" that no President should have to honor.

For workers and unions used to dealing with corporate executives, Bush's lexicon has sounded awfully familiar. Managers and CEOs talk incessantly about "flexibility" when they really mean outsourcing, wage-cutting, union-busting, and part-timing. Like the smooth-talking CEOs who say they need "flexibility" to protect their companies from financial danger, Bush claimed to need it to protect the country from terrorists.

While Bush never even tried to explain how labor rights aided terrorism, or how union busting would increase anyone's "security," the mainstream media rarely pressed him on the points. Instead, many news outlets regurgitated claims that workers and the labor movement threatened Americans and the country itself. When Republican members of the House made baseless accusations in 2002 that "more and more people are becoming victims of union violence," the Associated Press lent their story credibility with a matter-of-fact headline, "GOP Discusses Union Violence." In the face of such "dangers," no anti-union tactic was deemed excessive. When Bush threatened in 2002 to use the Taft-Hartley Act to crush a potential longshore strike on the West coast, reporters for the *Wall Street Journal* openly marveled at the "unusual caution exhibited by the White House."

In fact, Bush was anything but restrained: he soon became the first president in 25 years to invoke Taft-Hartley. Moreover, American workers aren't dying from "union violence"—although every year, 6,000 do die from workplace injuries and 50,000 more die from illnesses caused by exposure to workplace hazards. And so far as anyone has been able to tell, collective bargaining isn't an al Qaeda plot.

So why all the hubbub?

The recent crackdown on labor came at a time when the movement was gaining strength: after decades of decline, unions were adopting militant tactics, organizing new workers, and making common cause with groups working for immigrant rights, global economic justice, and environmental sustainability. Workers' centers were springing up throughout the country, organizing immigrant workers and challenging employers in court. And groups like Jobs With Justice were bringing together unions and communities to support worker struggles. Employers threatened by labor's revival, and an administration hostile to workers' demands, seized on "national security" as a pretext for putting a lid on the labor movement.

As David Bacon explains in this chapter, before September 11, 2001, organized labor had advocated pathways to legal residence and U.S. citizenship for undocumented immigrants. For the first time in their histories, unions representing hotel and restaurant workers, janitors, and garment workers—as well as the AFL-CIO itself—assailed "guest worker" programs that left immigrants vulnerable to firings and deportation, and won contractual clauses allowing workers time off to normalize their immigration status ("Braceros or Amnesty?").

Immigrant workers and the unions organizing them became some of the most militant elements of the U.S. labor movement, and came in for hard hits from both employers and the government. Abby Scher describes a 2002 Supreme Court decision which denied undocumented workers the back-wages that employers are required to pay workers who are illegally fired for union activity. The *Hoffman Plastics* decision has emboldened employer attacks on immigrants from Los Angeles to New York, and prompted a fightback among workers and unions ("When is a Labor Law Violation Not a Labor Law Violation?"). In a later article, Bacon surveys the terrifying environment that immigrant workers face nationwide today—from the Social Security Administration sending "no-match" letters to employers, to INS raids in workplaces, to airport baggage screeners losing their jobs simply because they are not citizens. As Bacon emphasizes, these attacks target both immigrants themselves and the unions they have recently formed ("Immigrant Workers in the Crosshairs").

Airline workers have also found themselves under fire since September 11. As Rodney Ward explains, terrorism and war created a "perfect storm" in which employers and the federal government could try to weaken or even dismantle airline unions. US Airways, United, and other industry giants have succeeded in extracting devastating concessions from workers and even shredding union contracts, all while enjoying billions of dollars in federal bailouts. As Ward makes clear, airline workers—like immigrants—are strategic targets for employers and a government seeking to weaken the entire labor movement. The airlines are one of the most densely-unionized sectors of the U.S. economy, and unions in other sectors will be more vulnerable if airline unions are weakened or broken ("September 11 and the Restructuring of the Airline Industry"). When labor is the target, the "War on Terrorism" doesn't shoot blindly.

BRACEROS OR AMNESTY?
By David Bacon
November/December 2001

At the end of Mexican President Vicente Fox's first state visit to Washington, D.C., in September, he left frustrated and empty-handed. It wasn't supposed to work out that way.

Months before, the occasion had been planned for Fox and U.S. President George W. Bush to unveil far-reaching proposals for immigration reform. Fox would return to Mexico City with much-needed proof of his effectiveness in office, and Bush would quickly introduce the package in Congress, enhancing his carefully crafted pro-Latino image.

Instead, Bush couldn't keep key members of his own party, who oppose any amnesty, on board. And without their votes in his pocket, he wasn't about to introduce anything. When a frustrated Fox told the Washington media that he expected to have a proposal negotiated by the end of the year, non-plussed Bush-administration officials made soothing public statements of general good intentions, but avoided any concrete promises.

Republicans are stuck on the horns of a dilemma. The industries that provide them with political contributions need workers to pick crops, clean hotel rooms, and do other hard work at low pay. These workers are increasingly undocumented immigrants. But a new immigration amnesty—allowing undocumented workers currently in the country (and conceivably those yet to come) to apply for legal permanent residence—carries the prospect of political upheaval. Many Republicans are loath to legalize the estimated 11 million undocumented immigrants in the United States—who might, as a result, join unions, become citizens, and vote (probably not for the GOP).

For Bush, the easy answer is "guest-worker" programs. These programs, which permit the recruitment of workers in other countries for temporary jobs in the United States, have a long history here. Widely known as *bracero* (laborer) programs, after the system that allowed growers to recruit farm workers from Mexico during the 1940s and 1950s, such programs have historically drawn opposition from unions and Latino and Asian/Pacific Islander communities. While guest workers have rights on paper, employers can not only fire those who protest bad conditions and organize, but in effect can deport them as well. César Chávez could only begin organizing the United Farm Workers (UFW) when workers became free of the *bracero* system. Despite the end of the original *bracero* program, two guest-worker programs still exist in the United States, supplying skilled workers to the high-tech sector and farm laborers to agribusiness.

This year, even Republican right-wingers like Sen. Jesse Helms (R-NC) and Sen. Phil Gramm (R-TX)—once opposed to any measures that would let more people into the United States legally—have changed their stance on guest-worker programs. Both now favor the programs' expansion to meet the rising labor needs of employers in their states. This sudden conversion makes the immigration debate clearer. The choice is not over what policy will or will not stop people from coming across the border, but over what happens to people when they're here in the United States. It is the age-old American dilemma—bondage (whether as slaves, indentured servants, or *braceros*) or freedom (even if that still means workers will have to organize and fight to improve conditions).

New Friends: U.S. Labor and Fox Join Hands on Immigration

As usual, the new fault lines in the immigration debate were more visible in Los Angeles than anywhere else. After laying siege to Santa Monica's Loews Hotel, where management has stalled its immigrant workers in their pursuit of a union contract, hundreds of delegates to the July convention of the Hotel Employees and Restaurant Employees International Union (HERE) marched to the Fairmont Miramar. There, in its cavernous ballroom, they welcomed Mexican Foreign Minister Jorge Castañeda with a standing ovation.

Just the appearance of a high official of the Mexican government at the convention of a major U.S. union is a sign of changing times. For decades, U.S. unions and the Mexican government have looked at each other across the border with deep suspicion and hostility. Unions have condemned Mexico's low-wage economic policies, while its government has accused U.S. unions of protectionism and racism toward Mexican migrants.

Ironically, President Fox is probably the most pro-business head of state Mexico has had since the Mexican Revolution (1910–1921). Yet his push for immigration reform in the United States, along with the new interest of U.S. unions in defending Mexican immigrants, has created a whole new relationship. "Finally the U.S. has accepted that both countries have to discuss immigration," Castañeda told HERE members. "And for the first time, Mexico has agreed that it has joint responsibility with the United States for it. These are enormous changes—we have to take advantage of them."

Just as Castañeda was addressing the HERE convention, the White House's Mexican Migration Working Group, headed by Secretary of State Colin Powell and Attorney General John Ashcroft, was leaking its own proposed recommendations. As soon as the press corps began reporting that the Working Group might recommend a legalization program for undocumented immigrants, the White House immediately made clear it would not support such a move.

The administration seemed anxious to show powerful Congressional Republicans like Sen. Gramm that they could still call the shots on immigration. During Fox's visit, Gramm made it plain that there would be no GOP support for an amnesty. As a result, the Working Group's report has yet to be released. In the wake of the crossed wires during Fox's visit, the panel seems unable to make a decision the administration can live with.

Unions interested in legalization have their own problems getting immigration-reform proposals on the table. Despite recent efforts by Bush to reach out to more conservative unions in the AFL-CIO, unions have little or no influence with the administration around guest workers and amnesty. Castañeda's appearance at the HERE convention highlights the newest twist in immigration politics. Increasingly, pro-legalization unions hope the Mexican government will represent their position in its negotiations with Bush.

In June, HERE President John Wilhelm and other labor leaders went to Mexico City to talk to Fox. "We said we were inalterably opposed to guest-worker programs," Wilhelm recalled. "We don't want any program in which a worker's immigration status is attached to their job, and where there is no realistic path to legalization."

The commitment of the Mexican government to legalization seems less clear. At the HERE convention, Castañeda described what he called "the whole enchilada," a package of proposals that the Fox administration is presenting to Bush—"regularization" of the status of undocumented Mexicans, more permanent visas for Mexicans to join relatives in the United States, greater cooperation to prevent the deaths of migrants crossing the border, and promotion of Mexican economic growth "to create more opportunities for Mexicans to stay and thrive in Mexico." The proposals are tied together, he emphasized, and Mexico won't allow the U.S. to negotiate just on the ones it likes.

The most controversial point was Castañeda's call for expanding guest-worker programs. The foreign minister even used a supposed labor shortage in the service sector as a justification. That drew strong objections from many delegates who hold service jobs in hotels and who see a tight labor market in the industry as an important bargaining advantage. "Just think what would happen if Loews could bring in a bunch of guest workers while we were fighting for this contract," grumbled one delegate as he left the ballroom. "We'd never get them to agree."

The key question is what the Mexican government means by "regularization" of the status of the undocumented. Does "regularization" mean Mexicans living in the U.S. should become guest workers to gain some form of legal status? While unpopular among Mexicans already here, that might be more acceptable to many people in Mexico considering the dangerous journey north. Fox already claims that expanded guest-worker programs will open the door to jobs and legal migration north.

That compromise has an additional huge attraction for Fox: It's the only arrangement the Bush administration will clearly support. Bush has explicitly stated he wants expanded guest-worker programs, not legalization. State Department spokesperson Richard Boucher explained that "it's really a question of an orderly guest-worker program, the safe and orderly migration, and in that context, obviously, looking at the status of people who are currently here."

Bush is looking over his shoulder at his fellow Texas Republicans, Sen. Phil Gramm, Rep. Lamar Smith, and Rep. Tom DeLay. "Anything that smacks of [amnesty] we'll oppose," warned Gramm Spokesperson Larry Neal. Smith, until last year chair of the House Immigration Subcommittee, warned that any amnesty proposal would encounter a lot of opposition. "I'd be surprised if the administration pushed it," he said.

What gives these Texans nightmares are the recent elections in southern California. In the recent Los Angeles mayoral contest, many HERE convention delegates walked precincts for former state assembly Speaker and union leader Antonio Villaraigoza, despite their lack of citizenship. "We called people on the phone, we went door-to-door," recalled Douglas Marmol, a delegate from Local 814. "It doesn't matter where you come from. We all have rights, and we need people in office who understand and respect that."

In 1997, members of HERE Local 681 working at Disneyland or at unionized hotels did the same thing in Orange County. As a result, Republican Rep. "B-1" Bob Dornan, who sat on the right wing of his party with Gramm, Smith, and DeLay, went down to defeat at the hands of Democrat Loretta Sánchez. Republicans are afraid that further opening doors to legalization and citizenship will leave them on the wrong side of the country's changing demographics.

Growers and Unions Negotiate Over Guest-Worker Programs

Agribusiness has pushed hard for expansion of the agricultural guest-worker program, which last year brought 40,000 workers into the United States. At the end of the 2000 Congressional session, California Democratic Rep. Howard Berman and Oregon Republican Sen. Gordon Smith proposed an amnesty, which would have granted legal status to hundreds of thousands of undocumented farm laborers. In exchange, requirements that growers provide housing to guest workers, and pay them a minimum wage adjusted annually for inflation, would have been relaxed.

The deal was crafted by farm-worker unions to get agribusiness support for amnesty. Unions argued that the existing glut of farm labor keeps rural wages below the minimum for guest workers in many areas, and therefore growers were unlikely to make much more use of the program. The program already exists, they argued, Congress is not likely to end it, and some expansion of the program was likely to pass in any case. But at the last moment then-Senate Majority Leader Gramm, who opposes any amnesty at all, killed the bill.

With Bush in the White House, growers scrapped last year's compromise. Idaho Republican Sen. Larry Craig introduced a new guest-worker bill, with no amnesty provision. Instead, undocumented farm workers currently in the United States would have to work 150 days in each of five years to qualify for permanent residence, a difficult feat for seasonal workers. Only work in the fields would count. The new bill requires only the minimum wage, and the government would no longer have to certify a labor shortage to permit importing workers—the growers' word would do. After meeting with Mexican President Fox, UFW President Arturo Rodríguez told the press, "We've made it clear that without legalization there will be no new guest-worker program or revision of the current guest-worker program."

Other industries now want guest workers, too. In Congress, the push comes from the Essential Worker Immigration Coalition, which includes the American Health Care Association, the National Association of Manufacturers, and the U.S. Chamber of Commerce.

HERE convention delegates unanimously rejected the idea of a *bracero* program in their industry. HERE President Wilhelm called an expanded guest-worker program "a terrible idea." "We need amnesty instead," said Pedro Navarro, an Anaheim delegate who works at Disney's Paradise. "It's the only way we'll be able to work securely, to face the police in our streets, or feel our kids will have real rights in school."

A first-ever HERE committee on immigration and civil rights reported to delegates that "tens of thousands of workers would be [made] hostage, and ultimately destroy wage and working conditions in the hospitality industry." Instead, the convention called for a broad legalization and citizenship program, and for repealing employer sanctions—the law which makes it illegal for undocumented workers to hold a job.

In an effort to solidify union ranks across racial lines, HERE also announced its intention to force hotels to begin hiring Black workers, alleging that in its eagerness to hire immigrants, the industry has erected discriminatory barriers to African-Americans. Wilhelm assailed the failure of the industry to hire Blacks in cities like Los Angeles as a "social catastrophe," while one of the union's highest ranking Black officers, National Executive Board Member Isaac Monroe, criticized the labor movement for "its failure to promote the leadership of African-Americans." But Monroe also warned delegates that "demographic changes are a wakeup call. The movement for immigrant rights is real, it's important, and it's our future."

The union's support for immigrant rights isn't just convention rhetoric. A majority of HERE members are immigrant workers. Two years ago, Los Angeles' Local 11 negotiated a master hotel contract allowing workers time off to normalize their immigration status, and requiring management to notify the union if the Immigration and Naturalization Service begins enforcement action against them. In San Francisco, Local 2 successfully won new legal protection for workers who in the past lost jobs when the Social Security Administration told employers their numbers were invalid. And Wilhelm heads the immigration committee of the AFL-CIO, pushing the labor federation to fight in Washington for immigration amnesty.

The Possibilities for Immigration Reform

Anti-immigrant fever has already begun to build in the wake of the September 11 terrorist attacks on the World Trade Center and the Pentagon. Calls for beefing up border enforcement and restricting immigration are appearing on the op-ed pages of major U.S. newspapers. Along with the economic downturn, that will complicate the future of immigration reform.

But the labor needs of employers are not going to disappear, and the strategic drive for a new relationship with Mexico, while not as high on the agenda as it was during Fox's visit, is still a centerpiece of Bush's foreign policy. Fox said Bush called him the weekend after the attacks, saying he "hasn't forgotten that we have commitments to work to regularize the situation of immigrants." In turn, Castañeda announced that "the United States has every right and reason to seek revenge.... We cannot deny them support." The statement made it clear that Mexico's foreign-policy independence—and frequent criticism of U.S. military intervention—was a thing of the past. Whether it will ease discussions of a guest-worker program, however, remains to be seen.

HERE President Wilhelm argues that a guest-worker proposal can be defeated, especially if employer groups take a long-range, enlightened view of their own self-interest. "Some have said privately that guest workers aren't the answer, just a temporary Band-Aid," he explained in an interview. "Everyone thinks the labor shortage will get worse over the next two decades, and there's no incentive to provide training, or even English classes, to guest workers. So if we can get a significant group of employers to reject the idea, we have a shot. Short of that, I'm very fearful."

The union, in any case, isn't waiting passively. HERE has already announced plans for an "Immigrants Freedom Ride" to Washington, D.C., next May "in search of legalization and immigrant rights." The union's call uses the language of the 1960s civil-rights movement, and refers to the time when people from the North rode busses to southern states to end segregation. "We want full and complete amnesty," Pedro Navarro emphasized. "We want the same rights everyone else has, nothing less."

Unfortunately, such an outcome now seems further away than ever.

WHEN IS A LABOR LAW VIOLATION NOT A LABOR LAW VIOLATION?
By Abby Scher
September/October 2002

Jesús Pérez owns a butcher shop in Washington Heights, a largely Dominican community in the northern section of Manhattan. Pérez's shop is not large but it is worth paying attention to, and not for the quality of his rib roast. It's because last

March, Mr. Pérez's lawyer invoked the ominous words "*Hoffman Plastics*" in a nasty letter he wrote refusing unpaid wages to one of Perez's workers.

Hoffman Plastics is a recent Supreme Court decision that denied back pay to a machine operator whom a California chemical company had illegally fired for union activity. Why? Because he was an undocumented immigrant. The National Labor Relations Board (NLRB) had told Hoffman Plastics to give this man 3-1/2 years of back pay—the wages he would have earned if he hadn't been illegally fired—saying he deserved the same remedy that a documented worker would receive in the same circumstances. But the Supreme Court countered that immigration law takes precedence over labor law. "Allowing the Board to award back pay to illegal aliens would unduly trench upon explicit statutory prohibitions critical to federal immigration policy … and encourage future violations," wrote Chief Justice William Rehnquist in the 5–4 decision.

Now, awarding back pay to someone who was fired is not the same as owing wages for work actually done, a distinction apparently lost on Jesús Pérez's lawyer. But other lawyers with less garbled ideas about the potential meaning of the *Hoffman* decision are also testing the waters in courts across the country, trying to use the decision to overturn workers compensation awards and end enforcement of minimum wage and overtime laws for undocumented immigrants. This is happening even though *Hoffman Plastics'* lawyer argued explicitly that minimum wage and overtime laws should not be affected by the Court's decision in the case.

So far, these attempts have been unsuccessful. But immigrant rights advocates fear they will spend so much time putting out little legal fires across the country that they will be kept off balance and stuck in defensive mode, never able to set the agenda themselves. "It stops cases from moving forward and distracts resources," says Michael Wishnie, a New York University law professor who worked on *Hoffman*.

Other lawyers have already blocked at least two of these cases and are fighting numerous others. In Los Angeles, a District Court judge foiled an attempt by Albertsons, a supermarket chain, to intimidate janitors who had filed a class-action suit seeking the minimum wage for their past work. *Hoffman*, the judge said, was irrelevant to the case, and the company could not investigate the immigration status of its workers. A federal judge in New York said the same thing in June to garment manufacturer Donna Karan/DKNY, which is the defendant in a longstanding suit for overtime pay in New York City sweatshops.

Greg Shell of Florida Legal Services is confident he can beat back Mecca Farms, a large agricultural producer trying to weasel out of paying the minimum wage to thousands of its packinghouse and field workers who are now waging a class action suit against the company. "It's probably one of the ten largest growers in the U.S. [and] uses virtually all undocumented workers. And they're saying the workers have no rights to sue!" said Shell. "*Hoffman Plastics* has given them new hope. Their heart soared!" Ironically, he added, the head of Mecca Farms is vice chairman of Florida Farmers, a trade association that decries conditions in Mexican fields to win trade barriers that support American growers.

But while minimum wage and overtime laws may be less vulnerable, other areas of labor law are at greater risk, particularly those involving money damages such as anti-discrimination and workers compensation cases, says Shell. In Michigan, a company called Eagle Alloy is claiming it does not need to provide workers compensation to an undocumented worker. That case is now in the District Court of Appeals.

In a move that would have nationwide impact, the Equal Employment Opportunity Commission in June said it was reviewing its stance that federal anti-discrimination laws apply to all workers, no matter what their immigration status.

Labor activists are not depending on the courts to save them. They are lobbying regulators to prevent the extension of the Supreme Court's interpretation in *Hoffman* to other areas of law. The Washington State Department of Labor announced it would continue to enforce state labor laws, including workers comp, for all workers. In California, a novel bill is now before the state Senate that would exact penalties on any employer engaging in unfair labor practices against undocumented workers, put the money in a state fund, and then pay it out to the workers. The California AFL-CIO is the lead sponsor, backed by the Mexican American Legal Defense and Education Fund, La Raza, and other civil rights and labor groups.

In Washington, D.C., the AFL-CIO is quietly pulling together a bipartisan coalition to promote legislation clearly stating that all workers are covered by labor law and that employers must pay penalties if they violate the law, no matter what the immigration status of the worker. The coalition was given a narrow opening by the Supreme Court itself. "The Supreme Court said in its decision that if Congress disagreed with its balance of labor law and immigration law to make it plain," said Josh Bernstein, senior policy analyst at the National Immigration Law Center, which is working with the AFL. "We argue there is no contradiction. If you enforce labor law there is less incentive to violate the immigration law. This is even what the Bush administration said. It is only the Supreme Court that says otherwise." According to Bernstein, the bill might come up in December. "We have a good shot at being successful," he added.

In this campaign, labor and immigrant advocacy groups may find themselves with strange bedfellows. Like the garment manufacturers and Latino business organizations who filed an amicus brief opposing *Hoffman* on the grounds that it would create unfair competition with companies underpaying undocumented workers. Or the anti-immigrant groups that fear *Hoffman* will encourage the sweatshop economy and its concomitant demand for undocumented workers. And the AFL-CIO must work with allies who remember the Federation's sorry history in defending immigrant rights—it was only in February 2000 that the AFL called for an amnesty program and opposed employer sanctions—as well as those who notice that major state labor federations, like New York's, remain conspicuously silent.

At the grassroots level, Mr. Pérez was not able to stop Make the Road by Walking, the Brooklyn organization representing the worker he was refusing to pay, from picketing his butcher shop. However, other employers may be more successful in silencing and intimidating undocumented workers—and their documented coworkers who fear exposing them to retribution—without even going to court. In July, an undocumented seamstress asked Ursula Levelt, a New York labor lawyer, why she should file an NLRB claim against a scofflaw employer, when she would never see an award. Levelt had no answer for her.

IMMIGRANT WORKERS IN THE CROSSHAIRS
By David Bacon
January/February 2003

Erlinda Valencia came from the Philippines almost two decades ago. Like many Filipina immigrants living in the San Francisco Bay area, she found a job at the airport, screening passengers' baggage.

For 14 years she worked for Argenbright Security, the baggage-screening contractor used by airlines across the country. For most of that time, it was a minimum-wage job, and she could barely support her family working 40 hours a week. Then, two years ago, organizers from the Service Employees International Union (SEIU) began talking to the screeners. Erlinda Valencia decided to get involved, and eventually became a leader in the campaign that brought in the union. "We were very happy," she remembers. "It seemed to us all that for the first time, we had a real future." The new contract the union negotiated raised wages to over $10 an hour, and workers say harassment by managers began to decrease.

Erlinda Valencia's experience reflected a major national shift in immigrant workers' organizing. In recent years, immigrant workers made hard-fought gains in their rights at work, and in using these rights to organize unions and fight for better wages and conditions. Despite the hostile reaction embodied in measures like California's Propositions 187 and 227, which sought to penalize undocumented immigrants and ban bilingual education, the political and economic clout of immigrants has increased, in large part because of successful labor organizing efforts. Some, like the janitors' strike in Los Angeles, have become well-known.

As a result, the AFL-CIO changed its position on immigration, and began calling for the repeal of employer sanctions, the federal law making it illegal for an undocumented worker to hold a job. The national movement for amnesty for undocumented workers began to grow, and the U.S. and Mexican governments started to negotiate over variants of the proposal. Under pressure from unions and immigrant rights organizations, the Immigration and Naturalization Service (INS) reduced the number of raids it carried out from 17,000 in 1997 to 953 in 2000.

Then the airplanes hit the twin towers in New York and the Pentagon in Washington. The mainstream media universally portrayed the September 11 attacks as the actions of immigrants. Political figures across the board proposed restrictions on immigration (by students, for instance) and crackdowns against undocumented workers, despite the fact that none of this would have prevented the attacks. The movement towards amnesty, and away from immigration raids and heavy-handed enforcement tactics, halted abruptly. Many public agencies, from local police departments to the Social Security Administration, which previously faced pressure to stop aiding the INS, took up immigration enforcement as a new responsibility. The Bush administration took advantage of the anti-immigrant fever to undermine the rights of workers, especially the foreign-born. The nativist scapegoating also provided a rationale for attacks on civil liberties, including the open use of racial profiling, indefinite detention, and other repressive measures.

Everything Changes—for Transportation Workers

Screeners like Erlinda Valencia were among the first, and hardest, hit. Media and politicians blamed the screeners for allowing terrorists to board airplanes in Boston and New York with box cutters and plastic knives, despite the fact that these items were permitted at the time. But the whispered undercurrent beneath the criticism, that the screeners were undependable, and possibly even disloyal, was part of the rising anti-immigrant fever which swept the country.

Screeners in California airports, like those in many states where immigrants are a big part of the population, are mostly from other countries. In fact, the low pay for screeners was one of the factors that led to the concentration of immigrants and people of color in those jobs. In the search for scapegoats, they were easy targets.

In short order, Congress passed legislation setting up a new Transportation Security Authority (TSA) to oversee baggage and passenger screening at airports, and requiring that screeners be federal government employees. That could have been a good thing for Valencia and her coworkers, since federal employees have decent salaries, and often, because of civil service, lots of job security. Federal regulations protect their right to belong to unions, as well—at least they used to.

The TSA, however, was made part of the recently established Homeland Security Department. Legislation passed after the November elections—and after some Democrats did an about face and voted for it—allows Homeland Security Czar Tom Ridge to suspend civil-service regulations in any part of the new department. By doing so, he can eliminate workers' union rights, allow discrimination and favoritism, and even abolish protection for whistleblowers.

In the anti-immigrant fever of the times, moreover, Congress required that screeners be citizens. Valencia had never become one, because of a Catch-22 in U.S. immigration law. She is petitioning for visas for family members in the

Philippines. As a citizen, however, she would actually have to wait longer to petition for them than she has to as a legal resident.

At the San Francisco airport, over 800 screeners were non-citizens. The INS, however, refused to establish any fast-track to citizenship, to help them qualify for the new federalized jobs. So just as she and her coworkers finally made the job bearable and capable of supporting a family, she lost it in November, when the citizenship requirement went into effect nationwide. "It's so unfair," she said. "I've done this job for 14 years, and we're all really good at it. Instead of wanting us to continue, they're going to hire people with no experience at all, and we'll probably have to train them too. You can fly the airplane, even if you're not a citizen, and you can carry a rifle in the airport as a member of the National Guard doing security, without being a citizen either. But you can't check the bags of the passengers."

In recent years, screeners working for private contractors like Argenbright have organized unions at airports in a number of cities, including San Francisco and Los Angeles. By federalizing the workforce, the government was also, in effect, busting those unions and tearing up their newly won contracts. The act creating the Homeland Security Department—which, with 170,000 employees, will be the largest in the federal government—may be invoked to prevent the new screener workforce from forming new unions and bargaining with the TSA. The American Federation of Government Employees, which represents federal workers, has protested against the exemption of the TSA from federal regulations recognizing employees' collective bargaining rights, and announced its intention of organizing the new workforce. But it does not challenge the citizenship requirement for screeners.

Taking the "War" to the Workplace

Valencia was caught up in a wave of anti-immigrant legislation and repression that has profoundly affected immigrants and workers across the country in the wake of the September 11 terrorist attacks. The INS has launched a series of large-scale raids—Operation Tarmac. In airports around the country, the agency has told employers to provide the I-9 form for their employees. Using this information, agents have organized raids to pick up workers, and demanded that employers terminate those it says lack legal status. Close to 1,000 workers have been affected.

Initially, the INS stated publicly that it would only concentrate on workers who had access to the planes themselves, using aviation security as a pretext (hence the name Operation Tarmac). But once the raids got going, the crackdown expanded to workers in food preparation, and even in food service within passenger areas of the airports. A late-August raid at the Seattle-Tacoma International Airport led to the arrest of workers at the Sky Chef facility, which prepares on-board meals for airlines. The Hotel Employees and Restaurant Employees International Union (HERE), which is negotiating a contract with the company, claims that workers were called to an employee meeting, where they were met by INS agents in company uniforms. Some arrested workers had worked as long as 10 years at the facility, which ironically is owned by a foreign airline, Lufthansa.

Another 81 airport workers were arrested in raids on the Los Angeles, Orange County, Ontario (Calif.), Palm Springs, and Long Beach airports on August 22. The detained immigrants were working in janitorial, food service, maintenance, and baggage-handling jobs. They were picked up because they apparently were using Social Security numbers which didn't match the INS database. While federal authorities admit that none of them—in fact none of the people arrested in any Operation Tarmac raid—are accused of terrorist activity, U.S. Attorney Debra Yang claimed that "we now realize that we must strengthen security at our local airports in order to ensure the safety of the traveling public." Eliseo Medina, executive vice-president of the SEIU, which has mounted organizing drives among many of the workers in Southern California airports, called the arrests unwarranted. "These people aren't terrorists," he fumed. "They only want to work." Unions like the Communications Workers of America (CWA) have protested Operation Tarmac raids in Washington, D.C., and elsewhere.

While the anti-immigrant campaign may have started at U.S. airports, it has now expanded far beyond their gates. The agency taking the new anti-immigrant attitude most to heart has been the Social Security Administration (SSA). Following the September 11 attacks, the SSA has flooded U.S. workplaces with "no-match letters," which the agency sends to employers informing them of employees whose Social Security numbers don't correspond to the SSA database.

In the last few years, employers have used no-match letters to fire immigrant workers during union organizing drives, or to intimidate those attempting to enforce worker protection laws. Until September 11, unions were making some headway in preventing these abuses. Two years ago, San Francisco's hotel union, HERE Local 2, won an important arbitrator's decision, which held that finding the name of a worker in a no-match letter was not, by itself, sufficient reason for terminating her. In addition, pressure on the SSA resulted in the inclusion, in the text of the letter, of a similar caveat, saying that inclusion in a no-match list was not to be taken as evidence of lack of immigration status.

In the wake of September 11, however, SSA has consciously embraced the no-match letter as an immigration-enforcement device. In 2001, the agency sent out 110,000 letters, and only when there were more than ten no-matches at a company or if the no-matches represented at least 10% of a company's total workforce. This year it plans to increase the number of letters to 750,000, and all it takes is one no-match to generate a letter. The pretext is September 11: "Concerns about national security, along with the growing problem of identity theft, have caused us to accelerate our efforts," according to SSA Commissioner Jo Anne Barnhart. The Internal Revenue Service has also sharply increased the number of letters sent to employers questioning incorrect numbers, and has threatened to begin fining employers who provide them. As in the case of Valencia and the screeners, however, there is no logic that connects a worker's immigration status with national security. And proponents of these changes don't even bother trying to produce an explanation that does.

The new attitude at Social Security marks an important change. In Nebraska in 1998, Operation Vanguard, a large-scale INS program to enforce employer sanctions, relied on the SSA's database to sift out the names of possible undocumented immigrants from the rolls of all the state's meatpacking employees. Over 3,000 people lost their jobs as a result. The INS had plans to extend the operation to other states, but was unable to do so when the SSA expressed misgivings about the INS's use of its database, and denied further access. The SSA had faced pressure from immigrants' rights groups and labor unions, who questioned why information intended to ensure that workers receive retirement and disability benefits was suddenly being used to take their jobs. After September 11, 2001, such objections were brushed aside.

The net effect of the new enforcement efforts has been to turn the Social Security card into a *de facto* national ID card, especially for employment, without any act of Congress creating one. Immigrant rights and civil liberties advocates have fought for years against the creation of a national ID, saying that it would inevitably lead to abuse by government and employers, and that it would eventually become a kind of internal passport. And Congress has been unwilling to establish such a national identification system, at least until September 11.

An Injury to All

The wave of repression against immigrant workers hasn't just affected immigrants themselves. Limitations on workers' rights affect all workers. But because immigrants have been in the forefront of organizing unions and fighting sweatshop conditions, the threat against them has increased the danger that such conditions will spread, and affect workers throughout the labor force.

INS enforcement has increased the pressure on undocumented workers to avoid anything that could antagonize their employers, whether organizing a union, asking for a raise, or filing a complaint about unpaid overtime. There are almost 8 million undocumented people in the United States—4% of the urban workforce, and over half of all farm workers—according to a recent study by the Pew Hispanic Trust. When it becomes more risky and difficult for these workers to organize and join unions, or even to hold a job at all, they settle for lower wages. And when the price of immigrant labor goes down as a result, so do wages for other workers.

Attacks on immigrant workers have an especially big effect on unions trying to organize industries where immigrants are a large part of the workforce. The Operation Tarmac raids, for instance, hurt hotel unions' efforts to organize food service workers. The unions organizing immigrants are some of the most progressive in the labor movement. Unions like the Hotel Employees and Restaurant Employees have been disproportionately hit by the anti-immigrant offensive. Other unions, like the Teamsters and Laborers, have also led immigrant rights activity in many local areas, and suffered the impact of no-match letters and raids. Although the Bush administration has courted these unions' national leaders, the relationship doesn't seem to have provided any political leverage for stopping anti-immigrant abuses.

Organizing a Fightback

Today, employers illegally fire workers for union activity in 31% of all union organizing campaigns, affecting immigrant and native-born workers alike. Companies treat the cost of legal battles, reinstatement, and back pay as a cost of doing business, and many consider it cheaper than signing a union contract. Labor rights for all workers need to be strengthened, not weakened. But, as former National Labor Relations Board chair William Gould IV points out, "There's a basic conflict between U.S. labor law and U.S. immigration law." In its recent *Hoffman* decision (see Abby Scher, "When Is a Labor Law Violation Not a Labor Law Violation?"), the Supreme Court has held that the enforcement of employer sanctions, which makes it illegal for an undocumented immigrant to hold a job, is more important than the right of that worker to join a union and resist exploitation on the job.

Despite the decision, however, and the growing anti-immigrant climate, immigrants workers are still organizing. In May, four hundred workers won a hard-fought union election at the ConAgra beef plant in Omaha, a city where INS raids destroyed immigrant-based union committees only a few years ago. New Jersey recycling workers at KTI also finally won a union vote, on their fourth attempt to join the Laborers Union, which is also organizing successful campaigns among asbestos workers on Long Island. HERE won a 22-year battle for a contract at San Francisco's Flagship Marriott Hotel, the hotel chain's first corporate-managed property to sign a union agreement.

The union-based efforts for amnesty and the repeal of employer sanctions were dealt a serious blow by the post-September 11 climate, but there are signs of renewed forward movement. SEIU Local 790, in cooperation with Filipinos for Affirmative Action and the Phillip Veracruz Justice Project, led efforts to fight for screeners' jobs at the San Francisco airport. The SEIU also initiated a national postcard campaign, called A Million Voices for Justice, to restart the national campaign for amnesty. In August, the SEIU and the ACLU sued the Department of Transportation over the citizenship requirement, and in mid-November Federal District Court Judge Robert Takasugi ruled the requirement illegal. The decision, however, only applies to the nine workers in whose names the suit was filed. Lawyers for the plaintiffs hope to broaden it to a class-action, while federal authorities predictably announced they would appeal.

Last summer, HERE announced plans for a Freedom Ride on Washington, D.C., for immigrant rights. The union deliberately chose the name and used the language of the civil-rights movement in an effort to establish a greater level of unity between African Americans, Latinos, and Asian-Americans. HERE officials also said they intended to challenge the color line—employers have kept African-Americans out of hotel employment, while hiring immigrants at lower wages—in hotels across the country. Massive layoffs and the economic downturn in tourism made plans to challenge hiring discrimination a moot point, but in the spring, HERE announced that it would again begin organizing its Freedom Ride, and set it for fall 2003.

And while Erlinda Valencia was one of the nine named plaintiffs in the suit against the citizenship requirement, the favorable court decision only means, at best, that she can take a test to qualify for her old job. If she takes it and passes, she will be put on a list of eligible potential employees. Her old job at the airport and those of her coworkers have already been filled. Preliminary studies indicate that many new hires are ex-members of the military and law enforcement agencies, and that the new workforce does not include nearly as many immigrants or people of color as the old one.

Valencia, like may other former screeners, has found herself looking for another job. The labor councils, unions, and immigrant rights activists who supported the screeners mounted food drives, tried to help former screeners get retraining, and tried to help them find stable new employment. But the larger challenge, they believe, is building a political movement to roll back the anti-immigrant atmosphere in which Valencia, and many like her, have become ensnared.

SEPTEMBER 11 AND THE RESTRUCTURING OF THE AIRLINE INDUSTRY
By Rodney Ward
May/June 2002, updated May 2003

On September 11, 2001, stunned flight attendants and pilots learned that workplaces just like theirs had been transformed into lethal missiles. Flight workers lucky enough not to be on one of the hijacked planes prepared frantically for orders to land at the nearest airport. Crews then worked to calm passengers and arrange for transportation and lodging. In some cases, school gymnasiums accommodated passengers and crew, while church buses provided rides to the nearest sizeable city.

Through the four-day grounding of the U.S. civilian airlines, airline unions' Employee Assistance Programs worked overtime to provide support for traumatized workers. Crews themselves huddled together in front of TVs, watching as the nightmare unfolded before them, worrying about their friends and future.

As the first flights began again on September 15, some crews refused to fly, not confident of airport security. Those who steeled themselves to work entered a strange new workplace. With no guidance from the airlines or the Federal Aviation

Administration (FAA) on how to handle potential future hijackings, flight attendants inventoried galleys for objects they could use as defensive weapons. Shell-shocked passengers sometimes hugged flight attendants as they boarded. Many crew members barely contained tears, often hiding in galleys to avoid alarming passengers.

But as airline workers returned to the skies, a new danger loomed: layoffs. On September 15, Continental announced that it would cut 12,000 jobs. One by one, the other airlines followed suit: United and American announced 20,000 layoffs each; Northwest, 10,000; US Airways, 11,000. Delta forecast eliminating 13,000. As the toll topped 140,000, *Washington Post* writer David Montgomery quipped: "What thanks are flight attendants getting? How does this sound: You're fired."

The September 11 catastrophe hit the airline industry hard, but it also opened the door for airlines to accelerate the restructuring they already had underway. Many airlines, including giants like US Airways, were in bad shape *before* September 11. And the industry's agenda already included layoffs, mergers, greater restrictions on airline workers' rights, and a global deregulation of air travel. If post-9/11 politics allow the airlines to impose these changes, this will hurt not only airline workers, but also working people beyond the aviation industry.

The Executive Response

Within hours of the September 11 hijackings, an army of airline lobbyists descended on Congress (whose members have received $12 million in airline-industry contributions since 1998). The mission: Demand a massive taxpayer bailout for the industry (as much as $24 billion). If Congress failed to pony up the cash, the airlines would become "a major casualty of war," argued Delta CEO Leo Mullin.

While pleading their case, the airlines neglected to request any aid for the airline workers they were preparing to dump. Both houses of Congress defeated amendments, proposed by House Minority Leader Richard Gephardt (D-MO) and Sen. Jean Carnahan (D-MO), to provide relief to laid-off workers. Greg Crist, the spokesperson for House Majority Leader Dick Armey (R-TX), rationalized his boss's opposition as "focused on getting the airline industry back on its feet and [thus] getting these people back on the job. An expanded unemployment insurance benefit won't do anything to get you back on the job." It took six more months for Congress to provide even meager aid supplements for airline workers. (Even then, the March 9, 2002 unemployment extension legislation tacked on $8 in corporate tax breaks for every $1 spent on aid to laid-off workers.)

Rather than simply neglecting workers, however, the bailout does worse—it encourages attacks on union contracts and working conditions. Office of Management and Budget regulations state that airlines getting bailout money should provide a "demonstration of concessions by the air carrier's security holders, other creditors, or employees...." Not surprisingly, it's the employees who are bearing the brunt.

With the war on Iraq, the airlines received yet another bailout of $3.2 billion, as well as commercial airlift contracts worth nearly half a billion dollars. Once again, the wartime bailout requires airlines to cut operating costs, which will certainly mean more pressure for concessions from workers.

Leaving aside tax cuts and new military contracts, Congress has handed the airlines $18.2 billion in taxpayer money since 2001: $8.2 billion in direct grants and $10 billion in loan guarantees. At the depressed prices of airline stocks, the government could have easily bought a controlling interest in the entire industry for $18.2 billion. In another place or another time, the airlines might have been nationalized under management by airline workers. But this is far from the reality in Washington, D.C., today.

Downsizing Stock Prices, Downsizing Airlines

September 11, of course, delivered a serious hit to the airlines' bottom line. Troubled Midway Airlines closed up shop on September 12, 2001. (The company has since resumed limited operations, aided by bailout money.) In the following weeks, airplanes flew mostly empty. As the airlines shed workers, they also mothballed planes. Today there are approximately 2,400 planes, about 11% of the world's civilian air fleet, parked in the Mojave Desert.

Airline shares plummeted when the stock markets reopened on September 17. US Airways and America West shares each lost over half their value in just one day. The rest of the airlines suffered declines as well. Recently, some airline stocks have recovered to pre-September 11 levels, but several, like US Airways, are still in the dumps.

Competitive pressure, already at a high pitch, intensified. While big carriers like United, American, and Northwest downsized, Southwest and startup carrier JetBlue refused to lay employees off and began to move into markets the industry giants had evacuated. The economic shockwaves rolled through the aviation industry globally. Sabena and Swissair collapsed. British Airways carried out massive layoffs. British and Japanese carriers sought mergers. Other carriers (including Iberia and Air India) announced capacity cuts and restructurings. So did aircraft manufacturers.

Not All Bad News, If You're An Airline Executive

Not all economic impacts on the airlines have been negative, however. The industry is extremely capital intensive, its two largest costs being airplanes and fuel. Deferrals on airplane orders, the retirement of older and less fuel-efficient planes, and a tremendous drop in global fuel prices have dramatically cut costs. Though labor costs represent a small portion of overall airline costs (flight attendants represent less than 4.5% of operating expenses at United, for example), slashing the workforce also cut airline expenses.

So far, over 300 airlines have collected over $8 billion in bailout money. The lion's share has gone to industry giants United, American, and Delta. Also, on

March 9, Congress passed a new tax break for the airlines. Airlines are now allowed to claim losses from 2001 and 2002 on their taxes over the last five years, a change that could mean $2 billion in cash for the companies.

In addition, the airlines routinely carry "business-interruption" insurance to cover losses due to weather, strikes, or other unforeseen circumstances. It's not clear how much airlines are collecting on claims stemming from the four-day shutdown of U.S. airports in September. The *Baltimore Sun* reported that, when asked about business-interruption insurance, US Airways spokesperson David Castelveter replied guiltily, "That's something I don't think we would publicly discuss with anyone." The insurance firm Swiss Re, however, estimated in March that September 11-related business-interruption claims (to all industries) will amount to $3.5–$7 billion. Undoubtedly, a big chunk will go to the airlines.

The Aviation World Before September 11

Deregulation Degradation

The airline industry's chaotic state is not just a result of the September 11 attacks, but also the culmination of a quarter century of deregulation. Advocates had touted the 1978 Airline Deregulation Act as a way to increase competition and bring down ticket prices. Indeed, deregulation initially enabled upstart carriers to get in the air and made flying affordable for many people who had never flown before.

But that was not the whole story. Since deregulation, service to smaller, less profitable cities has suffered and pricing has become a crazy quilt of discriminatory arrangements. Travel to and from many airports has become monopolized by one or a few airlines. Nonetheless, airlines operate on very tight profit margins compared to other industries. As airline bottom lines have been squeezed, argues author Paul Stephen Dempsey, so has the margin of safety.

Deregulation resulted in a host of problems for airline workers, too. New competitive pressures caused the airline industry to lose more money in a few years than it had made in all the years prior to 1978 combined. These losses led to mergers and bankruptcies, and set the stage for leveraged buyouts. Financier Frank Lorenzo took over both Continental and Eastern, and then used Chapter 11 bankruptcy to break union contracts at both airlines.

Consolidation or death became the choices for many carriers. The competitive carnage destroyed once-great airlines such as Braniff and PanAm, and saw many others gobbled up. USAir bought PSA and Piedmont (ultimately dismantling PSA's entire West Coast operation). Delta swallowed up Western and the remains of PanAm, while Northwest took over Republic. More recently, American Airlines absorbed the venerable TWA. Not only did these mergers lead to route disruptions, but they also destroyed thousands of jobs, as overlapping sections of newly merged companies created "redundancies." The mergers also created challenges for union workforces—how to integrate seniority lists, for example.

Conflicts over seniority in the American-TWA merger will likely sow internal union conflicts for years to come.

Management Mishaps

Spectacularly inspired mismanagement by airline executives actually deserves much of the blame for the state of the industry. Airline workers frequently complain that they could run the airlines better than the executives. Meanwhile, management jealously guards its decision-making prerogatives against labor input. Who's right? You be the judge.

Over a year ago, the Airline Pilots Association (ALPA), proposed to US Airways management "hedging" on fuel (purchasing options to buy fuel in the future at current prices) while prices were low. This would protect the airline against expected increases in fuel costs. Company management rejected the suggestion. After that, fuel prices skyrocketed and so did a major portion of the airline's costs. Several pilots have bitterly joked to me that the entire pilot group could work for free for a year and a half and still not make up for management's mistake.

In another case, in 2000, United Airlines stonewalled its pilots in contract negotiations to the point that pilots refused to volunteer for overtime. This led to 9,000 flight cancellations that summer. A key demand of the pilots was that the company hire more pilots (who wants exhausted pilots working overtime anyway?). Eventually the company gave in to the pilots' demands, but only after alienating huge numbers of passengers.

Frank Reeves of Avitas, a Virginia airline consulting firm, told the *Pittsburgh Post-Gazette* that the post-September 11 crisis has given management "a golden opportunity ... to write off all the bad decisions they made over the last 10 years."

September 11 and the Airline Labor Movement

Airline management, of course, still has workers—and their unions—to contend with. Despite working under the restrictive Railway Labor Act (RLA), 80–85% of airline workers are unionized. This makes the airline industry one of the most heavily unionized sectors in the U.S. economy. The airline unions operate along craft lines, with separate unions for pilots, flight attendants, baggage handlers, mechanics, customer service agents, and flight instructors. The Airline Pilots Association (ALPA) is the largest pilots' union, while the Association of Flight Attendants (AFA) represents most flight attendants. Most mechanics and baggage handlers belong to the International Association of Machinists (IAM).

Force Majeure

The most immediate impact of September 11 on workers throughout the airline industry, of course, was massive job loss. Most airline unions have job security or "no furlough" clauses in their collective bargaining agreements. Airline management, however, claimed that since the hijackings were an "act of war," the airlines could activate "*force majeure*" clauses in the agreements to escape their contractual obligations. *Force majeure* (literally, "greater power") is a commercial contract law doctrine that releases parties to a contract from their obligations due to circumstances outside their control (an "act of God," act of war, that sort of thing). There is little or no precedent for the use of *force majeure* in labor contract law. Nonetheless, several airlines invoked the phrase as an excuse to disregard seniority rights, severance packages, and advance notice as they laid off thousands.

The business press dutifully reported airline claims that the union contracts contained "little-known" *force majeure* clauses. In reality, the alleged "clauses" in union contracts were little known because they did not exist. The airlines are simply trying to use this doctrine in the same way Frank Lorenzo used bankruptcy in the 1980s: to smash union contracts and attack airline workers. Though subsequent uproar has forced airline management to reverse itself on seniority and severance pay, the violation of no-layoff clauses is still working its way through the arduous process of arbitration under the RLA (even "expedited arbitration" can take nine months or more).

Delta Union Election

Airline union elections are different from those in most of the private sector. Under the RLA, ballots only have a "yes" box. If a ballot is not mailed in, for whatever reason, the National Mediation Board (NMB), the body that oversees airline labor relations under the RLA, counts it as a "no" vote. To win, a union must get a majority of the eligible votes. (Under the National Labor Relations Act [NLRA], which governs most workers in the private sector, the union only needs a majority of the votes cast.)

On August 29, 2001, the Association of Flight Attendants (AFA) filed for an RLA election at Delta. Delta management had already been planning a sophisticated campaign of anti-union propaganda and interference in the election. The September 11 attacks, however, gave management the opportunity to claim that now was not the time to talk about a union. Now was the time to save Delta!

Delta was afraid to provoke workers by inflicting massive layoffs in the middle of a union campaign. So the airline offered "voluntary" leaves of absence to flight attendants. An estimated 4,000 to 5,000 accepted. In reality, many of the "voluntary" leaves resulted from management threats and harassment, so they might as well have been involuntary. Soon after, a management newsletter incorrectly stated that flight attendants on leave would be ineligible to vote in the union election. Management later corrected itself, but only in an email message to which on-leave flight attendants had no access. The airline also subjected workers to frequent captive meetings devoted to anti-union harangues. Many supervisors implied that union supporters were disloyal, in a time of crisis, to the company and the country.

During the election campaign, union activists spoke to many flight attendants who either said they wanted a union but that now was not the time, or that they just couldn't make up their minds. In the end, 5,609 flight attendants voted for AFA, about 60% of the 9,517 the union needed to win.

The story, however, does not end there. The AFA has filed a case with the NMB alleging illegal interference by Delta. If the board rules in favor of the union, it may order a new election. The board has no power to make Delta management follow the law, so the airline could certainly interfere again. A fairer election solution would be a "Laker Ballot" (named in honor of former British carrier Laker Air, which was once punished for interference with a new, simple-majority election). This would mean an election held along the lines of an NLRA election, with ballots that read "yes/no" and only ballots actually cast counted in the total.

A Blank Check for Concessions

In December, all the airlines turned their attention to United's negotiations with its International Association of Machinists (IAM)-represented mechanics, waiting to see how talks unfolded before demanding concessions themselves. The United-IAM contract, the first big one to be negotiated since September 11, would be the first test of the airlines' ability to extract concessions in the wake of the attacks.

The 15,000 mechanics (and related classifications), represented by IAM Lodge 141M, first voted on a Presidential Emergency Board Recommendation. The proposed agreement included a "linkage" clause, which would require mechanics to participate in any "recovery plan" (meaning concessions) to which other United employee groups agreed, or to make concessions if United declared there was a threat of bankruptcy. The mechanics soundly rejected it—over two thirds voted "no." When the IAM's international leadership endorsed an almost-identical agreement, however, it passed. The contract includes major wage increases for better-paid IAM members. By ratifying the agreement with "linkage" included, however, the IAM basically handed United a blank check for future concessions.

Some 23,000 other United Airlines ground workers (baggage handlers, customer service workers, and others) represented by IAM Lodge 141 still remain without a contract. In March, they requested the NMB formally declare an impasse so they could move towards a strike. The airline said it would conclude negotiations with the ground workers before demanding across-the-board wage cuts. (Union activists believe Lodge 141 and United will come to an agreement before the United board meeting in May.) Meanwhile, the independent Airline Mechanics Fraternal Association (AMFA) has challenged the IAM for representation of United machinists, and some workers at the airline have begun rank-and-file organizing in response to the mechanics' contract. (An excellent analysis can be found in the April 2002 edition of *Labor Notes* <www.labornotes.org>.)

Nonetheless, the IAM has set an important precedent for concessions. Other airlines already smell blood in the water. The current US Airways-ALPA contract includes a pay provision (a system demanded by management in the last contract talks) called "parity + 1." This means pilots' wages are adjusted every year to equal the average at other major carriers, plus 1%. Since US Airways adopted the system, pilots at Delta and United have made major wage gains, pushing up pay for US Airways pilots as well. In response, new US Airways CEO David Siegel declared that parity + 1 made no sense for the airline (despite the fact that it was management's idea to begin with). It is the opening volley in US Airways' attack on the unions.

The Challenges for Airline Labor

The long-term trend of airline consolidation continues to the present. American Airlines absorbed TWA in 2000, and United and US Airways proposed to merge. Though the United-US Airways merger was blocked by the Justice Department on anti-trust grounds, the question of consolidation lingered on before September 11. There was serious talk of a merger between Delta and either Northwest or Continental.

Delta CEO Leo Mullin spent last fall and winter parading around the country declaring that the government must shed its aversion to big airline mergers. Rumors now abound about new mergers in the works. According to Holly Hegeman of the business-news website TheStreet.com, Delta and America West may be in serious negotiations. Even if large-scale mergers fall through, it is likely that larger airlines will gobble up small to medium-sized carriers. Further consolidation would certainly result in layoffs for large numbers of airline workers.

Merger discussions have even contemplated treaties to allow international consolidation. Presently, U.S. regulations limit foreign ownership of airlines, as well as landing rights for foreign carriers. Some proposals to change this are bilateral, like the Transatlantic Common Aviation Area, which would allow mergers between airlines in the United States and the European Union. More ambitiously, the International Chamber of Commerce argues that the world airline industry should be deregulated all at once by including commercial aviation in the proposed General Agreement on Trade in Services (GATS). In addition to allowing global airline mergers, this would likely introduce the "flag of convenience" status for airlines. Carriers could formally register themselves in any country, potentially choosing those with lax labor laws and low wages (as cruise ships do).

Airline workers also face more direct attacks as part of the current industry restructuring. A chorus of industry voices has gone up advocating reforms to the Railway Labor Act. Though the RLA, through a maze of waiting periods, makes it extremely difficult for airline employees to strike, even this is too much for some in management and in Congress. Legislation sponsored by Sen. John McCain (R-AZ), proposes a binding arbitration system that would virtually eliminate airline workers' right to strike. Delta, United, and Federal Express are among the companies championing the legislative attack. Not surprisingly, all three are major contributors to both parties. Fedex made a $5,000 contribution to McCain in the 1999–2000 election cycle.

Airline unions are not quite ready for the challenges coming their way. Though the industry is highly unionized, the unions are extremely balkanized. For example, five different unions represent flight attendants (including the Teamsters at Northwest, the IAM at Continental, Transport Workers Union at Southwest, and the Independent Association of Professional Flight Attendants at American).

Moreover, while unions representing different work groups have formed coalitions, the craft structure of the unions and the dramatic pay disparities between different work groups represent barriers to building solidarity. Pilots represent the elite of the airline workforce, with jumbo-jet pilots at mainline carriers making up to $200,000 a year. Yet junior pilots at "regional jet" carriers (RJs) can make as little as $15,000 a year, hardly an elite salary. The mainline-RJ disparity also exists, to a lesser magnitude, for flight attendants. Even within the same bargaining units, mechanics get higher pay than other ground workers. Customer service agents, meanwhile, are among the lowest paid of all airline workers. Just go to any airline-worker electronic bulletin board to witness the sniping about pay differentials. This only gets worse among workers at different airlines.

The good news is that a coalition of flight-attendant unions has fought, in the wake of September 11, for safer workplaces, federal whistleblower protection for airline workers, and relief for laid-off airline workers. Within some airlines, coalitions of airline unions from different work groups are forming united fronts against management concession demands.

But much of the coalition building, even among union locals, takes place only within the leadership. Membership meetings at airline unions are rare—the constant travel inherent for pilots and flight attendants certainly contributes to this problem—and rank-and-file participation is generally reserved for contract-negotiation times. Rank-and-file members, meanwhile, generally regard their unions as service providers for negotiations and grievances. Many members assume that this is what they pay dues for and expect the union to function, in the words of one veteran activist, as "a giant grievance machine."

This "service" model, however, is completely inadequate in the current crisis. To build the necessary capacity for struggle, the unions need to become social movements again. We need greater rank-and-file participation, more member education, and greater mobilization (not just at contract negotiation time). We need more solidarity among different work groups, between workers at different airlines, among airline workers from different countries, and between the airline unions and the rest of the labor movement. And we need to fight for labor-law reform that makes it easier, not harder, to organize and strike.

Unless we rise to these challenges, we will see far worse than just the decline of the airline unions. The airline industry has been a bellwether for the labor movement as a whole since Reagan fired striking air traffic controllers in 1981. If management succeeds in weakening the unions and eroding working conditions in such a densely unionized industry, it will encourage further attacks on unions and workers far beyond the airlines. What happens next will depend upon how well airline workers and their unions understand these threats, and on the potential power of their solidarity.

Chapter 4

SEVEN YEARS OF WELFARE "REFORM"

INTRODUCTION

The poor are rarely big news. In recent years, most of the coverage of poverty that the mainstream press has mustered has focused on the 1996 Personal Responsibility and Work Opportunities Reconciliation Act, commonly referred to as "welfare reform." This law has been hailed by both Republicans and Democrats as a huge success, and perhaps the greatest policy achievement of the Clinton administration.

Policymakers and the press typically back up the "unqualified success" moniker by citing the dramatic drop in welfare caseloads since 1996. Indeed, the number of families receiving benefits under Temporary Assistance to Needy Families (TANF)—formerly Aid to Families with Dependent Children—fell by 52% between 1996 and 2000. And in photo ops around the country over the past seven years, both Bill Clinton and George W. Bush have found women to pose beside them and describe how they have transformed their lives for the better under welfare reform.

That sounds great. But here's what you won't hear in the conventional discourse about welfare reform. You won't hear much analysis of what the caseload drop actually means. Does it mean that the families in question have achieved self-sufficiency, or only that they're facing continuing hardship with no assistance? Is the fall in caseloads primarily a result of the new welfare law, or does the late-nineties economic expansion in fact deserve the credit? And what are the broader economic consequences of gutting "countercyclical" programs such as welfare—programs that used to automatically increase government spending during economic downturns, stabilizing the economy?

Likewise, you won't hear much detail about what is happening in welfare offices around the country under the new law—how states, which now receive federal welfare funds in the form of "block grants" with few strings attached, are spending the funds and administering the program. You won't hear much about the politics behind welfare reform—about the political alignments that undergird the welfare reform coalition and the political benefits it has brought them. You won't hear any analysis of how welfare programs both old and new are shaped so as to regulate and control the lives of poor people.

Finally, and perhaps most important, you won't hear from a wide range of recipients and former recipients themselves. You won't come to understand the lived experience of being a poor parent, of struggling to comply with the often-punitive requirements of the new law, or of fighting for a better program as the 1996 law comes up for reauthorization in Congress. You won't learn about the impact that welfare reform has had on particular segments of low-income America, particularly on immigrants.

Beth Brockland, whose perspective is informed by her work with low-income people around the country, begins to fill in some of these gaps. She explains the structural changes in welfare that the 1996 law brought about, and gives voice to actual recipients, making it clear that whatever others may believe, many low-income people see welfare reform as anything but an "unqualified success" ("Reforming Welfare Reform"). Economist Heather Boushey demonstrates how the apparent success of welfare reform was dependent on the very atypical late-nineties economy. Although welfare reform was "impeccably well timed," she notes, low-income families have still been unable to make ends meet. The outlook for poor families is even less rosy now that the economy is in recession; in fact, she argues, this recession has hit the service sector—and the many low-income women workers who toil in it—particularly hard. And when the next expansion gets underway, Boushey shows how it is unlikely to perform the magic that the last one did ("Good Times, Bad Times").

Welfare reformers tout the value of work—any work at any wage—for poor women; they play, more or less subtly, on racially-charged stereotypes of recipients as lazy and unwilling to work. Since even the go-go economy of the late '90s did not provide enough jobs to allow states to meet the new law's work requirements, many states created so-called "workfare" programs in which recipients "work off" their benefits in public works or community service jobs. Dan Feder describes a hidden agenda these programs serve: crippling public-sector unions by replacing well-paid union jobs with virtually unpaid workfare positions ("Work First—Where Are the Wages?"). James Ridgeway outlines another untold story: how welfare reform has drawn disparate corners of the Republican tent together by privatizing the provision of welfare-related services, in particular by contracting with religious groups. Thus does welfare reform appeal to two conservative constituencies who do not often see eye to eye: the Christian right, which enjoys seeing public funding diverted to religious charities, and libertarians, who oppose the government social safety net on principle and are happy to see it shrink ("Ministering to the Poor").

Tami J. Friedman questions the structure of welfare spending under the new law. The federal government now hands block grants to states with little regulation, producing dismal results: during the 1990s, states failed to build up rainy day funds to prepare for the next economic downturn. Instead, they substituted federal dollars for their own welfare expenditures, freeing up those state dollars to spend elsewhere. And under welfare reform, since welfare is no longer an entitlement, the federal government has no obligation—and, apparently, no plans—to fill the gap by increasing its own welfare expenditures during a recession, when more families need help ("How States Are Spending Their Welfare Money—Or Not").

The point of any change in welfare programs should be to reduce poverty, not just caseloads. The U.S. poverty rate did fall during the late 1990s, but has crept back up during the recession—and there's some evidence that the number of people living in extreme poverty has risen. However the statistics rise and fall, it's critical to ask questions that go beyond changes in caseload numbers. The authors in this chapter provide the tools to understand the welfare-reform debate in depth and to develop a realistic assessment of this monumental change in U.S. social policy.

REFORMING WELFARE REFORM
By Beth Brockland
September/October 2002

Catrina Weber never made enough at her fast-food jobs to be able to pay her rent and still have enough left over to provide a good life for her three-year-old son. Without a high-school diploma, however, she found it difficult to land higher-paying jobs. Like many parents who are trapped in the low-wage labor market, Catrina often relied on public assistance for extra help while she was in between jobs or when she was working but simply earning too little to make ends meet. Enter President Clinton, who, along with a Republican Congress, passed a bill in 1996 "ending welfare as we know it." In doing so, they replaced the decades-old Aid to Families with Dependent Children (AFDC) program with a new block grant to states called Temporary Assistance to Needy Families, or TANF. Unlike AFDC, which guaranteed a minimal level of help to all poor families, TANF requires low-income parents like Catrina to meet strict work requirements and subjects them to a new maximum five-year lifetime limit on assistance.

Last fall, Catrina was earning $8.50 an hour at a temp job when her 3-year-old son fell seriously ill. Since she had no choice but to stay home and care for him, she was immediately fired and was forced to reapply for assistance. Hoping to escape the low-wage labor market once and for all, she asked her caseworker about GED classes; she was refused and told she would need a doctor's statement proving she had "good cause" for not meeting the work requirement. A few months later, in August 2001, Catrina hit her lifetime limit and lost all her benefits.

Unfortunately, Catrina's story is not unique. Six years after welfare reform, caseloads have declined by more than half, but poverty rates—particularly among people of color—remain high. Now, Congress is considering changes to the 1996 law, which expires this September. Much is at stake in the legislative scramble: different reauthorization bills, if passed, could either improve the prospects of low-income parents or sink them even deeper into poverty.

In this new round of welfare wars, low-income parents like Catrina are making their voices heard. What's more, they are raising challenging questions about how our nation's public policies can and should promote justice, equity and opportunity for all low-income Americans.

The War Against Welfare

The conservative assault on federal entitlement programs climaxed in the mid-1990s when Republicans, led by then-Speaker of the House Newt Gingrich, won back control of Congress and made overhauling the welfare system the bedrock of their Contract With America. The notion of welfare reform was, however, nothing new.

Ironically enough, at the height of the welfare-rights movement of the 1960s, "welfare reform" actually meant making the system more accessible to greater numbers of needy families. Grassroots groups, many of whom organized under the banner of the National Welfare Rights Organization (NWRO), helped tens of thousands of low-income parents to enroll in AFDC. The low-income black women who comprised nearly 90% of the NWRO's membership insisted that the need for welfare was the result of an unjust economic system, not personal failure. At its peak in 1969, NWRO had more than 22,000 members and chapters in nearly every major city.

But the 1970s ushered in a series of dislocating events— the costly ongoing war in Vietnam, a faltering economy—as well as an increasingly effective conservative political movement. Together, these political and economic forces converged to weaken the public consensus about the need to combat systemic poverty that had flourished a decade earlier. By the time President Reagan took office in 1980, public opinion about the poor had done a complete about-face. Now, welfare recipients *themselves* were the problem. Many Americans became convinced that the welfare system encouraged dependency on the federal government, and reform efforts were now aimed at changing poor women's behavior instead of attacking the real roots of poverty—systemic racism, sexism, and inequality.

Ending "Welfare As We Know It"

In this new era of welfare bashing, the debate centered on how to get welfare recipients off the rolls as quickly as possible. As a result, on August 22, 1996, President Clinton signed into law the Personal Responsibility and Work Opportunity Reconciliation Act (PRWORA), called welfare reform.

The law's passage did indeed end welfare as we knew it. It eliminated the 60-year entitlement to some minimal level of assistance for our nation's most vulnerable parents and children. The new system makes it extremely difficult to get help, even for people in desperate circumstances, and uses sanctions and time limits to push people off the rolls. The strategy is working. Since 1996, welfare caseloads have fallen by more than half. At the same time, poverty among single mothers—the population most affected by changes in welfare policy—has actually *increased* from 19.2% to 19.4% since the mid-1990s, in spite of the decade's booming economy.

The block-grant structure of TANF gave broad new authority to states to implement their own welfare programs, subject to little federal oversight. This has led to rampant lawlessness in welfare offices; in one notorious case, the State of Oregon told applicants to go "dumpster diving" instead of seeking assistance. And, as has been the case throughout American history, "states rights" has resulted in discrimination against people of color in access to services and benefits.

The result is a patchwork of state policies that have done little to address the root causes of poverty in America. Volumes of data and anecdotal evidence gathered since 1996 paint a sobering portrait of joblessness, low wages, lack of support and increased hardship for parents who have left the welfare rolls. Approximately one-third of former welfare recipients do not leave welfare for work at all, and those who do often work low- or minimum-wage jobs without paid vacation, sick leave or health benefits. Many are single mothers caring for young, sick or disabled children, who are forced to make impossible choices between being with their children when they are most needed and doing what the welfare system demands in order to keep their meager income.

Now, as the economic boom of the 1990s sputters to a halt, the safety net for low-wage workers is in tatters. Unemployment Insurance, our nation's first recourse for laid-off workers, reaches at most 40% of unemployed workers. Due to antiquated eligibility rules, low-wage and part-time workers are least likely to qualify when they become unemployed.

Moreover, under welfare reform, legal immigrants can no longer qualify for most federal public-benefits programs if they arrived in the country after 1996. Yet immigrants comprise a growing portion of the low-wage workforce; currently, one in four poor children lives in an immigrant family. While some states have picked up the slack and created their own programs for immigrants, millions of hardworking, tax-paying immigrants still have no safety net to rely on.

Welfare reform 1996-style raised a lot of questions about work, family and immigration that it is simply not equipped to answer. Rather than advocating for a return to a system that provided a limited safety net but otherwise did little to address the problem of poverty in America, progressives are fighting for a new framework for our nation's anti-poverty policy—one that promotes meaningful wages, job opportunities, and supports for all low-income Americans.

A New Grassroots Movement for Economic Justice

For decades, grassroots organizations of low-income people have been fighting for living wages, affordable housing, adequate health care and decent jobs in their communities. In the mid-1990s, as welfare reform spread out into the states, poor people had new battles to fight.

Many groups got actively involved in shaping the way welfare reform was implemented in their states. Groups like the Philadelphia Unemployment Project organized low-income workers and welfare recipients to press their states to create publicly-funded transitional jobs programs that provide welfare recipients with wages, training, and supports as they move from welfare to work. These programs have proven successful in giving low-income parents with little education or work experience the tools they need to get and keep good jobs.

Others have fought to break down some of the barriers at the state and local level that prevent millions of otherwise eligible families from accessing safety-net programs like food stamps, Medicaid, and child care. Employing a model pioneered by the Northwest Federation of Community Organizations, grassroots organizations around the country launched highly visible campaigns to simplify and improve the way these services are delivered. Victories include improved benefit levels, less burdensome application procedures, and greater accountability in local welfare offices.

Some focused on making welfare policies more responsive to parents with young children. Members of Working for Equality and Economic Liberation, a welfare-rights group in Montana, succeeded in pushing their state to create a model At-Home Infant Care program, which allows low-income mothers with infant children to receive child care grants to stay home and care for their children. This innovative program so impressed Senator Max Baucus (D-Mont.), the chair of the committee that oversees welfare programs, that he is now pushing to create a similar program at the federal level.

In May 2000, hundreds of these organizations came together in Chicago to launch the first national grassroots movement of low-income people fighting for economic justice since the welfare-rights movement of the 1960s. Building on dozens of local and state victories, they are now working under the banner of the National Campaign for Jobs and Income Support to make federal policy more responsive to the needs of low-income communities.

Together, in 2001, the members of the National Campaign teamed up with other national organizations like the Children's Defense Fund, RESULTS, and the National Council of La Raza to extract a partly refundable child tax credit out of President Bush's otherwise disastrous tax cut. The tax credit, which will deliver approximately $8 billion a year directly to low-income families, represents the largest federal investment in poor families since the expansion of the Earned Income Tax Credit in the early 1990s.

Most recently, in the spring of 2002, grassroots activists worked with allies in the anti-hunger and immigrants' rights communities to restore food-stamp benefits to all legal immigrants. This victory represented the first major crack in the architecture of the punitive 1996 welfare reform law, and set the stage for the battle over TANF reauthorization this summer.

The Next Round of Welfare Wars

The 1996 welfare reform law is set to expire this September, and a bitter debate over the next phase of welfare reform is underway. President Bush threw the first punch earlier this spring, when he introduced a welfare plan that would drastically increase work requirements for recipients, restrict access to education and training programs, provide no new money for child care or work supports, and do nothing to restore benefits to legal immigrants.

The Bush plan sparked outrage even among Republican governors and state welfare officials, who argue that it would force them to abandon successful job training and education programs in favor of costly "workfare" programs. These programs, which force welfare recipients to work off their benefits in unpaid jobs with no training or benefits, have never been proven to improve recipients' long-term earnings or employment. Moreover, because workfare workers do not receive a wage for their labor, they cannot qualify for Unemployment Insurance benefits or the Earned Income Tax Credit and are not protected by worker and civil rights protection laws. In one instance, a federal court recently ruled that a participant in New York City's Work Experience Program, the nation's largest and most notorious workfare program, was not protected by federal sexual harassment laws because she was "not a real worker."

In March, just one week after the President released his plan, the National Campaign convened 2,000 low-income parents in Washington, D.C. to push for a very different kind of welfare plan. There, grassroots activists from around the country rallied for education and training, benefits for legal immigrants, fair and flexible time limits for working families, racial equity and due process in welfare offices, and family-friendly policies that allow parents to balance the competing demands of work and family life. After rallying on the National Mall, the group marched to the headquarters of the Department of Health and Human Services to protest President Bush's punitive proposals.

Minutes later, the group boarded dozens of buses and headed over to the Heritage Foundation, a right-wing social policy think tank, to pay a surprise visit to Robert Rector. They demanded that Rector, the nation's leading conservative scholar on welfare and a primary architect of the Bush welfare plan, spend a day "walking in the shoes" of poor parents to see first-hand what it's *really* like to live in poverty in America. He consented, and a month later joined National Campaign leaders in Little Rock, Arkansas, to learn about their struggles to balance work, school and their families without adequate support from the system.

Maybe coincidentally—or maybe not—the very next day after the D.C. rallies, the Bush administration publicly recanted an earlier proposal to allow states to pay workfare workers less than the minimum wage.

Low-income activists are not just making waves in Washington. In more than 40 states, grassroots organizations are pressuring their senators and representatives to support a progressive anti-poverty agenda. By sharing the stories of their struggles—through lobbying, media work, coalition-building, and creative direct action—these leaders are changing the very way decision-makers and the public *think* about the problem of poverty in this country.

Congress Revisits Welfare Reform

Clearly, a fierce debate is underway. In May, the House of Representatives passed a welfare bill that mirrors the President's punitive plan. It increases work requirements for welfare recipients from 30 to 40 hours a week. It severely limits parents' ability to build skills that will lead to better jobs, trimming the amount of time education and training activities can count as "work" to only three months—down from twelve months under current law. It does nothing to address the strict five-year lifetime limit on assistance, which has already caused more than 150,000 parents to lose needed benefits. It provides for only a $1 billion increase in funding for child care—compared to the additional $9.5 billion that the Congressional Budget Office estimates would be needed to meet the 40-hour work requirement without cutting services to families already receiving child care assistance.

Not surprisingly, the Republican-controlled House passed its bill on a highly partisan basis. Fortunately, moderates from both parties are leading the debate in the Senate. Under the leadership of a "tri-partisan" group of Finance Committee members, including Senators Snowe (R-Maine), Hatch (R-Utah), Jeffords (Ind-Vt.), Lincoln (D-Ark.) and Breaux (D-La.), the committee voted out a welfare bill that is much closer to the principles for which grassroots leaders have been organizing.

The Finance Committee's bill maintains the current 30-hour work requirement and significantly improves parents' ability to get an education while on TANF. It adds $5.5 billion in new money for child care, restores TANF benefits to legal immigrants and Medicaid benefits to immigrant pregnant women and children, and provides much-needed flexibility for parents with disabled kids. It creates a new federal fund to support local transitional jobs programs and a pilot program that will allow parents with infant children to stay home and care for them.

The Finance Committee's plan is an important step forward, but a number of important issues remain unresolved as the bill moves to the Senate floor in September. If they are serious about helping families move out of poverty, activists contend, senators must add still more money for child care, further expand opportunities for education and training, and address the persistent problem of strict time limits.

The Next Chapter

A significant challenge still lies ahead as the two sides come together to hammer out a compromise that the President is willing to sign before the current law expires this fall. This is no small task and a great deal is at stake; the 1996 law caused untold hardship for millions of low-income families, and the House bill, if it prevails, will only push many of them deeper into poverty. No one can predict what will happen if action on the bill is delayed until next year, as the two parties vie for control of Congress this November and as the fiscal environment—both federally and in the states—continues to deteriorate.

Whatever its outcome, the welfare reauthorization campaign has been a victory for thousands of low-income parents who have, for the first time, been able to speak out at the national level about the policies that affect their lives. It's unlikely they will succeed in constructing an entirely new paradigm on poverty in 2002—largely because many Washington elites are stuck in the tired welfare-bashing debates of the 1990s—but a new platform of ideas and a new constituency have emerged for the long-term fight for economic justice.

GOOD TIMES, BAD TIMES: RECESSION AND THE WELFARE DEBATE
By Heather Boushey
September/October 2002

When President Clinton signed the welfare reform bill in August 1996, he could not have predicted that the next five years would bring such a rapid fall in welfare caseloads and such strong growth in employment among single mothers. The economic expansion of the late 1990s brought wage gains to workers across the wage spectrum—including those at the bottom end of the pay scale—and boosted employment among groups of traditionally disadvantaged workers (single mothers, workers of color, immigrant workers). The strongest labor market in decades meant that many women who came off the welfare rolls in search of a job were able to find one. In this sense, welfare reform—at least according to its proponents—was impeccably well timed.

However, the late 1990s boom was unusual compared with earlier expansions, and there is no guarantee that future upturns will benefit those at the bottom of the earnings scale. Although studies from around the country show that nearly two out of every three women who have left welfare have found a job (for at least a while), their wages are too low to support a family—even during a period of economic growth. Most jobs that former welfare recipients have found don't pay living wages and don't offer employer-provided health insurance. Part of the problem is that women continue to earn far less than men, both because of wage discrimination and because women tend to be concentrated in lower-paying "female" jobs. This continuing gender gap becomes a larger problem as more and more women are responsible for the economic viability of their families.

Now, as the economy moves through a recession, job losses and projected slower (or negative) wage growth next year mean that it will be even tougher for low-wage workers to secure employment at wages adequate to support their families. The very sectors of the economy where former welfare recipients found jobs have been hit hard by the economic downturn. Employment rates—the proportion of Americans with a job—have fallen, and wage gains are already eroding as workers are forced to compete for jobs, instead of employers having to compete for workers. The fortuitous timing of welfare reform has now come to an end, raising urgent questions about how working single moms are going to make ends meet, not only during the slowdown but in more typical periods of economic expansion as well.

The Good Times Weren't So Good

The late 1990s economic expansion was atypical in several respects. In contrast with the economic expansion of the 1980s, low-wage workers in the late 1990s experienced low unemployment, increased job retention, and sustained (and significant) wage gains. These positive labor market trends were a result of historically low unemployment rates that lasted longer, without driving up inflation, than economists generally had thought possible.

While every demographic group saw low unemployment rates, the declines were most pronounced for minority workers, including many who had been receiving welfare. After remaining above 10% for more than 25 years, the unemployment rate for African Americans fell to 7.6% in 2000, its lowest since the Bureau of Labor Statistics began tabulating unemployment rates by race in 1972. (Even so, the 2000 unemployment rate among African Americans was still more than twice that of whites.) For Hispanic workers, the unemployment rate also reached an historic low, falling from 9.3% in 1995 to 5.7% in 2000.

Because of tight labor markets in the late 1990s, many more women, especially women of color, entered the workforce. In 2000, 60.2% of women were working—more than at any other time. While white women's labor force participation rose by less than a percentage point during the peak years of the economic expansion—1995 to 2000—African-American and Hispanic women increased their participation rates by 3.7 percentage points and 4.3 percentage points, respectively.

The tight labor market meant that workers in all wage groups earned more money. During the second half of the 1990s, workers' wages, on average, grew by 9.4%. Between 1995 and 2000, the lowest-paid women workers saw their wages rise by the same proportion as women earning high wages—about 10%. Men near the bottom of the earnings scale saw slightly higher percentage gains compared to men near the top (11.6% compared to 10.6%). In addition to favorable labor-market conditions, increases in the minimum wage in 1996 and 1997 helped to raise wages. Expansion of the Earned Income Tax Credit in 1993 further boosted incomes for the working poor. Because of these gains, women and men across the wage spectrum were able to improve their living standards.

But this picture isn't as rosy as it sounds. For example, the strong wage gains of the late 1990s were not enough to compensate for the wage declines that occurred between the late 1970s and the early 1990s. In 2001, men near the bottom of the wage scale were still earning 2.6% less than in 1979. And for women at the bottom, wages in 2001 were 2.2% below 1979 levels.

Further, although women's wages did rise during the late 1990s, this did not lead to a closing of the gender gap. In 1979, women earned only 65 cents for every dollar men earned. When male wages fell during the 1980s, men's and women's wages moved closer together, and the gender wage ratio hit a peak of 81 cents on the dollar in 1993. But the gap narrowed because men's wages were falling, not because women's wages were going up. And since wages then rose for both men and women during the remainder of the 1990s, the ratio is still hovering around 80 cents on the dollar.

Finally, in spite of low unemployment and high wages, low-income families still were not able to make ends meet. About a third of former welfare recipients did not find employment in the second half of the 1990s. Those who did find jobs—usually in low-wage sectors such as child care, home health care, and temporary help—were earning, on average, $6-8 per hour. For full-time, year-round employment, this comes out to between $12,480 and $16,640. Those earning closer to $8 per hour may have been pushed above the official poverty line of $14,269 for a family of three. However, researchers at the Economic Policy Institute have calculated that a family of three (with one school-age and one pre-school child) needs an annual income of between $21,989 (in rural Hattiesburg, Mississippi) and $48,606 (in high-priced Nassau-Suffolk County, New York) to afford the basic necessities (including food, housing, health insurance, child care, transportation, and taxes). Most former welfare recipients come nowhere near this income range.

The Bad Times Hurt Women

The economic recession, which began with job losses in manufacturing in 2000, spread across the economy last year. During the first three quarters of 2001, the economy contracted and unemployment rose.

There are a few features that make the current recession atypical. In some ways, this recession has not been as hard on low-wage workers as earlier recessions. For example, during the early 1980s recession, unemployment for workers without a high-school diploma rose by nearly four times as much as for workers with a college degree or more. During the 2000-02 recession, however, the ratio was less than two to one.

The terrorist attacks of September 11 have made this recession unusual as well. Although the recession had already begun prior to the September 11 attacks, these events wreaked havoc on certain segments of the economy, particularly hotels, air travel, and retail. As a result, the recession's impact on services, transportation, and wholesale and retail trade—sectors of the economy that usually provide more employment growth during recessions (or at least smaller employment losses, in the case of transportation)—has been especially harsh.

For example, typically in recessions, employment in the service industry (which employs about one out of every three workers) keeps growing. During the second part of the early 1990s recession, the service sector grew respectably, and transportation and wholesale trade fell at about the same rate as in the first eleven months. Retail trade actually grew in the latter part of the early 1990s recession. (See Figure 1.)

But that hasn't been the case during the current recession. From October 2000 (when unemployment began to rise) through September 2001, services continued to grow while transportation fell slightly. Since September 2001, however, services have barely grown, and transportation and retail trade (which employ about one out of every 20 and one out of every five workers, respectively) have seen sharp drops in employment. (See Figure 2.)

Figure I: Employment change over the first and second halves of the 1990-92 recession

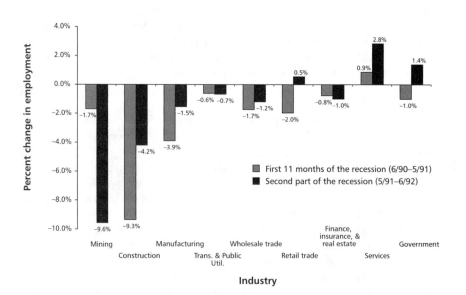

Source: Lawrence Mishel, Jared Bernstein, and Heather Boushey, *The State of Working America 2002-3* (Ithaca, N.Y.: Cornell University Press, 2003).

Figure 2: Employment change pre- and post- September 2001 during the 2000–02 recession (through July 2002)

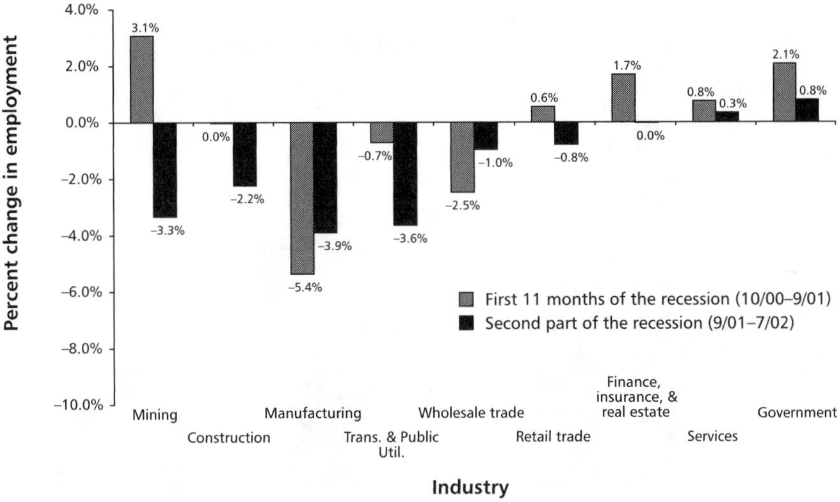

Source: Lawrence Mishel, Jared Bernstein, and Heather Boushey, *The State of Working America 2002-3* (Ithaca, N.Y.: Cornell University Press, 2003).

These job losses have made the 2000–02 recession harder on women, compared to prior recessions, since they are more likely to work in services and retail trade than men. Typically in recessions, men experience higher unemployment rates than women. That was true during the early 1980s and early 1990s recessions, and in the current downturn as well. During the current recession, however, women have nearly "caught up" with men. Because of slower growth and greater job losses in the service sector, women's unemployment increases look more like men's than in earlier recessions. (See Figure 3.)

For former welfare recipients, the consequences have been especially severe. About a third of former welfare recipients who found employment work in the retail industry, which has seen no job growth over the course of this recession. Other sectors where women formerly on welfare found employment, such as the temporary help sector (about 5% of welfare recipients) and hotels and lodging (about 4%), have also seen employment drop substantially over the course of this recession.

Along with fewer job prospects, former welfare recipients now face slower wage growth as well. For women at the bottom of the earnings scale, wages grew by 4.3% from the first half of 2000 to the first half of 2001, but rose by only 2.7% from the first half of 2001 to the first half of 2002. For men at the bottom, wage growth fell even further, from 4.2% to 2.1%, over the same periods. If high unemployment continues, it is likely that wage growth will continue to be slow, or even negative, next year.

Figure 3: Women's unemployment has risen nearly as much as men's during the 2000-02 recession.

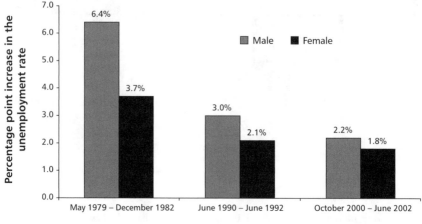

Source: Lawrence Mishel, Jared Bernstein, and Heather Boushey, *The State of Working America 2002-3* (Ithaca, N.Y.: Cornell University Press, 2003).

Reauthorization of What?

The fortunes of working families rise and fall with conditions in the labor market. During the strong economy of the late 1990s, jobs were plentiful and wages went up. Even during the economic expansion, however, low-wage families still struggled to make ends meet.

That was especially true for families that once relied on welfare because the mid-1990s "reform" limited poor women's access to welfare. During the boom times, many were able to find employment, so that leaving welfare for a job was a viable option. Now that economic circumstances have changed, former welfare recipients will find it much more difficult to find and keep jobs.

Congress must reauthorize the 1996 welfare reform legislation by October 2002. In May, the House passed a reauthorization bill calling for stricter work requirements—in the form of more welfare recipients required to work, and at more hours—and only a marginal increase in child care spending, adding $1 billion over the next five years to the currently allocated $4.8 billion per year. In June, the Senate Finance Committee issued a different bill, which does not require welfare recipients to work more and also increases spending on child care by $5.5

billion over the next five years. Even this higher figure, however, is at most *one tenth* of what advocates believe is necessary to provide sufficient child care.

What neither bill does is recast welfare as a program that puts cash in the hands of people who need it—and will spend it—during economic contractions. When unemployment rises, families need a safety net they can rely on. But it's not just families that need the safety net; the economy needs fiscal policies that sustain demand when unemployment rises so employers will have an incentive to maintain production. Welfare—and other programs that provide assistance to families during economic slowdowns, such as unemployment compensation and Food Stamps—helps to smooth out the economy's ups and downs. With that in mind, the impact of the recession on low-wage workers should be an important part of the current welfare debate.

Resources: Heather Boushey et al., *Hardships in America: The Real Story of Working Families* (Washington, D.C.: Economic Policy Institute, 2001); Lawrence Mishel, Jared Bernstein, and Heather Boushey, *The State of Working America 2002-3* (Ithaca, N.Y.: Cornell University Press, 2003).

"WORK FIRST"—WHERE ARE THE WAGES?
By Dan Feder
November/December 2002

After Bill Clinton signed the 1996 "welfare reform" law, people working off their welfare benefits became a ubiquitous sight in New York City. "You'd see these ragtag groups of people all around the city," recalls Gregory Heller, a welfare policy associate at the New York Association of Community Organizations for Reform Now (ACORN), "in just their ordinary clothes with orange vests that said WEP."

WEP is the "Work Experience Program," in which New York City welfare recipients are required to do unpaid work for city agencies or risk losing their benefits. They do jobs that heavily unionized municipal workers once performed, but for a lot less money. Even if WEP workers' paltry monthly welfare checks are considered wages, these workers are making far below the federal minimum of $5.15 an hour. The average benefit of $450 a month (in rent allowances, food stamps, and cash benefits) comes to about $3.75 an hour for a 30-hour work week. A union park or sanitation worker might have made $16 an hour.

Although WEP actually started in the early 1990s, welfare reform greatly increased the scope of welfare-to-work, or workfare, programs. Under Temporary Assistance for Needy Families (TANF), as the new version of welfare is called, recipients must spend 30 hours per week in work-related activities (like job training or looking for work, in addition to actual labor) to receive their benefits.

Conservative ideologues have defended "work first" welfare reforms by claiming that traditional welfare rewards laziness and fosters dependence, which cause poverty. But critics say these policies also serve a budget-slashing agenda: reducing the cost of public services by destroying public-sector unionism and creating a large pool of unpaid labor for the city and state. "At Pelham Bay Park, you had sixty union workers and five WEP workers when the program started," said Heller. "Now, it's ten parks employees and seventy WEP workers."

Community groups, welfare-rights advocates, and labor unions in New York and across the country have been fighting both to win for workfare workers the protections that other government workers enjoy and, ultimately, to abolish workfare altogether. ACORN has been organizing WEP workers since 1997. That year, the organization held an "election" asking WEP workers to vote for or against union representation. About 17,000 people—nearly half of the workfare workers at that time—voted, 99% of them in favor of a union. Since the city does not recognize the workers' right to bargain collectively, the election did not result in the formation of a bargaining unit—but it did send a strong pro-union message. This was not lost on the city government. Shortly after the election, Mayor Rudolph Guiliani obtained a court order against WEP workers unionizing.

At its height, the WEP program had 80,000 workers under its control. Today, it enrolls about 20,000. Workfare advocates say the drop shows how many people the new system has moved into the regular workforce. However, the current workfare system has no mechanism for tracking names that drop off the rolls. Heller believes that, while many people do find jobs, countless others drop off the rolls for more troubling reasons. Some cannot fulfill the work requirements due to such problems as a lack of child care. Others are forced out by sexual harassment or unsafe working conditions at their workfare assignments. "What happens," said Heller, "is that because of a perceived lack of caring on the part of the welfare bureaucracy, a woman doesn't show up for her assignment, gets taken off the welfare rolls. But that's recorded as a success."

In San Francisco, where welfare-to-work experiments started back in 1985, 2,500 of the city's 12,000 welfare recipients are enrolled in workfare. An agreement between the city government and the Service Employees International Union (SEIU) locals that represent most city workers prevents the city from eliminating a worker's job and then replacing it with a workfare assignment. Nonetheless, as municipal workers have retired or earned promotions, the city has replaced their vacant positions with unpaid workfare slots. "What you can see over the course of 15 years is a massive reduction in the number of city employees," said Steve Williams, executive director of People Organized to Win Employment Rights (POWER). "In 1985, we had 300 city-employed street sweepers. We now have 16. But those 16 supervise about 1,000 workfare workers."

Despite the threat workfare poses to public-sector unions, Williams says the labor movement has been sluggish in responding to the issue. Even though workfare workers endured conditions the unions presumably would not have tolerated for their own members—Williams cites such abuses as the lack of safety equipment when handling dangerous chemicals and the denial of access to employee bathrooms and lunchrooms—union leaders were unwilling to speak up. When POWER started organizing workfare workers in the late 1990s, leading a successful campaign to win state OSHA coverage for the workers, some union officials actually took it as a threat, Williams says: "Initially, they felt that this could be a situation of dual unionism," with the public employees unions representing traditional workers, and organizations like POWER representing workfare workers. "It took months, if not years, to develop what the relationship [between welfare advocates and the unions] would look like."

The relationship between POWER and the SEIU locals in San Francisco has begun to improve since the two worked together to gain passage of a city living-wage ordinance in 2000. Real cooperation is still limited, and Williams still perceives union indifference to workfare issues, an attitude that "POWER's working on that, so we don't really have to do anything." He believes that could change, however, as POWER pressures the city to move more welfare recipients towards high-skilled apprenticeships and training programs. POWER is working with the unions to develop those programs, through which welfare recipients could move into union jobs.

Josie Mooney, the executive director of SEIU Local 790, a major San Francisco public employee union, is enthusiastic about apprenticeships and training programs for workfare workers. "Twenty or thirty years ago, the public sector was one place where people of color could count on good union jobs with real benefits." Now, she says, the tightening of budgets nationwide and the creation of workfare programs threaten to erode this resource. The apprenticeship program, unlike most pointless state "job training programs," could actually put poor people first in line for high-paying public-sector jobs.

Mooney and Williams hope that activists in other cities learn from their recent collaboration. Mooney says that by working together on the living-wage ordinance campaign, which in San Francisco included language that applied directly to workfare workers, the SEIU and POWER gained the leverage to make demands on the city. "Unions and welfare groups in other cities don't have it so well."

MINISTERING TO THE POOR: CHURCH AND STATE, TOGETHER AGAIN
By James Ridgeway
March/April 2001

For years, mainstream politicians have used poor people as a political football, excoriating them for their supposed moral failings and attacking them as a drain on the public treasury. From Bill Clinton, we got "personal responsibility." Then came George W. Bush with "compassionate conservatism," or "faith-based" initiatives to help the poor.

Clinton's "welfare reform" program gave public and private social-service agencies new latitude to impose moral conditions on poor people, and to deny aid to those who fail to comply. Under Bush's faith-based proposal, the poor will fare even worse. Bush's plan, like Clinton's, isn't really about helping poor people. It's about controlling them. And it's about killing off what's left of the New Deal state and divvying up the remains.

Private Charity and Christian Morality

Bush may accomplish what the Right has been trying to achieve for years—the replacement of a state-run system of entitlements with a voluntary program of moral charity rooted in the Victorian era. In her 1996 book, *The De-Moralization of Society: From Victorian Virtues to Modern Values*, leading conservative Gertrude Himmelfarb criticized the current welfare system. "We have so completely rejected any kind of moral principle," Himmelfarb claimed, "that we have deliberately, systematically divorced poor relief from moral sanctions and incentives." For inspiration, she looks back to the Victorians, who—steeped in the traditions of Methodism and Evangelicalism—offered moral and spiritual discipline as well as material aid.

In the world of private charity, the Victorian ethos is alive and well. The conservative American Enterprise Institute touts the Mormon Church's "bishops' storehouse," a system for doling out food and other essentials to the "truly needy" (as determined by the bishops) in exchange for services rendered to the Church. A recently-published essay collection, *Loving Your Neighbor: A Principled Guide to Personal Charity*—edited by informal Bush adviser Marvin Olasky, who coined the phrase "compassionate conservatism"—highlights "success stories" like a New York soup kitchen that promotes "personal responsibility," and "pregnancy care centers" in Maryland that offer low-income pregnant women moral ministration along with a place to stay.

Bush himself has been a master at mixing Christian piety and public funds. As governor of Texas, he helped to set up the first Christian-run wing inside a state jail, and he even supported making Christian conversion an "explicit goal." Don Willett, the governor's director of special projects, told Joe Loconte of the conservative Heritage Foundation that the state of Texas did not intend to "merely duplicate the weaknesses of government style aid." Rather, Willett explained, "we are trying to create a safe harbor for explicitly religious programs."

Now that conservatives have destroyed the federal welfare apparatus, they plan to replicate these models nationwide. The 2000 Republican Party platform praised charitable and faith-based organizations for "making great strides in overcoming poverty and other social problems." During the presidential campaign, Bush pledged to "allow private and religious groups to compete to provide services in every federal, state and local social program." "Wherever we can," he added, "we must expand their role and reach." If Bush has his way, that reach will extend to homes for unwed mothers, federal after-school programs, drug treatment centers, shelters for battered spouses and children, homeless shelters, prisons, and even medical insurance for the poor.

Bush has wasted no time getting his program underway. He already has set up a White House Office on Faith-Based and Community Initiatives. He also plans to create a "compassion capital fund"—costing $1.8 billion over ten years—that will help small charities, including religious organizations, to obtain federal funds.

Poor People: A Tax Deduction

The poor already represent a major source of tax deductions for rich people and large corporations. In recent decades, private groups have taken over the job of channeling food from agribusiness to the poor. Last year, America's Second Harvest—a network of more than 200 food banks and services that distributes free food through 50,000 charitable agencies—provided 26 million people with a billion pounds of food. Much of that food comes from companies like Nabisco, which get substantial tax write-offs in return.

Bush's brand of "compassionate conservatism" will offer incentives for individuals and corporations to donate even more. Currently, only taxpayers who itemize deductions can write off charitable contributions. Bush wants to allow non-itemizers (taxpayers who claim the standard deduction) to deduct their charitable donations too. Another scheme would let people over age 59 withdraw money from their Individual Retirement Accounts (IRAs) for charitable giving, without paying the tax penalty that would normally apply. The Bush plan would also permit corporations to deduct up to 15% of their taxable income for charitable donations, instead of the current limit of 10%.

It's not at all clear, though, that Bush expects rich people to do all the spending. In 1999, charities reported donations totaling $190 billion—up 41% from 1995. Much of that money came from wealthy households: According to the National Committee for Responsive Philanthropy (NCRP), 90% of those with incomes over $100,000 made charitable contributions. But Bush's other tax proposals will reduce incentives for rich people to give. For example, the wealthy often donate to charity in order to reduce their estate taxes. If Bush succeeds in repealing the estate tax, charitable donations could decline by at least $1 billion, according to one Treasury Department report. NCRP officials worry that nonprofits will suffer if the repeal goes through.

If the rich stop giving, then who will fund the faith-based initiatives to help the poor? Why, the poor themselves. Already, half of all households with incomes below $10,000 give to charity. Under Bush's charitable deduction proposal, low-income contributions would undoubtedly rise. According to a study commissioned by Independent Sector, a group of Washington-based charities, the Bush plan could bring in another $14.6 billion for charity each year—most of it from low- and middle-income people.

And if that happens, the churches will be most likely to cash in. In 1999, 43% of all charitable donations went to support religion; the next-biggest category, education, got less than 15%. Right now, religious groups get 70% of all charitable contributions made by low- and middle-income people who don't itemize their deductions. In the Heritage Foundation's *Mandate for Leadership*, published in 1996, Adam Meyerson reported that weekly churchgoers gave a higher proportion of their incomes to charity than those who attended church less than once a month. "Religious revival," Meyerson said, "dwarfs tax incentives as a means to encourage more involvement with charity." Maybe so, but greater tax incentives are bound to boost that involvement even more.

What's Wrong With This Picture?

Currently, government regulations require faith-based service providers to keep their religious and social-service activities distinct. Bush's aim is to bring the two missions closer together. If he succeeds, churches could infuse social-service programs with religious zeal. That's a major concern for the Rev. C. Welton Gaddy, executive director of the Interfaith Alliance, which opposes the religious right. Speaking to the *New York Times* last December, Gaddy warned that, under the Bush proposal, organizations "could turn food or clothing or counseling or rehabilitation into a tool for proselytizing," with government support. The results could be devastating for poor people, who might be denied services for failing to adhere to a certain religious affiliation or set of moral codes. People in need might simply avoid programs that offer spiritual salvation along with material assistance, out of discomfort or fear. If right-wing fundamentalists—Bush's favored constituency—fare best in the contest for federal dollars, these problems will be especially acute. Bush aides say they will work to ensure that secular alternatives are available, but they don't say how they will make this happen.

Under the Bush program, it seems unlikely that the government will be able—or willing—to keep churches from misusing public funds. Writing in the *New York Times* last December, Forrest Church, senior minister of All Souls Unitarian Church in Manhattan, admitted that the lure of public aid was "tempting." But, he added, "I've been tempted before." He described how, 16 years earlier, a state senator had given his church, along with 11 others, $10,000 each in public funds for community outreach. "When I received this manna from Albany," Church said, "I immediately turned it back—for a good reason. It would have been too easy to spend the money on religious programs, instead of charitable ones, and not be caught."

Finally, the level and quality of services will undoubtedly decline. Social-services funding is already grossly inadequate, and Bush's plans to cut taxes for the wealthy will reduce federal revenues even more. On top of that, his charitable deduction scheme, according to the Joint Congressional Committee on Taxation, will cost an estimated $75 billion over ten years. All of this means fewer resources for social programs, whether they are publicly- or privately-run. Even if there's a simultaneous jump in charitable donations, there's no guarantee that the money will go to help the poor. As a result, even well-meaning churches will have to cut corners. And since Bush supports alternative licensing requirements for church-based programs, the quality of services will probably suffer too.

Since 1996, when "welfare reform" was enacted, the number of unemployed, childless adults receiving food stamps has dropped by 59% nationally, and in New York City, by nearly 70%. Without soup kitchens and food pantries, many of which are operated by churches, millions of people would have no food. But the need is so great that private agencies—even those with no religious affiliations or motivations—cannot possibly fill the void. Nor should they be asked to do so. As a society, we have an obligation to provide people with the basic necessities of life. That's the job of the state, not the church.

Private Charity as a Political Tool

Quite aside from the moral rituals, the Bush camp is using religion to pull together previously warring factions under the Republican big tent. This is no easy task. The Republicans are divided when it comes to a central theory of governance. By far the most boisterous and aggressive branch of the party on economic issues advocates a straight-up libertarian-style approach, aiming at every turn to cut back the functions of the federal government, reduce or eliminate taxes, and push programs and policy-making towards the local level. Libertarian-minded Republicans don't much care about abortion or other "moral" questions.

Opposing this libertarian tendency is the Christian Right, which wants to harness the power of the central government to implement such pet social policies as banning abortion, outlawing same-sex marriage, and stigmatizing divorce. In short, the Christian Right wants to enforce a return to the so-called nuclear family—with criminal penalties if need be.

During the Reagan era, the two factions set aside their differences to unite under the banner of anti-communism. Since the Berlin Wall came down, they've been trying to paper together alliances under the banner of the drug war, the threat of rogue states, and the income tax. Although those campaigns have succeeded, they still haven't managed to unite the party into one juggernaut.

"Compassionate conservatism" offers a rationale for getting everyone together again. By encouraging the churches to take over welfare, Bush is promising them federal money and an arena in which they can proselytize and construct a Disney-like replica of Victoriana. They may not get to administer a whole state under Bush, but they'll have a chance to become the gestapo of the underclass. Under Bush's program, churches will be able to raise their own money in a unique situation, fishing for donations with the lure of massive tax write-offs and the knowledge that, should they fall on hard times, the federal government will back them up. As for the libertarians, they will get reduced taxes, a diminution of federal programs, and hence a reduced federal budget. In this equation, moral charity replaces anti-communism as the Republican Party's unifying theme.

If the Republicans play their cards right, they can also bring some of their historic adversaries into the fold. There was evidence of this at last summer's Republican convention, where the fire and brimstone of the Christian Coalition was replaced by a scene many Republicans have been dreaming of—a nice, clean, black Greater Exodus Baptist Church in the heart of Philadelphia, with a neatly-attired choir singing religious tunes to an audience of nervous but friendly white people, and then enthusiastically applauding as officials from the conservative Manhattan Institute read off polling data showing that people who go to church make good citizens. On hand to extol "compassionate conservatism" were such dignitaries as the church's pastor, Herbert H. Lusk II (the former "Praying Tailback" for the Philadelphia Eagles) and the city's former Democratic mayor-turned-preacher, Wilson Goode.

The courtship didn't end there. Last December, Bush met in Austin with about 30 religious leaders—including a dozen black ministers—to discuss his plans for expanding the role of the church. At the gathering, Bush talked openly about needing to win over the black community. Clearly, he sees faith-based programs as a route to that goal.

Not everyone finds the overtures convincing. Yvonne Scruggs, executive director of the Black Leadership Forum, criticized Bush for not inviting the eight largest black denominations—representing 65,000 churches and ten million members—to Austin. "We are a little skeptical of the sincerity of his claim he's reaching out," she told the Albany, N.Y., *Times-Union* in January. Bishop John Hurst Adams, head of the Church and Society Committee of the Congress of National Black Churches, told the *Times-Union* that the Austin meeting was "an affront to the black church, its leadership, and all African Americans."

Some progressive clergy, though, are cautiously optimistic. Rev. Jim Wallis, of the liberal-minded *Sojourners*, attended the Austin meeting. "Perhaps," said Wallis, "a Republican preaching compassionate conservatism, working with Democrats who want to fight for poor working families, and both joined by faith-based organizations at work on the streets, could accomplish things that neither Democrats and Republicans have been able to do."

But as the record shows, neither party is much interested in helping poor people. It's hard to see how this latest scheme—which will further diminish access to public services in the guise of moral instruction—signals a change of heart.

Resources: American Association of Fundraising Counsel <www.givingusa.org>; American Enterprise Institute for Public Policy Research <www.aei.org>; America's Second Harvest <www. secondharvest.org>; Heritage Foundation <www.heritage.org>; National Committee for Responsive Philanthropy <www.ncrp.org>; *Sojourners* <www.sojourners.com>.

HOW STATES ARE SPENDING THEIR WELFARE MONEY—OR NOT

By Tami J. Friedman
March/April 2002

The destruction of "welfare as we knew it" dramatically transformed how the U.S. government assists poor families. Under the old entitlement program, Aid to Families with Dependent Children (AFDC), the federal government matched a percentage of state welfare spending, which fluctuated according to the number of families in need. Under the new system, Temporary Assistance for Needy Families (TANF), which Congress approved in 1996, the states receive annual block grants pegged to the amount of federal money they received under AFDC—and not adjusted for inflation. (To qualify for their block grants, the states have to spend some of their own money—but less than what they spent in the final days of AFDC.)

The new system has raised some important questions. First, because so many families have been kicked out of the welfare program under TANF, states have spent much less on basic assistance to poor families than they have received in the form of block grants. How are they using the leftover funds? Second, since caseloads have risen due to the recession, the block grants may be inadequate to meet growing demand. How will states ensure that they have enough resources on hand?

In a report issued last August, the U.S. General Accounting Office (GAO) examined how ten states were allocating their TANF resources and whether they were setting funds aside for a "rainy day." At the same time, the Center for Law and Social Policy (CLASP) released an evaluation of how all states reported using their TANF money in fiscal year 2000 (FY2000).

Here's how the picture looked at the start of FY2000. The states had a total of $24.2 billion in federal TANF funds to work with—$17 billion in current funding, and $7.2 billion carried forward from previous years. By the end of FY2000, the states had spent a total of $12.5 billion—slightly over half of the available funds. (See Chart 1.)

Chart 1: How states used federal TANF funds in FY2000 (Total funds available = $24,162,964,924)

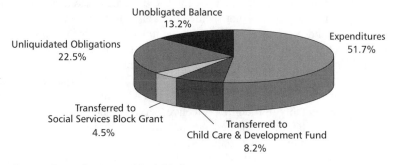

Unobligated Balance
13.2%

Expenditures
51.7%

Unliquidated Obligations
22.5%

Transferred to
Social Services Block Grant
4.5%

Transferred to
Child Care & Development Fund
8.2%

Source: Center for Law and Social Policy

How did the states spend their federal TANF money? Based on CLASP's findings, it seems like about 41% went for *basic assistance*, and another 11.3% toward *child care*. Less than 4% of total spending was reserved for *transportation and supportive services*, and *education and training* accounted for a paltry 1%. (See Chart 2.) These figures may not be accurate, though, because states can fiddle around with prior-year funding in their current spending reports.

Chart 2: How states spent federal TANF funds in FY200 (Total Expenditures = $12,483,172,895)

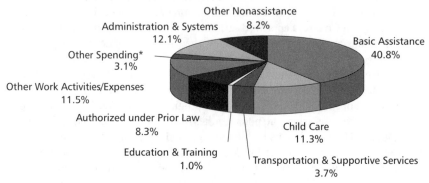

Source: Center for Law and Social Policy

* Includes work subsidies, individual development accounts, refundable Earned Income Tax Credit or other refundable tax credit, nonrecurrent short-term benefits, pregnancy prevention, and two-parent family formation.

Some spending categories are not clearly defined. For example, 8.3% of spending went for activities *authorized under prior law*—activities that may not be TANF-related but were approved under earlier programs like AFDC—and states don't have to give details about how they spent those funds. (According to the California Budget Project, some of California's "prior law" money was used for juvenile probation camps.) The states spent another 8.2% on *other nonassistance*, a miscellaneous catch-all for TANF-related activities that neither qualified as actual "assistance" nor seemed to fit elsewhere. (See Chart 2.)

To understand how states really spent the money, we have to know what's happening on the ground. For example, nine of the ten states in the GAO study were using federal TANF dollars to pay for state programs formerly financed with state funds—and then using the freed-up state funds for other purposes. The state of Texas used at least $320 million in federal TANF money to replace state spending, most notably for child protective services and foster care. While advocates for poor families consider such programs vitally important, they think the state should commit its own resources, not federal welfare funds.

Texas officials claim that they're now spending more money across the board on social services, but Eva De Luna Castro, a budget analyst with the Austin-based

Center for Public Policy Priorities (CPPP), disagrees. "The state general revenue is about the same," she says, "and in some cases it actually went down." Spending per client, she adds, has "gone down dramatically." At the same time, she says, the state funds freed up by federal TANF spending helped to pay for $2.3 billion in tax cuts to homeowners and businesses over five years.

There is other dubious spending that the official data don't reveal. In Wisconsin, for example, welfare contractors (counties and private agencies) can keep profits from unspent funds. Contractors have also misused welfare money. One agency, Maximus, agreed to return $1 million as compensation for spending abuses (although the state didn't require the company to pay back $6 million that went to corporate expenses in 1997–99). Another agency, Employment Solutions (a division of Goodwill Industries), was forced to reimburse the state for nearly $500,000 in misspent funds. Employment Solutions also paid out $1.7 million in bonuses to its executives and staff. In the glare of negative publicity, it is now quitting the welfare business, and Wisconsin will spend $3.8 million in—what else?—TANF funds to transfer Employment Solutions cases to other private contractors.

What about the federal TANF funds—nearly half of the total available for FY2000—that weren't spent at all? The states transferred $3 billion, or nearly 13% of what was on hand, to two other block grants: the Child Care and Development Fund, and the Social Services Block Grant. That left $8.6 billion, or nearly 36%, in unspent balances, consisting of *unliquidated obligations* (funds that were committed but not yet expended) and *unobligated balances* (funds that hadn't been committed at all). (See Chart 1.)

Just because the states reported unspent balances, however, didn't mean they had additional money on hand. Some 63% of the "leftover" funds was already obligated (but unspent), and even the "unobligated" category can include funds already slated for future use. Moreover, according to CLASP, 11 states reported no uncommitted funds at all.

Of course, economic conditions have worsened since the end of FY2000, so any unspent balances won't last long. Texas finished out FY2000 with 25% of its federal TANF funds reported as unspent. But in fiscal year 2001, says CPPP's De Luna Castro, there was "no room" to replace state funds with federal dollars, because Texas was "spending TANF money faster than it was coming in." At the end of FY2000, Wisconsin reported unspent balances totaling 46% of its available federal TANF funds. But the welfare caseload rose by 25% in 2001, and it is still climbing fast. According to the state's Legislative Fiscal Bureau, the actual balance of TANF funds will fall to 10.5% for the 2001–02 budget period, and to less than 1% for 2002–03. Wisconsin is projecting a TANF deficit of $107 million each year in 2003–05.

How will these deficits affect poor people? Under TANF, Wisconsin has committed considerable resources to subsidize child care. But that's a costly investment: Even though most eligible families aren't receiving child care benefits, the state still faced a child care budget shortfall for 2001-03. And in Texas in 1999, state officials decided to tie cash benefits to the federal poverty level (the monthly grant had remained constant for 15 years). As a result, monthly cash benefits have risen from a shocking $188 for a family of three to a barely less shocking $208—but before long, the state may not be able to sustain even that. Advocates for poor families fear that, as the demand for basic assistance increases, such "extras" will be the first to go.

Alternatively, the states could find other resources to close the fiscal gap. Last year Wisconsin lawmakers managed to avert the coming child care budget crisis, partly by reducing administrative spending and allocating more state funds. But as the competition for shrinking state revenue heats up, it's not at all likely that welfare will win. In Texas, even policymakers who want to help poor people are constrained by their state constitution—which limits state general revenue spending on cash assistance to 1% of the total biennial budget.

States have funneled federal TANF dollars into activities not geared for poor families. But even when states have tried to help poor people, the available resources still don't meet existing needs. The only solution, it seems, is to compel states to drastically alter their spending priorities—and to force the federal government to do the same.

Special thanks to Kelly Bablitch, Office of Wisconsin State Sen. Gwendolynne Moore; David Carroll, California Budget Project; and Eva De Luna Castro, Center for Public Policy Priorities.

Resources: U.S. GAO, *Welfare Reform: Challenges in Maintaining a Federal-State Fiscal Partnership*, GAO-01-828, August 2001; Mark Greenberg, "How are TANF Funds Being Used? The Story in FY2000," 14 August 2001 (revised October 2001) <www.clasp.org>.

Chapter 5

THE ARTIFICIAL SOCIAL SECURITY "CRISIS"

INTRODUCTION

There is a looming pension crisis in the United States today. In the last two decades, U.S. companies have discontinued tens of thousands of pension plans. Today, fewer than half of all U.S. workers have any kind of pension plan at work. And so-called "defined-benefit" plans—the classic pension plans under which, after working for some number of years, a retiree receives a guaranteed annual pension until death—are rapidly becoming extinct. Today, only 22% of full-time employees in the private sector have a defined-benefit pension; the five years from 1991 to 1995 alone saw a 15% drop in the rate of defined-benefit coverage. The newer "defined-contribution" plans that now cover 42% of full-time workers in the private sector offer much less security. They depend on employees' own contributions, which employers may or may not match. Furthermore, their value at retirement depends on the vagaries of the stock market or other investments, and many workers will outlive their accounts.

On top of all this, the pension plans that do still exist in the private sector are massively underfunded—to the tune of about $240 billion. In other words, corporations that offer defined-benefit plans are not putting aside enough money to meet their financial obligations to their retirees down the road. Some public-employee pension plans are similarly underfunded. If a company goes bankrupt or is unable to meet its pension obligations, the Pension Benefit Guaranty Corporation (PBGC) steps in. In 2001, the PBGC paid out more than $1 billion in benefits to nearly 269,000 retirees. And in that one year, the PBGC became trustee of 104 terminated pension plans covering nearly 89,000 people, its largest one-year increase ever. In 2002, it expects to take on twice as many new payees.

This certainly sounds like a crisis. But if you've heard anything about a crisis of retirement income, it's probably been the "Social Security crisis" that policymakers and pundits have been touting for years now. Retirees are said to depend on a three-legged stool: personal savings, employer pensions, and Social Security. Of the three legs, Social Security has gotten the most attention for being in danger, but in fact, it is unquestionably the most solid. You just wouldn't know it from the way mainstream commentators typically address the issue.

As Ellen Frank explains in this chapter, Social Security is not in a crisis, and will not be any time soon. You may have heard that Social Security is going to go bankrupt in such-and-such a year: a few years ago it was 2024, today it's 2038. But in "Social Security Q&A," Frank shows just how misleading such statements are. Social Security has a lot of excess revenues today, which it is in essence loaning to the federal government by buying treasury bonds. The aging of the U.S. population may lower the ratio of workers to retirees; if so, a day will come when Social Security will need to "cash in" these bonds in order to pay benefits. When the bonds are used up, Social Security will be back to relying solely on the payroll tax to meet its obligations to retirees. At that point, either the payroll tax rate will have to be raised or else the federal government will have to cover some portion of Social Security benefits out of general personal and corporate income tax revenues. This is what critics refer to as "bankruptcy."

Frank cogently explains that whether we think of the federal obligation to Social Security as legitimate or an accounting gimmick, the financial security of retirees now and in the future simply depends on the ability of the U.S. economy to produce enough goods and services to meet everyone's needs. And she clarifies the politics behind loaded terms like "crisis" and "lockbox." The payroll tax that currently funds Social Security is a regressive tax that falls hardest on low-income workers. Whether the more progressive income tax should pay for part of the nation's pension system is—like any number of other questions—a ground for political struggle. Words like "crisis" and "bankruptcy" merely serve to provoke fear and prevent the public from recognizing the terms of the struggle and what is at stake.

Right now, a related struggle is playing out over whether Social Security should be privatized. Under various privatization schemes, some portion of workers' payroll taxes would be placed in individual accounts and invested in the market. Then, the guaranteed Social Security retirement income would be cut on the basis that the accruals in these individual accounts would make up the difference. Of course, repeating the word "crisis" like a drumbeat helps persuade Americans that some dramatic change like this is necessary, although big losses in the stock market since 2000 have chilled many people's enthusiasm for the idea. Nonetheless, the Bush administration is pressing forward.

Dean Baker analyzes the report of the president's Social Security Commission and finds one idea to endorse: individual, portable retirement accounts administered by the federal (or state) government. He describes how such accounts would go at least a small way toward meeting the need of a majority of U.S. workers who have no private pension. In that sense, they could bolster the employer-pension leg of the stool ("Taking One From the Bush Team"). But as for the idea of using such accounts to replace Social Security, Ellen Frank shows it to be unworkable and a threat to most Americans' retirement security. Ultimately, she explains, privatizing Social Security would be a gift to Wall Street fund managers, not workers and retirees ("The Hidden Costs of Private Accounts").

SOCIAL SECURITY Q&A

By Ellen Frank

November/December 2001

Q: Is there or is there not an actual Social Security trust fund?

A: Since the mid-1980s, the Social Security Administration (SSA) has been collecting more in payroll taxes each year than it pays out in pension, survivor, and disability benefits. The difference between receipts and payments grew significantly in the 1990s, and now amounts to some $160 billion each year. The Social Security system is expected to continue running annual surpluses at least through 2025.

Each year, SSA turns over any surplus funds to the U.S. Treasury, which spends the funds. In return, SSA receives special-issue, non-negotiable U.S. Treasury securities, which represent an implicit promise by the U.S. government to repay Social Security when and if additional money is needed to cover benefits. These bonds are what we call the "trust fund." In 2000, the trust fund contained bonds valued at $1.2 trillion; by 2025, the accumulated surpluses should top $3 trillion.

These, of course, are projections—the surpluses (and thus the trust fund) could be larger or smaller than anticipated, depending on wage growth, population changes, the overall state of the economy, and so on. Under the SSA's "low-cost" (or best-case) scenario, the Social Security trust fund will grow continuously until late in the 21st century.

So, yes, there is a trust fund, representing the excess of payroll taxes over benefit claims, and it is "invested" in promissory notes issued by the government.

Q: Is there actually money in the Social Security trust fund? And if not, where is it?

A: There is not actually "money" in the trust fund, any more than there is actually "money" in your bank account. When you open a bank account, the bank lends your money out. You exchange money for a promise from the bank to repay you, subject to whatever limitations and provisions you may have agreed to in advance. Your money is replaced with a piece of paper laying out those terms and obligations—a bank statement, passbook, quarterly notice, whatever. Your money has become a claim on a financial firm and is as good as the stability of that financial firm.

Similarly, the surplus revenues flowing into Social Security over the years have all been lent to the Treasury and spent—all, that is, except this year's $160 billion surplus. Before the attacks in September, Congress was still arguing over this money. By December, the surplus is almost certain to have disappeared in any case.

Some critics of Social Security use alarmist rhetoric in discussing the trust fund: The SSA is bankrupt, our hard-earned money is gone, the government has blown it all. They're right that there's no money in the trust fund. But there's nothing duplicitous in this. All money gets lent or spent and replaced with other kinds of paper claims. Banks and other financial firms don't keep money lying around either.

Q: Then why do I keep hearing about a "crisis" in Social Security?

A: The problems with Social Security are not really financial in nature. They stem from the fact that, over the last 30 years or so, birth rates have declined in the United States, while life expectancies have increased. If these trends continue (and there's no reason to suppose they will not), the ratio of retirees to workers will rise. Unless the economy grows faster than the SSA predicts—unless those future workers are more productive than the SSA projects, or the workforce grows faster than expected due to immigration—the cost of supporting all these retirees will exceed the revenues that would accrue from current tax rate of 12.4% on payroll.

According to SSA's none-too-optimistic projections, the Social Security system will have enough revenue from payroll taxes alone to cover benefits at their current levels (adjusted for inflation) up until 2016. For seven years after that, there will be enough revenue from payroll taxes and interest on the bonds held by the trust fund to cover benefits at current levels. Then, in 2023, SSA will need to begin redeeming the bonds. When that happens, the system will have enough revenue—from payroll taxes, interest, and bond redemption combined—to cover legislated benefits for another 15 years or so.

The problem is this. Once we reach a point where payroll tax receipts fall below projected benefit payments—once the SSA actually needs the interest and principle from the bonds to meet its obligations—the U.S. Treasury will have to find resources to pay the SSA, just like it has to find resources to pay back any other creditor. They can do this by raising taxes, cutting spending on other federal programs, or borrowing from the private financial markets.

Q: But if the government has to raise money to pay the SSA in the future anyway, then what's the point of collecting these surpluses today?

A: Good question. From a purely economic perspective, there is no point. The federal government is collecting surplus payroll taxes and then spending them, and will have to raise revenue somehow in the future to pay Social Security benefits. The bonds in the trust fund do nothing to alter this.

Realize that the bonds are non-negotiable, and SSA cannot redeem them for cash unless Congresses allocate money for this purpose. But if future Congresses choose not to repay Social Security, they can simply raise payroll taxes or cut benefits and avoid altogether the need to redeem the bonds. Understanding this, some Democrats have insisted in recent years that Social Security surpluses be used exclusively to repay debts that the government currently owes to the financial markets. This is the idea behind the so-called Social Security "lockbox."

In fact, it makes absolutely no difference to the trust fund whether the surpluses are used to repay public debt, cut taxes, or pay for expanded federal programs, any more than you, as a depositor, need concern yourself with where a bank lends your deposits. But the defenders of the trust fund apparently feel that using the surpluses to repay debt will harden the federal government's commitment to the security of future retirees. If the money has purportedly been "saved" in a rhetorical "lockbox," the reasoning goes, it will be pretty hard for opponents of Social Security to turn around 10 or 20 years from now and argue that benefits need to be cut.

Now look at this from the perspective of anti-government Republicans. They oppose higher taxes, have little faith in the ability of government to cut spending (and plenty of ideas on how to raise spending for defense and corporate subsidies), and object to the government borrowing cash from the financial markets. They are also none too keen on the idea of workers retiring into extended periods of idleness. Back in the 1930s, when Social Security was established, conservative business groups vehemently opposed it. They gave their support grudgingly, and only when then-President Roosevelt assured them that the system would be funded entirely by payroll taxes on working stiffs. General tax revenues, which are paid largely by upper-income groups, were never to be tapped for Social Security.

But if governments of the future are to honor the commitment implicit in the trust fund, then general revenues will have to be tapped. Real resources will need to be transferred to retirees, above and beyond the 12.4% payroll tax, so that retirees can survive without a paycheck. The amount needed is not that large, but it's large enough to worry those corporate and wealthy taxpayers who neither need nor want Social Security and who are likely to be asked to foot the bill.

This is why proponents of privatization are claiming that the Social Security trust fund is on the verge of collapse. The trust fund was designed to solve a potential economic problem—transferring resources to seniors in the future so that American workers can continue to enjoy retirement—with a political accounting device. Privatization boosters are today exploiting the contradictions inherent in that accounting device to attack Social Security and to justify regressive policies such as raising current payroll taxes or cutting current benefits.

Q: But there will be a shortfall in Social Security at some point in the future. What can we do about that?

A: It's difficult to say for sure whether the projected shortfalls will materialize. But they may. And if they do, privatization is definitely not the answer. The economic problem of caring for a large number of retirees in the future cannot be solved with private accounts. Even if they worked as their boosters claim (and they won't—see Ellen Frank, "The Hidden Costs of Private Accounts," page 92), private stock accounts are just another sort of accounting device. Eventually, all those private account holders are going to retire and try to sell their stock for the cash needed to buy real resources—food, shelter, health care. If the economy has not grown sufficiently to provide the resources, the stocks will rapidly become worthless.

The only real investment we can make today to strengthen Social Security is in economic growth and enhanced economic well-being. Next time your Congressional representative talks about Social Security, ask her what she's doing today to ensure that America's future workers will be healthy enough, happy enough, secure enough, and skilled enough to care for their aging parents. That's the only security we can count on.

THE HIDDEN COSTS OF PRIVATE ACCOUNTS
By Ellen Frank
November/December 2001

As Bush's handpicked commission on Social Security grapples with the details of diverting Social Security revenue into private accounts, it will almost certainly confront a knotty little logistical problem—an issue that so stumped privatization boosters in the past that most either finessed the problem or threw up their hands entirely. The problem is how to actually manage the 150 million plus personal accounts even a partially privatized system would require.

When privatization was initially floated several years back, advocates had in mind something along the lines of the current employer-sponsored 401(k) programs. In a 401(k) plan, employers contract with a fund manager to invest employee contributions. To minimize paperwork and oversight costs, they limit the number of available investment options, generally to around 10 funds, though sometimes to as few as three or four, so that workers are not wholly free to actively manage their own portfolios.

Even so, tracking this money is neither easy or cost-free. Employers need to set up accounting and compliance systems, select investment options, and monitor fund performance. The U.S. Department of Labor estimates that administrative costs run somewhere between $100 and $200 per year for each person enrolled in a plan. On top of that, fund managers rake off fees—usually 1 to 2% of the balance—to cover costs and leave some profit. And the system doesn't work seamlessly. Contributions get lost, delayed, misdirected; sometimes willfully, sometimes by accident.

Consider, then, how a national 401(k)-type program, funded out of payroll taxes and covering every single worker in the United States, would operate. Each and every employer in the country would need to set up a monitoring system and contract with financial firms to manage the accounts of even part-time, transient workers. The plan Bush put forth during his presidential campaign would divert two percentage points of the 12.4% payroll tax to personal investment accounts. Presumably, the law would require employers to offer some minimum array of investing options. Let's say they would have to offer five options, and let's imagine further that the typical employee would choose to allocate her savings equally among the five funds.

Consider, as an example, the local donut franchise with several part-time employees, typically working 20 hours each week at $7.50 an hour. Currently, the business owner sends $18.60 per worker to the Social Security Administration (SSA)—the combined employee and employer share of payroll taxes. Now, though, the donut shop will need to send out two checks—$15.60 to the government, and $3 to the financial contractor managing the employee's investment accounts. That's 60 cents in each of the five funds. The cost to the donut shop owner of setting up and monitoring these accounts could add up to thousands of dollars each year.

Now, imagine that our representative fast food worker quits after 10 weeks and takes a job with the pizza shop down the road. Does she shift her $30 in accumulated savings to the pizza maker's plan? Must the pizza shop owner offer the same five investment options as the donut franchiser? If not, who will arrange for the transfer of her funds from one financial contractor to another?

Or can the worker simply leave her miniscule balances—$6 in each of five funds—where they are, opening new funds with new financial firms as she shifts from part-time job to part-time job in the low-wage sector of the economy? If so, who will pay the administrative costs of maintaining all these accounts? The donut shop? The pizza store? The worker herself? Will the typical U.S. teenager complete high school with perhaps 20 different accounts, each containing a few dollars apiece, and those few dollars destined to be eaten away by annual management fees and administrative costs? And what happens if funds are lost, or deliberately withheld, or sent to the wrong fund manager? Would the federal government oversee this? Would the grocer, the baker, and the pizza maker pay for independent oversight? Would the mutual fund industry want this headache? Would anyone?

Chewing over this logistical nightmare, earlier advocates of privatization proposed to streamline the process. To ease the burden on small businesses, employers would instead send all payroll tax money to the SSA, as they do now, and the SSA would place two percentage points in privately managed accounts, nominally owned by the covered workers. Acting like a centralized human resources office for the entire U.S. labor force, the SSA could offer a wider array of investment choices and set up a system, similar to those offered today by a number of large employers, that would allow workers to actively manage their savings.

This is undoubtedly much simpler. But it is not cheap. The SSA would now be responsible for two major administrative functions—managing the flow of funds to current pensioners, and handling the mutual fund monitoring and record-keeping for 150 million private accounts. Economists estimate that this would at least double the administrative costs of running Social Security, raising the annual cost of administration from nearly 1% to just under 2% of payroll taxes. Will these costs be paid by workers? If so, nearly half of the projected returns from private accounts will be lost to administrative costs—and this is before we even talk about fees charged by the finance industry.

Or will Social Security's extra costs be paid by the Treasury out of general tax revenues? In this case, the government could save itself the trouble. If general revenues amounting to an additional 1% of payroll taxes were shifted to the SSA, that would go a long way towards solving Social Security's long-range financing problems, adding a number of years to the life of the trust fund.

Then there's another question. If all the money targeted for private accounts must, in any case, flow through the SSA, why bother with private accounts in the first place? Why not let the SSA invest the same share of its own revenues in private assets, manage its own portfolio, and use the presumably higher returns to fund higher benefits, or close future operating deficits?

"Absolutely not!" say privatization boosters. Allowing a federal agency to manage billions in private assets in its own name on behalf of 150 million taxpayers is socialism. Allowing the same agency to contract with financial firms to manage those same stocks in the name of said taxpayers is free-market capitalism. So does ideology trump common sense in the Social Security debate.

Last year, the conservative Federalist Society invited me to debate Charles Rounds, Suffolk University law professor and supporter of private accounts. The audience questioned Rounds closely on how the accounts would operate. Would workers actually own their own savings? If so, could they withdraw funds and spend them as they chose? Or invest them in anything at all—say, Florida real estate or an Internet start-up? And what would happen if their investments went sour or they spent down their savings before retiring?

These are the sorts of questions privatization boosters prefer not to address. A libertarian and Cato Institute researcher, Rounds criticized Social Security as a big-government welfare scheme which, disguised as a pension plan, coerces American workers to support retirees. Yet he conceded that a privatized system would itself necessitate quite a lot of federal coercion—workers would be required to save, to place their savings in a few pre-selected stock funds, and to keep them there until retirement. He also acknowledged that Congress might need to saddle the SSA with yet another task—administering a supplementary welfare program for those who outlived their savings.

That is the dirty little secret of privatization. A system of private accounts would be so expensive to set up and monitor, and would expose workers to so much risk and so many fees, that the federal government would almost certainly have to manage the whole mess, from choosing investment options and monitoring accounts, to establishing a parallel welfare system for those whose investments prove unprofitable.

So the push for privatization is not about freedom and individual choice after all. It's about diverting the money now going to SSA into the coffers of Wall Street.

TAKING ONE FROM THE BUSH TEAM

By Dean Baker

November/December 2002

Implausible as this may seem, President Bush's Social Security commission came up with a good idea. While no single proposal could possibly fix all the problems of the private pension system, the commission designed a scheme that could get part of the way there.

Granted, the members of the "President's Commission to Strengthen Social Security" were selected by the Bush administration for their allegiance to the myth of the Social Security crisis and their support of privatization. The commission's 2001 final report was remarkable not so much for its recommendation of partial privatization (that came as little surprise) but for its cynical errors and omissions of fact. For example, its inflated stock return projections conflict with the slow economic growth rates projected by the Social Security trustees. The commission's case for an imminent Social Security meltdown, and for partial privatization, is founded on fiction.

But one commission idea merits serious consideration. It proposed establishing a national system of pension accounts for every worker in the country. Of course, Bush's commission wanted to *divert* a portion of the Social Security payroll tax from Social Security into these accounts. This would not only place at risk the only guaranteed income many Americans can bank on having at retirement. It would more than double the administrative costs of the current Social Security system, and strain Social Security finances (which despite the hyperbole are on sound footing at present).

The commission has it backwards. Its proposed system of individual accounts makes no sense as a replacement for Social Security. It does make sense, however, as a supplement to Social Security. *Without* drawing on Social Security payroll deductions, a system similar to that envisioned by the Bush commission could serve as a nationwide alternative to private 401(k) plans. (See box, "401(k) Defined.")

A bare bones 401(k)-like pension modeled after the Thrift Savings Plan for federal

401(k) Defined

The 401(k) plan takes its name from section 401(k) of the Internal Revenue Code. Now one of the most common types of pension in the private sector, 401(k) plans are employer-sponsored tax-preferred retirement savings vehicles. They are financed primarily by voluntary employee contributions—in other words, out of employees' own paychecks. Some employers match employee contributions up to a cap (with cash or, less often, with company stock). The contributions are invested in one or more funds chosen by the employee from a limited menu. Employees bear the risk of their 401(k) investment choices in full.

employees, the national pension plan would offer workers three or four basic funds (for example, a stock index, bond index, and money market) and allow them to divide their accounts among these funds and to switch their holdings periodically. The accounts would be administered by a central authority.

A Universal Solution

The benefits from such a system would be substantial. Currently, about half of the nation's workers have no access to a pension. Coverage rates for low-wage workers are far lower. Only about 13% of workers in low-income households are eligible for employer-sponsored pensions. Among the hardest hit are people who work for small businesses and short-term and part-time workers. Under a national pension system, every individual in the country would immediately have access to a low-cost, fully portable, retirement plan. This means that workers could contribute to the fund on their first day at a job, even in part-time or temporary positions. They could also keep the same account no matter how frequently they changed jobs.

Employers would have the option to contribute to this fund on behalf of their workers, just as they do now with 401(k) plans. Because the plan would be low-cost and simple, many employers would probably replace their existing 401(k) plans with the national system. Small businesses that now see pension administration as burdensome might begin to make contributions to their workers' accounts at very little administrative cost. In this sense, a national voluntary 401(k)-type system may actually prove to be something of a boon to small businesses, since they would be able to offer the sort of pensions provided by larger companies.

The fact that a national pension system will cost far less to administer than the current system will also bolster workers' asset accumulations. The Bush commission estimated (probably optimistically) that the administrative fees on a national pension system would average 0.3% of the account values, more than 1.1 percentage points below the cost of a typical employer-sponsored 401(k) plan at present. Over time, the fee reduction (whatever the exact amount) would have a large impact on the size of retirement wealth.

Taking the commission's fee estimate at face value for the moment, if a worker puts $1,000 per year for thirty years into a typical 401(k), the account would grow to just $50,000. But with the lower-cost national system, it would grow to more than $60,000 (at a 4% rate of return). Over a forty-year period the difference would grow still larger: $80,000 under the existing system, compared to $104,000 under the national system.

A national pension system will not address all or even most of the problems of the existing system. There are tens of millions of workers just making ends meet now. Most low-income workers will not be able to contribute to a national pension system regardless of how good a deal it is. Once a national pension system were put in place, it would be imperative for working people to push for a federal subsidy or tax reimbursement, similar to the one President Clinton proposed in 1999 and Vice President Gore proposed in his 2000 presidential campaign. Under Gore's proposal, federal government contributions would be paid into the accounts of low-income individuals. Such a federal match could amount to a sizable transfer of wealth to the working poor.

It is also worth noting that this system of accounts need not be established at the national level to reap economies of scale. A relatively large state would have enough workers to push down the costs close to that of the national system. (As the number of workers in a system gets larger, the costs per worker decline.) Since most workers don't often move across state borders, they could expect to stay with a single fund for much of their working career. Already, there is substantial interest in the Washington State legislature for setting up a system of "Washington Voluntary Accounts." If Washington or any other state successfully adopted a centralized system of accounts, it could serve as a model for other states and for the nation.

As a side benefit, a national system of voluntary accounts should provide a bit of a shake-up to the financial industry in a time when the public doesn't think very highly of Wall Street. The banks and brokerage houses that have been charging workers administrative fees equal to 1.4% of 401(k) holdings will suddenly be forced to compete with a system that charges less than one quarter of this amount. In order to keep their place in the market, the banks and brokerage houses would have to reduce their fees. Such a reduction in fees would benefit all workers with 401(k)s, even those who opt not to take part in the national system.

In short, a national pension system could be a good first step toward repairing the holes in the private pension system. (And a federal match or tax reimbursement for low-income workers' contributions would be better still.) There seems little not to like about the Bush commission's plan for a national system of pension accounts, so long as it has *nothing* to do with Social Security.

Chapter 6

TAX WINDFALLS FOR THE WEALTHY

INTRODUCTION

During the Gilded Age, the late 19th and early 20th centuries, capitalists such as Andrew Carnegie, John D. Rockefeller, and J. P. Morgan amassed unheard-of fortunes (in steel, oil, and banking, respectively), and their class displayed its vast wealth with conspicuous excess. At the same time, millions of Americans lived in squalid districts and toiled in hazardous mines, fields, and factories for poverty wages.

There is evidence that the United States today is in a new Gilded Age. Although Americans' lives as workers and consumers have changed dramatically since the original Gilded Age, the vast gap between rich and poor that was a defining feature of that era has returned. In particular, the distribution of wealth and income in the United States is the most unequal it has been since the years before the Great Depression. For example, as of 1998, the latest year for which such figures are available, the wealthiest 1% of U.S. households owned 38.1% of the nation's wealth, while the bottom 40% of households jointly owned less than 0.3%. (That's less than three out of every thousand dollars!) The top 1% of households held more wealth than the entire bottom 95%.

U.S. society has always been characterized by significant economic inequality. However, even 25 years ago, the problem was not as severe as it is today. Between the end of the Great Depression and the mid-1970s, the benefits of the U.S. economy's massive growth were distributed relatively equally among families at all income levels. Beginning in the mid-1970s, however, this forty-year trend reversed. The United States moved into a period of growing inequality which accelerated in the 1990s. Between 1983 and 1998, for example, the average net worth of the wealthiest 1% of U.S. households *grew* by 42.2% in real terms while the poorest 40% saw their average net worth *fall* by 76.3%. Income inequality has followed a similar trend. Between 1979 and 1998, the average income of the wealthiest 5% of U.S.families grew by 64%, while the income of the poorest 20% fell by 5%.

In the face of such growing inequality, we might imagine that a democratic (small "d") government would use tax policy to redistribute money from the rich to the poor. In fact, many Americans no doubt believe that the current tax system does just that. After all, doesn't the federal government spend billions of dollars every year on programs like welfare? So it may come as a surprise that the distribution of *after-tax* income is actually slightly more unequal than the distribution of *pre-tax* income. And over the past 25 years, the inequality of after-tax income has grown faster than the inequality of pre-tax income. In other words, tax changes since the late 1970s have indeed redistributed wealth—from the poor and middle class to the rich!

Today, the Bush administration is accelerating the trend. After successfully pushing through a huge tax cut in 2001, of which 38% will go to the wealthiest 1% of families, the administration is pressing for further cuts, including dropping the tax on corporate dividends and making the repeal of the estate tax permanent. Part of the explanation for the administration's success, perhaps, lies in the language it has used to describe these policies—language that the media has largely, and often uncritically, adopted. This language includes phrases like "double taxation" and "death tax," which economist John Miller ("Double Taxation Double Speak") and researcher-activists Rosie Hunter and Chuck Collins ("'Death Tax' Deception") deconstruct in this chapter.

Wealth and its owners claim their share of space on newspaper pages and television screens. But the news coverage, while extensive and not always positive, is limited by underlying assumptions that the material in this chapter calls into question. Recent corporate financial scandals have made well-publicized villains of the likes of Enron's Ken Lay, Salomon's Jack Grubman, and Tyco's Dennis Kozlowski. But by focusing on those whose abuses are so extreme, the media only reinforce the underlying assumption that everything would be fine if only everyone would play by the rules—that the rules themselves are reasonable and fair. President Bush travels the country telling audiences that his proposed tax cuts are justified because "It's your money." That sounds reasonable and fair.

But the rules—like tax policy—that govern how wealth is distributed are often neither reasonable nor fair. For example, as John Miller points out in "Getting Back More Than They Give," the wealthiest 1% of families actually got a larger share of the 2001 tax cut than the share they pay of federal taxes. Meantime, payroll taxes, which are a greater burden for a majority of taxpayers than the income tax, were not cut at all. The other two selections by Miller, "The Bush Tax Cut" and "Red Ink, Blue Bloods, and Bad Policy," analyze the Bush administration's tax policies further, showing how they have given windfalls to the wealthy, and squandered federal surpluses that could have met pressing social needs.

"DEATH TAX" DECEPTION
by Rosie Hunter and Chuck Collins
January/February 2003

The federal estate tax, or "death tax," isn't dead yet, but a powerful clique of wealthy families and interest groups will stop at nothing to kill it. Their movement makes small business owners and family farmers its poster boys. But those who stand to gain the most from repeal are a few thousand very wealthy households. The effort to turn the public against the estate tax, and ultimately abolish it, is a case study in conservative movement tactics—the campaign uses distorted facts, dirty tricks, and front groups, and it's bent on repealing the nation's only tax on inherited wealth.

The decade-long public relations and lobbying campaign seemed to pay off when President George W. Bush signed his $1.35 trillion tax cut into law in 2001. The bill included a gradual phase-out of the estate tax over ten years (see box). But because the tax bill—a bizarre assortment of delayed activation dates and gimmicks that money guru Jane Bryant Quinn called "a contemptible piece of consumer fraud"—was structured to "sunset" at the end of 2010, the estate tax will

---

The Estate Tax: The Basics

The federal estate tax is the only tax on accumulated wealth in the United States. It is a transfer tax, levied at the time of death when assets transfer to heirs. It falls on the country's wealthiest households—less than 2% of all estates—but still generates significant revenue (currently $30 billion annually, or about 9% of the non-military discretionary budget).

Under the 2001 tax cut, the amount of wealth exempted from the estate tax rises from $1 million ($2 million for a couple) to $3.5 million in 2009 ($7 million for a couple). As a result, the number of households subject to the estate tax will shrink from 50,000 to about 6,000 a year.

Even at its current level, the estate tax affects only a small percentage of businesses and farms. This is in part because family-owned businesses and small farms receive special treatment under the tax, including large deductions when the business or farm represents at least 50% of the estate, and assessments that reduce the estimated value of assets. These special rules frequently allow family own businesses and farms to pass on $5 to $8 million, tax-free, to heirs.

Those family-owned businesses that are subject to the estate tax rarely pay the top marginal rate, and are given a generous 14-year payment schedule. The estate tax is a graduated tax with a rate structure that starts at 32% and increases to a top rate of 55% on estates exceeding $3 million. The 2001 tax bill reduces the top rate to 45% between now and 2009. The "effective rate," the percentage of the total value of the estate actually paid in taxes, averages about 30%.

be fully repealed for only one year, after which tax rules revert back to what they were before passage of the bill.

The anti-estate tax lobby is now pushing hard to make repeal permanent. With Republicans back in control of both houses of Congress, repeal proponents on both sides of the aisle are emboldened. And they understand that they must move quickly because as the budget deficit grows, permanent repeal will become politically more difficult to justify.

Can this juggernaut be stopped? Perhaps, but only if progressives take a hard look at the anti-estate tax campaign, debunk its claims—and its "grassroots" façade—and then organize like never before.

The Case for Preserving an Estate Tax

Abolishing the estate tax would further concentrate the nation's wealth in the hands of the super-rich at a time when the distribution of wealth is already more unequal than at any point since the 1920s. It would also drain resources from strapped states and charities. Among the pressing budgetary reasons to preserve the tax are these:

- Making the repeal of the estate tax permanent would contribute to a fiscal train wreck, draining government coffers of $850 billion between 2011 and 2021.

- Repeal would eliminate one of the few progressive taxes in our federal system, resulting in the transfer of hundreds of billions of dollars to the trust funds of the nation's wealthiest families while shifting the burden of taxation (or cuts in services) onto those less able to pay.

States—already straining to balance their budgets—stand to lose $9 billion a year in state-linked revenue by 2010 as a result of the planned estate tax phase out.

Estate tax repeal would also shrink charitable giving and bequests, particularly from estates in excess of $20 million. Without the incentives provided by the estate tax (which encourages charitable bequests during life, in anticipation of the tax, as well as at death), the Treasury Department estimates that charitable giving may decline as much as $6 billion a year.

But the estate tax was meant to do more than bolster budgets and aid charities. From its inception, it was meant to ward off the emergence of a hereditary aristocracy in the United States. Established in 1916, the tax was a populist response to the excesses of the Gilded Age. President Theodore Roosevelt justified it by arguing that society has a claim upon the fortunes of its wealthy. Roosevelt pointed out that "most great civilized countries have an income tax and an inheritance tax. In my judgment both should be part of our system of federal taxation." Such taxation, he noted, should "be aimed merely at the inheritance or transmission in their entirety of those fortunes swollen beyond all healthy limits."

A number of modern-day millionaires—who are themselves subject to the tax—understand its historical importance. As part of the opposition to repeal, over 1,200 wealthy individuals signed a petition calling for preserving—but reforming—the tax. The signers (who include William H. Gates, Sr., George Soros, and Ted Turner) argue that the tax is an essential means to moderate the excessive build-up of hereditary wealth and power. Investor Warren Buffett argued in the *New York Times* that repealing the estate tax would be comparable to "choosing the 2020 Olympic team by picking the eldest sons of the gold-medal winners in the 2000 Olympics…Without the estate tax, you in effect will have an aristocracy of wealth, which means you pass down the ability to command the resources of the nation based on heredity rather than merit." Petition-signers and other activists say they support raising the cap on exemptions to further reduce the already-miniscule number of small businesses and farms affected by the tax. For some, the call to raise exemption levels is in part tactical—a means to gain congressional support for tax preservation.

The Push for Repeal

How did legislation benefiting only a narrow slice of the wealthiest Americans advance so far? Who is behind the push to abolish the estate tax?

Repeal backers describe their movement as "grassroots," but peek behind the curtain and you find a well-funded public relations, lobbying, media, and research apparatus (led by sophisticated operatives, many with deep connections to the Republican Party).

In the early 1990s, a group including the heirs to the Mars and Gallo family fortunes embarked on a long-term effort to eliminate the tax. They enlisted the help of Patricia Soldano, an Orange County, California, advisor to wealthy families. She formed a lobbying organization (the "Policy and Taxation Group") to provide an "outlet" for wealthy families "interested in communicating their concerns to members of Congress." Soldano channeled funds to congressional backers of repeal and hired the powerful lobbying firm Patton Boggs.

By the mid-1990s, Soldano's outfit and other early pro-repeal groups had joined together with a veritable anti-tax industry of think tanks, lobbying firms, and interest groups in Washington, D.C. to form a powerful "death tax elimination" lobby. Conservative think tanks, including the Heritage Foundation and the libertarian National Center for Policy Analysis, produced "policy backgrounders" criticizing the estate tax, and made the requisite op-eds and TV appearances as well. The anti-government group Citizens for a Sound Economy encouraged its members to lobby their senators and representatives against the tax. Other groups involved in the anti-estate tax crusade include the private campaign organization Club for Growth; the political arm of the libertarian Cato Institute; the American Conservative Union; Grover Norquist's Americans for Tax Reform; and the 60 Plus Association, a self-styled conservative alternative to the American Association of Retired Persons. At the center of the lobbying effort is the National Federation of Independent Businesses (NFIB), a business trade association and one of the most influential organizations in Washington. The NFIB's lobbying web site <www.YesToGrammKyl.com> sends faxes to Congress urging estate tax repeal.

In 1993, U.S. Representative Christopher Cox (R-Calif.) introduced the first repeal legislation with just 29 co-sponsors. Soon, Sen. Jon Kyl (R-Ariz.) became a chief ally, along with Reps. Jennifer Dunn (R-Wash.) and John Tanner (D-Tenn.). Within a year, elimination of the "death tax" occupied a central plank of the G.O.P.'s 1994 "Contract with America." By 1998, repeal legislation had over 206 House sponsors including the entire Republican leadership.

At NFIB's 2002 Small Business Summit, Bush strategist Karl Rove said "the NFIB and the Bush administration work hand-in-hand because we see eye-to-eye." Referring to NFIB's failed effort in June 2002 to make the repeal of the estate tax permanent, Rove assured his audience, "Don't look at it as a defeat. This is a war, and we need to make an ongoing commitment to winning the effort to repeal the death tax."

Death Tax Lingo

In perhaps its greatest public relations feat, the pro-repeal lobby has managed to portray the estate tax as a "death tax" on most Americans. The phrase suggests a tax imposed upon death itself, although over 98% of those who die go untaxed. The "death tax" label has proven a major asset to the campaign, yet its authorship is disputed. James L. Martin, president of the 60 Plus Association and Bush family friend, credits himself. Rep. Dunn credits *Seattle Times* publisher Frank Blethen.

Whatever the origin of the tag, Republican pollster Frank Luntz masterminded its widespread use. Luntz urged conservative legislators and candidates to exclusively call the estate tax a "death tax," and in a 1994 memo he suggested legislators hold anti-estate tax press conferences at local funeral homes. Republicans employ the "death tax" label so effectively that the term is now used in the mainstream press.

Martin has thought up plenty of other labels for the tax as well, including "grim-reaper's tax," "grave robber's tax," "cruelest tax," "pine-box tax," and "success tax." Martin travels the country to spread the word that "taxing cadavers is gross public policy," and to ask the public, "Should Uncle Sam, rather than a blood relative, be the first in line when you die?" At one point Martin ran a contest to generate new catch phrases; the winner—"last-grasp tax"—got $100. Martin, Luntz, and other Republican spin-doctors recognize that success hinges on how the debate is framed. Martin told *The American Prospect,* "it's all a matter of marketing."

Deception Down on the Farm

Pro-repeal literature is packed with claims that the estate tax forces working farmers to sell their farms. When Congress passed legislation to repeal the tax in 2000, it delivered the bill to President Bill Clinton on a tractor to symbolize the "down on the farm" effects of the bill. On the campaign trail later that year, George

W. Bush declared, "To keep farms in the family, we are going to get rid of the death tax!"

Starting in the spring of 2001, a number of investigative reports began to question the veracity of these claims. They found that stories of farmers losing the farm to the estate tax are so rare that experts and investigators have been unable to find any real examples. Neil Harl, an Iowa State University economist whose tax advice has made him a household name among Midwest farmers, said he searched far and wide but never found a case in which a farm was lost because of estate taxes. "It's a myth," said Mr. Harl, "M-Y-T-H."

The *New York Times* reported that when the pro-repeal American Farm Bureau Foundation was challenged to produce one real case of a farm that was lost because of the estate tax, it could not cite a single example. In April 2001, the Bureau's president sent an urgent memo to its affiliates stating, "it is crucial for us to be able to provide Congress with examples of farmers and ranchers who have lost farms ... due to the death tax." Still, no examples were forthcoming.

Disabled Americans Against the Death Tax?

In early 2001, Responsible Wealth (a project of the popular education organization United for a Fair Economy) initiated the petition of wealthy individuals calling for preservation of the tax. The petition prompted a swift counterattack by the pro-repeal lobby, which issued a barrage of advertising and media events to undermine the Responsible Wealth effort. One example provides an illustration of pro-repeal tactics.

In March of 2001, full-page advertisements appeared in several daily newspapers around the country including the *Wall Street Journal* and the *Washington Times*. The advertisements were produced by a new organization, dubbed "Disabled Americans for Death Tax Relief." Its leader, a young woman from Austin, Texas, named Erin O'Leary, claimed she had just formed the organization two weeks earlier and already had over 1,000 members.

O'Leary was "deeply offended by the callous and heartless comments made by 125 so-called 'millionaire' signers of the Responsible Wealth ad that appeared in the *New York Times*." She alleged that there are "2.5 million disabled people who are family members of millionaires, a number that would grow to 8 million over the next thirty years," and that with rising medical costs, these individuals needed their inheritances. The text of the advertisement continued:

> In order to live a full life, these Americans may require medical help, nursing and living assistance far beyond that which is covered by medical insurance. Warren Buffet, Bill Gates, Sr. and George Soros believe that these people should be denied full financial help from their parents.

The "Disabled Americans" stunt was the creation of conservative communications maven Craig Shirley (whose public relations firm represents the National Rifle Association, the Heritage Foundation, and the Republican National Committee). Fox News and several conservative talk shows kept O'Leary busy with interviews, but most other news media recognized O'Leary's advertisement for the charade that it was.

Disabilities experts responded, including author Marta Russell, who felt that "using disabled people to front for the interests of the wealthiest members of our society is an outrage and a disgrace." Russell disputed the claim that millions of disabled people could be adversely affected by the tax. O'Leary's figures made no sense given the economic profile of the disabled population in this country. The disabled are one of this country's poorest groups, and highly dependent on the very tax-funded social services that repeal of the estate tax could put at risk.

Shaping Public Perception

Print and radio advertisements are key weapons both in molding public perception and attacking members of Congress who vote against full repeal. The owner of the *Seattle Times*, Frank Blethen, sees estate tax repeal as his personal crusade. (Blethen believes that the estate tax is responsible for the decline of family-owned newspapers.) He started a website <www.deathtax.com> and organizes an annual "Death Tax Summit" in Washington, D.C., to mobilize other independent newspapers and business groups to lobby Congress.

Blethen has used the *Seattle Times* as a vehicle for his anti-estate tax cause, both on the editorial page and through advertisements, stirring concerns from the paper's editors about his lack of impartiality. Further, he circulated the anti-death tax ads he developed to other newspaper owners; they were published in over one hundred independent newspapers nation-wide.

The estate tax is also a favorite issue for conservative groups seeking to exercise political influence through issue ads. In the months prior to the 2002 election, pro-repeal organizations ran estate tax issue ads in South Dakota, Missouri, Minnesota, Iowa, and Arkansas. In Missouri, the United Seniors Association and Americans for Job Security (phony grassroots organizations fronting for corporate interests) targeted former Senator Jean Carnahan's position on the estate tax. In Minnesota, Americans for Job Security ran full-page newspaper ads attacking the late Senator Paul Wellstone for voting against full repeal, and flew a banner at the Minnesota state fair: "Wellstone Quit Taxing the Dead!"

Dividing Diverse Constituencies

Another pro-repeal strategy has been to thwart progressive and diverse groups that might be inclined to preserve the estate tax. Over the past five years, pro-repeal forces worked to convince the public that the estate tax is particularly detrimental to women and people of color as well as farmers. In doing so, they spin an illusion of a rainbow coalition in opposition to the tax.

For example, the NFIB and front group called the Small Business Survival Coalition recently organized press conferences with women business owners and alleged that "women—not men—are the chief victims of the tax" because women generally outlive men. They mobilized women's business organizations including

Women Impacting Public Policy and the National Association of Women Business Owners in support of repeal.

But claims that the estate tax burdens women business owners are misleading. The great majority of all businesses fall below the taxable level. Relatively few businesses of any kind face the tax, and because women-owned (and minority-owned) businesses are smaller than average, they are affected even more rarely. As for the argument that women outlive men, the only families subject to the tax are those who own assets at least 20 times greater than the net worth of the median family. Therefore few widows lose any inheritance to the estate tax. And those who do are among the wealthiest 2% of households, not hard luck cases. On the other hand, women—and people of color—benefit disproportionately from social programs (including small business loans and education spending) funded by the tax.

Anti-estate tax groups have similarly put forward minority business groups, such as the Hispanic Business Roundtable and the National Black Chamber of Commerce, as visible allies. Frank Blethen enlists minority-owned newspapers in opposing the tax. He tells readers of the <www.deathtax. com> newsletter that it is important to "educate" members of Congress that the estate tax is "a minority and female-owned business issue and an environmental issue."

In April 2001, billionaire Robert Johnson of Black Entertainment Television and a group of other African-American business people ran ads in the *New York Times* and the *Washington Post*. Johnson invoked race in his ads, claiming to speak for African Americans broadly. The ads asserted that the estate tax unfairly takes wealth away from the black community and that repeal would help African Americans gain economic power. Although there are no statistics available on the number of African Americans subject to the estate tax, African Americans are clearly far less likely than white people to inherit fortunes large enough to face taxation. The median net worth for African-American households (excluding homeownership) is $1,200, compared to $37,600 for white households. (The median Hispanic household is lower still, with zero net worth.) One in four African-American households own no positive wealth at all, compared with one in seven white households. And there are only two African Americans on the Forbes 400: Oprah Winfrey and Robert Johnson himself.

Nevertheless, President Bush moved quickly to quote Johnson in his speech to the Council of Mayors, saying "as Robert Johnson of Black Entertainment Television argues, the death tax ... weighs heavily on minorities."

Soon after, Bush tried to convince the members of the National Council of La Raza, a major Latino advocacy group, to join him in supporting estate tax repeal. Bush described a Mexican-American taco-shop owner who said he wanted "to get rid of the death tax so I can pass my business from one generation to the next." It turned out, as even the *Wall Street Journal* noted, the taco shop Bush described was valued at $300,000, far below the over $1 million exemption the current law allows owners of businesses. George W. got it wrong. The taco shop would pass to heirs untaxed, just as the vast majority of small businesses do.

Like the allegations about small farms and family enterprises, pro-repeal forces repeat these allegations about women and people of color over and over through their media work and lobbying efforts.

A principal tactic of the campaign has been to get the minnows to front for the whales.

But the truth is, few or no folks are losing their taco shops—or their farms—to the estate tax. In fact, in 1998, only 776 estates where family-owned business assets represented over half the value of the estate were "taxable" under estate tax rules, out of 47,482 total taxable estates, and 2.3 million individual deaths. So the great majority of estates taxed under the estate tax are not estates built on family-owned businesses and farms, but other forms accumulated wealth—stock investments, nonproductive assets, fourth homes, art collections, luxury items, etc.

All or Nothing Repeal

The architects of the repeal effort are zealots. They advocate nothing short of complete repeal and consistently oppose any reform or compromise. They understand that partial reform will not benefit the principal patrons of the repeal effort—the very wealthy interests who bankroll the campaign would not be covered by exemptions. (Their wealth is so great it would exceed even a very high cap.)

But this strategy may backfire when the groups that have bought into the misrepresentations realize that, rather than family farmers or small business owners, the vast majority of whom will never owe any estate tax, the windfall of estate tax repeal will go to the heirs and heiresses of the country's 3,000 wealthiest estates. This elite group will inherit billions in appreciated stock and real estate, enormous capital gains that have never been subject to taxation. The *Wall Street Journal* has estimated that George W. Bush's heirs alone would stand to gain from $6 to $12 million if the tax is repealed, assuming his estate remains the same size up to his death. Cheney's heirs would save between $10 and $45 million. And the heirs of the Gallos and Marses stand to make even more.

Conclusion

In the bid to eliminate the estate tax, anti-repeal forces have used slick advertising, explicit falsehoods and deception. But we should not have to endure the triple whammy of lost federal revenue, state revenue and charitable giving in order to give a handful of millionaires and billionaires a tax break, no matter how well disguised in a misinformation campaign.

With Republicans back in control of the U.S. Senate, the push is already on to permanently repeal the federal estate tax. For now, even with their new majority and Democratic party supporters, repeal proponents fall short of the 60 votes they need under budget rules that expire in April 2003. If the budget rules are not extended, however, they will be able to advance their anti-estate tax agenda with only a simple majority. This juggernaut can be stopped, but time is running out.

STILL A BAD IDEA: THE BUSH TAX CUT
By John Miller
March/April 2001

We said we didn't want it. Most people didn't even vote for it. In survey after survey, public opinion polls rank a large tax cut as one the least desirable uses of the federal budget surplus. And Republican and Democratic leaders alike have warned the President-select that his tax cut package will never emerge whole from Congress.

But all to no avail. George W. Bush has yet to back off from the monstrous, surplus-draining tax cut proposal that was the cornerstone of his campaign. Now he's even telling us that it's for our own good: His tax cut will cure our softening economy and stave off the threat of recession by "encouraging capital formation, economic growth, and job creation." Even Alan Greenspan, chair of the Federal Reserve Board and a debt-reduction hawk, is prepared to accommodate the Bush plan.

At least one group is happy to swallow the Bush tax cut medicine—"the haves and the haves-more," as Bush referred to his supporters during a fundraiser last year. After all, it is their taxes he will cut. Together, lower income tax rates (with the biggest drop at the top) and the repeal of the estate tax account for nearly three-quarters of the Bush tax cut. Nearly three-fifths of the total benefits of the tax cut package will go to the richest 10% of all taxpayers, and some 43% will go just to the top 1%, those who make more than $319,000 a year and showed average income of $915,000 in 1999.

But no matter what Bush says, his tax giveaway to the wealthy will not inoculate us against recession. Nor are well-to-do taxpayers suffering from over-taxation, as the Bush team insists. One thing is sure. If the Bush tax cut goes through, social programs that have already been neglected for more than two decades will continue to suffer.

Defending the Indefensible
The editors of the *Wall Street Journal* never met a pro-rich tax cut they didn't like. And the Bush tax cut is much to their liking. Last December, they argued the case for a massive tax cut on three grounds:

- "Taxes are too high. Last year [1999], federal tax revenue as a percentage of the economy reached an historic peak—20.4% of GDP."
- "For the past couple of years, our tax overpayments have put the federal budget in surplus. And Congress, incited by this surplus, has exceeded its own

budget caps and increased its spending beyond the rate of inflation. And they've just done it again, passing a humongous budget."

• "The economy is beginning to wobble. Economic forecasters are sniffing a recession; they are busily lowering growth projections for next year. And for good reason; some of the data are starting to look scary."

On closer inspection, none of these arguments holds up. First, let's look at what the *Journal* editors had to say about government being too large and taxes too high.

Federal tax revenues—as a percentage of Gross Domestic Product (GDP), or national output—are currently, as the editors suggest, at their highest levels since World War II. But that is not because government got bigger during the 1990s or because today's federal budget is "humongous" in historical terms.

The economic boom of the 1990s—faster economic growth and a skyrocketing stock market—did enlarge the tax base and allow the federal government to collect more tax *revenues*. Those added tax dollars closed a $300 billion deficit in the federal budget and then generated the current surplus. But that surplus hasn't translated into bigger government, as the *Journal* editors claim. During the 1990s, federal *spending* as a share of GDP actually got smaller, not bigger, slipping below 20%. In 2000, it reached just 18.2%, the lowest mark in 35 years. (See Figure 1.)

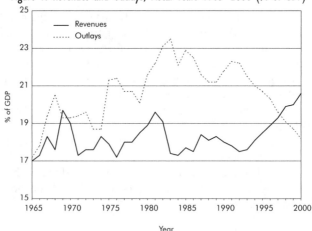

Figure 1: Revenues and Outlays, Fiscal Years 1965–2000 (% of GDP)

Source: Congressional Budget Office.

Even some conservatives, if not the *Journal*'s editorial writers, noticed the drop. "The good news of the Clinton presidency," says Stephen Moore of the Cato Institute, a libertarian think tank, is that "the federal government is getting smaller, at least relative to the size of the economy."

So much for the government being too big by historical standards. But what about the beef about "over-taxation"? It misses the mark as well.

The *Journal* editors are fond of pointing out, in their paeans to the "New Economy," that any serious assessment of the 1990s should take into account the wealth amassed through the stock market boom and other investments. But tax revenue as a share of GDP is a misleading measure of the decade's tax burden precisely because it fails to do this.

Here's how. According to economists Alan Auerbach and William Gale, about one-third of the surge in tax revenues during the 1990s came from taxes on the capital gains realized when stockholders and other investors cashed in their holdings. The calculation of taxes as a share of GDP counts capital gains tax revenues but ignores gains in wealth that have not been cashed in. From 1989 to 1999, the total wealth or net worth of households (their total assets minus debt) more than doubled. Had all of that new wealth been included in the *Journal*'s calculation, then taxes as a share of economic activity would have shown a decline.

Economists have long argued that, for tax purposes, changes in net worth should be counted as income. Even conservative economists agree. For instance, Bruce Bartlett, former Reagan administration Treasury official, says that today most people regard increases in net worth as "the equivalent of increases in income," even before they realize their investments. When Bartlett calculated taxes as a share of economic activity, he adjusted his measure for changes in net worth and found that the tax share declined during the 1990s. In 1990, tax revenues measured 18.3% of the sum of GDP plus year-to-year changes in household net worth, but were just 15.1% in 1998. (See Figure 2.)

Figure 2: Federal Revenues as a Percentage of GDP and of GDP Plus the Increase in Net Worth

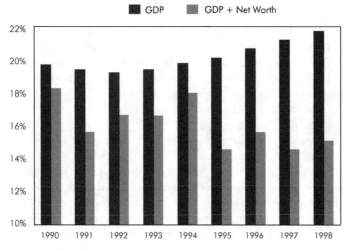

Source: Bruce Bartlett, "The Trouble with Tax Cuts," *Policy Review* (Dec. 1999/Jan. 2000).

For Bartlett, that downward trend goes a long way toward explaining why "tax cuts have fallen sharply as an issue of concern to voters" and why "the tax revolt went into hibernation." When the Heritage Foundation, the Washington-based conservative think tank, published Bartlett's study in 1999, they distributed it to journalists with a cover letter instructing "conservatives who favor tax cuts" to "wake up and smell the apathy."

The *Journal* editors weren't listening. Rather than face up to the implications of an intellectually honest analysis of federal taxes by a fellow conservative, they prefer to spend their time spinning data in a desperate attempt to awaken the tax revolt from its slumber.

No Recession Fighter

Crying recession is the *Journal* editors' and the Bush team's latest attempt to resuscitate the tax revolt. The threat of recession is genuine enough. Slower economic growth abroad, higher oil prices, stagnating stock prices, and jacked-up interest rates have already damped down U.S. economic growth and surely could bring the current expansion to an end. Still, that is no reason to give in to the chicanery that we must bribe the rich with a tax cut if we want to forestall a recession.

The Bush tax cut is no recession fighter. First off, it will do little to combat slower growth in a timely way. Even if Congress passes the proposal intact, none of the cuts would be enacted before 2002. In truth, much of the Bush proposal would be slowly phased in over ten years, with just 11% of the tax cut coming in the first three years. Worse yet, the later and larger tax cuts would take place regardless of economic conditions—and in all likelihood well after the end of the next recession.

Aside from its poor timing, the Bush tax cut is ill-designed to jumpstart the economy. The immediate effect of lower taxes comes from increasing consumer spending. But by targeting the rich, who consume less of their income than others, the Bush tax will offer little of this stimulus. That holds for both the repeal of the estate tax—whose benefits will go exclusively to the richest 2% of the population—and the across-the-board cut in income tax rates, which is weighted heavily in favor of the wealthiest taxpayers.

Nor are repealing the estate tax and cutting income taxes likely to provide the long-term stimulus to capital formation and job creation that Bush promises. Tax-cut backers can't point to a single credible economic study showing that eliminating the estate tax will boost investment. The track record of cutting income taxes is problematic as well. The Reagan administration reduced income tax rates across the board and lowered capital gains taxes—cuts that supply-side economists claimed would encourage people to work, save, and invest. But when mainstream economists, such as Barry Bosworth and Gary Burtless of the Brookings Institution, checked out the effects of the '80s tax cut, they found quite different results. Male workers put in about the same number of hours after the tax cut as before it, and while women did work more hours, their earnings failed to improve. Not only that, relative to the size of the economy, savings plummeted and net investment declined. That hardly fits with the claims of the Bush team.

Finally, if slower growth is now the justification for cutting taxes, then the budgetary implications of the Bush tax cut are even more alarming than when it was originally proposed. In January, the Congressional Budget Office (CBO) projected that the federal budget (except for Social Security) will run a surplus of $3.1 trillion over the period 2002 to 2011. The CBO projection assumes brisk economic growth averaging 3.1% over those ten years (comparable to that of the 1990s), no recession this year, a continuation of the rapid productivity gains of the last five years, and a hot stock market. But deteriorating economic conditions, let alone a prolonged recession, could compromise each of those assumptions and leave a surplus far smaller than the amount of the Bush tax cut, pushing the budget back into deficit.

Even if the CBO projections hold up, financing the Bush tax cut out of the surplus will be difficult. A recent study by the Center on Budget and Policy Priorities (CBPP), a liberal think tank, found that much of the surplus was unavailable for a tax cut. Some $400 billion of the projected surplus comes from the Medicare Hospital Insurance Fund, and there is overwhelming bipartisan consensus that those funds, along with the Social Security surpluses, should be set aside, not used for tax initiatives. Another $600 billion of the projected surplus disappears if current spending policies are maintained; the bulk of that would go to adjust discretionary spending for inflation and changes in the U.S. population. That still leaves about $2 trillion unallocated. But at least $500 billion, according to the CBPP, would be needed to help restore the long-term solvency of Social Security and Medicare, if Bush intends to keep that campaign promise.

Finally, an honest accounting of the cost of the Bush tax cut reveals that it will drain at least $1.9 trillion from the projected surplus, not $1.3 trillion, as his campaign claimed. According to Citizens for Tax Justice director Robert McIntyre, the Bush figure is based on nine years, not ten, because it starts its projection in 2001, a year before the tax cut would go into effect. On top of that, the government would have to borrow money to finance the Bush tax cut in its first years (before the larger surpluses kick in), but the Bush calculation doesn't include the cost of the interest on that borrowing. Those interest payments will be even larger if the economy slows, drying up projected tax revenues. Not only that, McIntyre now estimates that the total cost of the tax cut could be as high as $2.5 trillion, due to a quicker phase-in of the proposed cuts, new CBO revenue projections, and a likely reduction in the 26% minimum tax that upper-income taxpayers are now required to pay on their taxable income.

We Can Do Better

How might we make better use of the projected surpluses in the federal budget? On that score, the Democrats are not much help. In reaction to the extremism of the Bush tax cuts for the wealthy, they are offering up a warmed-over Eisenhower-moderate-Republican proposal from the 1950s—use the surplus to pay down the debt.

But devoting the surplus to retiring government debt is unlikely to produce a more robust economy. Reduced government borrowing is intended to lower interest rates and thus juice up capital investment, which accelerates economic growth. In practice, however, government borrowing and interest rates are not closely correlated, and lower interest rates are seldom by themselves sufficient to coax balky investors to part with their money. But if lower interest rates are the goal, the Federal Reserve can bring them down without expending the surplus. In fact, the Fed furiously lowered interest rates in the first two months of this year. Fed action makes sense, since it's the Fed's numerous hikes of the interest rate during 1999 and 2000 that helped to jeopardize the current economic expansion in the first place.

It's not hard to enumerate better uses of the budget surplus. To begin with, if a tax cut is needed to bolster the economy, then why not use the surplus to pay for a cut in the payroll taxes paid by wage workers? The majority of taxpayers now pay more in payroll taxes—deductions from paychecks to fund Social Security and Medicare—than in income taxes. Reducing payroll taxes would have a greater impact on most families than an income tax cut of the same size, while disproportionately favoring low-income earners. Also, by targeting wage workers, who are often strapped for cash, a payroll tax cut—in effect an across-the-board raise—would immediately boost consumer spending. A 10% reduction in Social Security and Medicare tax rates would cost about $60 billion in fiscal year 2001, according to the CBO, and could be funded from the projected budget surplus (leaving much of the surplus to meet other demands).

But what we really ought to do with the projected surplus is dedicate it to pressing social needs. In the United States today, 32.3 million people are living below the official poverty line, 44 million go without health insurance, and perhaps as many as seven million have no place to live. Our public schools are deteriorating, the state of public transportation is abysmal, and decent, affordable housing is practically impossible to find.

Even if we simply maintained current spending levels, adjusted for inflation and population growth, we could inject badly-needed funds into a large swath of government activities, including education, environmental protection, food and safety inspection, the National Park Service, and Head Start. While we're at it, we could shore up the Medicare trust fund. That would still leave vast resources to provide universal health care coverage, combat childhood poverty, renew public investment, and support numerous other social programs that the federal government has ignored. Even if the entire $3.1 trillion projected surplus were used for public spending, federal outlays in fiscal year 2011, according to the CBO, would be just 18.4% of GDP—smaller than at any point during the 1970s, 1980s or 1990s.

With budget surpluses now projected for the rest of the decade, these proposals are hardly beyond our means. It's just a matter of political will. In the last 20 years, social programs have been slashed almost beyond recognition. Squandering the surplus on a tax giveaway for the wealthy, while continuing to turn our backs on those in need, would be a criminal act.

Resources: Alan Auerbach and William Gale, *Does the Budget Surplus Justify Big Tax Cuts? Updates and Extensions* (The Brookings Institution, 1999); Bruce Bartlett, "The Trouble With Tax Cuts," *Policy Review* (December 1999/January 2000); Barry Bosworth and Gary Burtless, "The Effects of Tax Reform on Labor Supply, Investment, and Savings," *Journal of Economic Perspectives* (Winter 1992); "The Bush Tax Cut," *Wall Street Journal*, 19 December 2000; Congressional Budget Office, *The Budget and Economic Outlook: An Update*, 18 July 2000; James Horney, Isaac Shapiro and Robert Greenstein, "How Should the Surplus Be Used?" (Center on Budget and Policy Priorities, September 2000).

GETTING BACK MORE THAN THEY GIVE:
THE BUSH TAX CUT SHOWERS BENEFITS ON THE RICH
By John Miller
September/October 2001

By now your $300 tax rebate must be long gone. If you got one, that is. Some 34 million mostly low-income taxpayers didn't. If you did get a rebate, don't go looking for much more. For the vast majority of taxpayers, the 2001 tax "rebate" is most of what they will get from legislation that cuts taxes by over $1.8 trillion over the next ten years. But for the rich, the Bush tax cut is the gift that keeps on giving.

The tax cut—by cutting income tax rates, especially in the upper income brackets, and repealing the estate tax—overwhelmingly benefits the well-to-do and the super-rich. When fully enacted, the majority of the benefits of the tax cut will go to the richest 10% of taxpayers, with a whopping 38% going to the richest 1%. Those 1.3 million taxpayers, all with incomes in excess of $373,000 per year, will save an average of $53,123 a year on their federal tax bills. Meanwhile, the average tax cut for the bottom 60% of taxpayers is $347 a year, less than $1 a day. These 78 million taxpayers, each earning less than $44,000 a year, will get less than 15% of the benefits of the tax bill. (See Table 1.)

The passage of a tax cut that squanders an unprecedented federal budget surplus on those who need it least is an astonishing triumph of conservative rhetoric and public relations. The tax bill came cloaked in deception and distortion—including false claims that the "death tax" was unfair to small businesses and family farmers and that the budget surplus could simultaneously accommodate a large tax cut, expanded social spending, and paying down of the

TABLE 1: Effects of the House-Senate Conference Version of the Bush Tax Plan
(Annual effects when fully in place, at 2001 income levels)

Income Group	Income Range	Average Income	Income Tax Cuts ($billions)	Estate Tax Repeal ($billions)	Total Tax Cuts ($billions)	Average Income Tax Cut	Average Total Tax Cut	% of Income Tax Cut	% of Total Tax Cut
Lowest 20%	Less than $15,000	$9,300	$-1.7	$-0.0	$-1.7	$-66	$-66	1.2%	0.9%
Second 20%	$15,000–27,000	$20,600	$-9.8	$-0.0	$-9.8	$-375	$-375	6.6%	5.3%
Middle 20%	$27,000–44,000	$34,400	$-15.6	$-0.0	$-15.6	$-600	$-600	10.5%	8.5%
Fourth 20%	$44,000–72,000	$56,400	$-26.7	$-0.0	$-26.7	$-1,026	$-1,026	17.9%	14.5%
Next 15%	$72,000–147,000	$97,400	$-43.6	$-0.0	$-43.6	$-2,234	$-2,234	29.2%	23.7%
Next 4%	$147,000–373,000	$210,000	$-14.3	$-3.1	$-17.4	$-2,744	$-3,345	9.6%	9.5%
Top 1%	$373,000 or more	$1,117,000	$-37.4	$-31.8	$-69.1	$-28,722	$-53,123	25.1%	37.6%
All		$57,000	$-149.1	$-34.9	$-184.0	$-1,137	$-1,404	100.0%	100.0%
Addendum									
Bottom 60%	Less than $44,000	$21,400	$-27.1	$-0.0	$-27.1	$-347	$-347	18.3%	14.7%
Top 10%	$104,000 or more	$256,000	$-69.0	$-34.9	$-103.9	$-5,301	$-7,981	46.3%	56.5%

Source: Institute on Taxation and Economic Policy Tax Model; Citizens for Tax Justice

national debt. But perhaps no rhetorical device did more to sell such an inequitable tax cut than the Bush campaign mantra: "The surplus is not the government's money. The surplus is the people's money." As Bush would have it, the tax cut does nothing more than "share the surplus with the people who pay the bills." Of course, by "the people who pay the bills" Bush means the wealthy.

Even if you agree that the federal government should refund the budget surplus through tax cuts—rather than increasing spending on health, education, or other constructive uses—and that taxpayer refunds or tax cuts should based on how much they paid toward the federal tax bill—and not, say, on the basis of need—the Bush tax cut still hands over far too much of the surplus to the rich. A closer look at who pays federal taxes shows that the Bush tax cut is not just unfair, but unfair on its own terms.

The Bush approach seems to suggest that the federal government running a budget surplus is like a group of friends going out to dinner and realizing that they have contributed too much toward paying the check. The excess over the bill, or the surplus, should, according to Bush's reasoning, go back to each of member of group according to what they contributed toward the bill. Those who contributed the most get the most back; those who contributed less get less back. And those couple of down-on-their-luck friends who the rest are treating to dinner, of course, don't get anything back.

But who does pick up the tab for the federal government? The well-to-do and the rich, in fact, pay the bulk of federal taxes. This year, before the 2001 tax cuts were enacted, the richest 1% of taxpayers will pay just over one-quarter of all federal taxes and, altogether, the top 20% will pay about two-thirds of federal taxes, estimates Robert McIntyre, director of Citizens for Tax Justice, the Washington-based tax equity group. That is mostly because two federal taxes, the personal income tax and the estate tax, are two of the most progressive taxes in the U.S. tax code. The burden of those taxes fall most heavily on the well-to-do and the rich. The best-off fifth of taxpayers pay four-fifths of personal income taxes and the estate tax fall exclusively on the richest 5% of taxpayers. (See Table 2.) And these are the very taxes most on the chopping block with the Bush tax cut.

Nonetheless, the Bush tax cut can't manage to conform to its own mantra when it comes to the share of the tax cut going to the super-rich. The richest 1% of taxpayers, with an average income over $1 million, get nearly two-fifths (37.6%) of the benefits of the tax cut, while they pay little more than one-quarter (or 26.3% to be exact) of federal taxes. For the bottom 60% the Bush tax cut is far stingier, refunding a share of the tax cut that just about matches its 14% share of the federal tax burden. (Compare Table 1 and Table 2.) Many of those taxpayers, who pay sizable federal payroll taxes and excise taxes, but no personal income taxes and of course no estate taxes, will get no tax cut at all. (See Table 2.) As these figures show, the Bush tax cut does not so much pay out the federal budget surplus to taxpayers according to what they contributed to the federal tax bill as it pays off those at the top.

Table 2: Distribution of Pretax Income and Federal Taxes in 2001
(Figures are before the 2001—enacted tax cuts)

Income Group	Income Range	Average Income	Percent of All Pretax Income	Personal Income Taxes	Payroll (OASDHI) Taxes	Corporate Income Taxes	Excise Taxes	Estate Taxes	All Federal Taxes
Lowest 20%	Less than $15,000	$9,300	3.2%	-0.9%	2.9%	0.9%	12.5%	0.0%	1.1%
Second 20%	$15,000–27,000	$20,600	7.1%	1.0%	8.3%	2.9%	17.6%	0.0%	4.2%
Middle 20%	$27,000–44,000	$34,400	11.8%	5.8%	14.7%	5.8%	16.6%	0.0%	9.2%
Fourth 20%	$44,000–72,000	$56,400	19.4%	14.3%	25.9%	9.5%	20.1%	0.0%	17.6%
Next 15%	$72,000–147,000	$97,400	25.1%	25.0%	31.6%	14.6%	19.7%	0.0%	25.6%
Next 4%	$147,000–373,000	$210,000	14.4%	19.5%	11.9%	16.4%	4.2%	9.0%	15.8%
Top 1%	$373,000 or more	$1,117,000	19.2%	35.3%	4.5%	49.6%	3.5%	91.0%	26.3%
All		$57,000	100.0%	100.0%	100.0%	100.0%	100.0%	100.0%	100.0%

Source: Cititzens for Tax Justice
*Old Age, Survivors, Disability, and Health Insurance (OASDHI) is the fund for Social Security.

It's not like the super-rich need tax relief. Their incomes have grown more quickly over the last two decades than any other income group's. Corrected for inflation, the top 1% saw their incomes increase 142% from 1979 to 1997, while the incomes of the middle quintile increased just 9% and the bottom fifth suffered an 4% decline in their incomes. Nor have federal taxes taken a larger bite out the growing income of the super-rich. Their effective federal tax rate, the percentage of their total income the richest 1% pay in federal taxes, was 33.3% in 1997, well-below the 37.3% rate in 1979, and would have fallen to 32.7% had the 2001 tax cuts been enacted in that year. Nor have federal taxes been able to counteract the unprecedented inequality produced by this lopsided growth. A recent Congressional Budget Office study found that in 1997 the 2.6 million people who made up the richest 1% of the population had as much after-tax income as the 100 million Americans with the lowest incomes, or over 38% of the population.

Fortunately, there is still time to act. The most disastrous provisions of the Bush tax cut can still be averted. To force the $1.8 trillion Bush tax cut into the $1.35 trillion budget guideline approved by Congress, the bill relied on budget gimmicks and a bizarre tax-cut timetable: The income tax cuts for the upper income brackets are left until the later years of the tax cut, while the estate tax is gradually reduced over the bill's first eight years, repealed in the ninth year, and then reinstated in the tenth.

Meanwhile, the slowing economy and the budget process have exposed more fully the costs of the Bush tax, which will all but drain the budget surplus of the money available for new budget initiatives. Late in August, with an economic recovery still in doubt and a recent downward revision in official productivity growth figures, it seems almost certain that the Congressional Budget Office will cut its ten-year projection of the budget surplus. Popular social-spending proposals, such as universal prescription drug coverage for seniors, have also thrown into sharp relief the cost of the Bush tax cut. That program would cost little more than what the tax cut bestows on the richest 1%.

Re-centering federal budget policies towards national needs and genuine tax fairness will require, first, that we defeat the phony tax rhetoric coming out of Washington and the conservative think tanks and, second, that we build broad-based political support for constructive uses of what remains of the budget surplus. Until then Federal tax policy will continue to insure that those who feasted during the economic boom of the 1990s escape paying the bill for their night out on the town.

Resources: "Final Version of Bush Tax Plan Keeps High-end Tax Cuts, Adds to Long-Term Cost," Citizens for Tax Justice, 5/26/01 <http://ctj.org>. "Historical Effective Tax Rates, 1979–1997," Congressional Budget Office, May 2001, <http://www.cbo.gov>. Robert McIntyre, "The Institute on Taxation and Economic Policy Tax Model," 6/14/2001.

DOUBLE TAXATION DOUBLE SPEAK: WHY REPEALING DIVIDEND TAXES IS UNFAIR

By John Miller

March/April 2003

Concerned that the most well off in our society might be suffering a bout of the post-holiday blues, the *Wall Street Journal*'s day-after-Christmas editorial urged the Bush Administration to end the "double taxation" of dividends—payments of corporate profits to stockholders. Nothing lifts the spirits of the wealthy like yet another tax giveaway.

But for the editors of the *Journal*, making dividends tax exempt is not just psychotherapy for stock investors. It's a matter of economic justice and sound economic policy. (See excerpts.) In their hands, however, notions of a fair and effective policy response to today's stagnant economy become "double taxation" doublespeak. Let's try to set the record straight.

> The equity argument [for ending the dividend tax] is that it is unfair to tax anything twice, even at the highest levels of income. Americans will favor repealing the double tax on dividends because it offends their sense of fair play.*

The "double taxation" of dividends is the heart of their argument. But there is nothing about double taxation that ought to offend Americans' sense of fair play. True enough, the government collects income taxes on dividends paid out of the profits of corporations that have already been taxed. But being taxed more than once on the same income is a fact of life for every taxpayer, not just dividends collectors. Most workers, for instance, pay Social Security payroll taxes and income taxes on their wages, and then sales taxes when they spend what remains of their paycheck.

Beyond that, the claim that dividends are "double" taxed is an exaggeration. To begin with, in the year 2000 more than half of corporate dividends went to tax-exempt pension funds, individual retirement accounts, and non-profit foundations or to individuals who owed no income tax. In addition, corporate *income* is hardly taxed the first time around. Relative to GDP, U.S. corporate income taxes are no more than half those of other wealthy industrial (OECD) countries. By our own historical standards, corporate income taxes have fallen from 4.1% of GDP in 1960 to just 1.7% of GDP in 2001. In addition, the average rate of taxation on corporate profits currently stands at 15%, far below the top corporate tax rate of 35%. Worse yet, in 1998, twenty-four highly profitable major corporations, including Pfizer, PepsiCo, MCI Worldcom, General Motors, and Texaco, paid no corporate income taxes—and received a tax rebate. Robert

---

All quotations are from the editorial "Ending Double Tax Trouble," Wall Street Journal, *December 26, 2002.*

McIntyre, director of Citizens for Tax Justice, estimates that "barely more than half of corporate profits are subject to tax at any level."

More importantly when it comes to fairness, the issue is not *how often* we pay taxes, but *how much* we pay in taxes. By that standard, eliminating taxes on dividends would surely violate most people's sense of fair play. As even the *Wall Street Journal* allows, the beneficiaries would be those "at the highest levels of income." Some 42% of the benefits from repealing taxes on dividends would go to the richest 1% of taxpayers, and three-quarters of the tax benefits would go the richest 10%, reports the Tax Policy Center of the Urban Institute and the Brookings Institution. The top 1% of taxpayers, those with yearly incomes greater than $373,000, also benefited most from the economic growth of the last two decades. After adjusting for inflation, their real average before-tax income more than doubled (a 138% increase) from 1979 and 1997, according to the Congressional Budget Office, while their tax burden, much like that of large corporations, has declined. By 1997, the richest 1% of U.S. families paid out about 1/3 of their income in all federal taxes, far less than the 2/5 they paid in 1977. These figures will only get worse due to the 2001 Bush tax cut or the elimination of dividends taxation.

> [Taxing dividends] creates huge distortions in both corporate and investor behavior... [O]n the corporate side, taxation creates incentives for companies to finance themselves via debt (interest on debt is tax deductible, dividend payouts are not). Increased debt can of course result in increased financial fragility for the company and risk for investors.

The *Journal* editors argue that repealing the taxation of dividends might reduce corporations' reliance on debt financing. Interest payments are currently tax-exempt. By putting the taxation of interest payments and dividends on an equal footing, the government would take away the incentive for corporations to finance themselves through borrowing. But so too would several other changes in the tax code that would not result in a tax windfall for the super wealthy. For instance, to eliminate the tax bias in favor of "growth stocks" (which benefit investors by increasing in price), we could just remove the 20% cap on income taxes on capital gains (the sale of stocks and other assets). But the editors of the *Wall Street Journal* are loathe to consider any proposal that would boost government revenues and arrest the decline in the tax burden of the rich or large corporations.

> The tax penalty also prompts companies to retain earnings ... rather than paying profits to investors. This can freeze capital—rather than allowing investors to reinvest cash in other businesses where rates of return might be higher, thus permitting capital to flow to more productive uses.

Cutting taxes on dividends is surprisingly less than popular with corporate managers. Both Carter and Reagan administration proposals to reduce or eliminate the double taxation found little support among business elites. Joel Slemrod, a former Reagan administration White House aide and tax economist, told the *Wall Street Journal* that business executives dismissed the Reagan proposal to cut dividend taxes as "just for shareholders," saying that they preferred tax relief that comes directly to corporations. While the *Wall Street Journal* editorial touts dividend paying corporations as a good investment in today's bear market, some economists are not convinced. Economist Alan Auerbach argues, for instance, that with lower dividend taxes, investors would expect corporations to pay out more of their earnings in the form of dividends, reducing the cash available for new corporate investments.

Finally, repealing the tax on dividends is unlikely to provide the stimulus necessary to counteract today's economic stagnation. As Slemrod's comments suggest, business investment is unlikely to pick up in response to cutting dividend taxes, especially in face of the overcapacity in today's economy. Even if shareholders do pour new money into stocks paying dividends, that will do little to spark new corporate investment. The vast majority of stock sales are not new issues, but resales of existing stock from one stock investor to another, which do not provide corporations with new funds for investment. During the 1990s stock boom, economists Robert Pollin, Dean Baker, and Marc Schaberg put the ratio of stock resales to new stock sales at 113.8 to 1.

If fairness and effectiveness are the issues, then a cut in the Social Security payroll taxes will do more to spread widely the benefit of cutting taxes and do far more to get the economy going again than eliminating dividend taxes. Today, three quarters of taxpayers pay more in payroll taxes than income taxes. In addition, we can count on those middle- and low-income households, many of them strapped for cash with the economic slowdown, to spend more of their income than the super-rich who would make out with the repeal of taxes on dividends.

A one-year payroll-tax holiday on the first $10,000 of wages would give workers a tax cut of up to $765, with much of the benefit going to middle- and low-income taxpayers. The AFL-CIO, the Business Round table, and the Economic Policy Institute all support proposals similar to this one. The Tax Policy Center estimates that 45.4% of the benefits of a Social Security payroll-tax holiday would go to the bottom 60%, as opposed to 4.7% of the benefits from repealing dividend taxation.

A payroll tax holiday would do as much to lift the spirits of most people as repealing dividends taxation would do to buck up the super-rich. It's the right thing to do. Don't let all the double taxation doublespeak make you doubt that for one minute.

RED INK, BLUE BLOODS, AND BAD POLICY: BUSH SQUANDERS THE BUDGET SURPLUS

By John Miller
May/June 2003

It's worse than we thought.

In January 2001, when George W. Bush took office, the bipartisan Congressional Budget Office (CBO) projected federal budget surpluses as far as the eye could see. Some $5.6 trillion in budget surpluses would accumulate over the next decade. This was Dubya's post-Cold War "peace dividend," a sum with the potential to reverse decades of neglect of the nation's pressing social needs.

By the spring of 2002, two-thirds of that projected surplus was gone. The largest single share went to the first round of Bush tax cuts. Now, one year later, the rest of the projected surplus is gone, and then some. Current federal tax and spending policies will saddle the federal government with budget deficits through fiscal year 2007, according to the latest CBO study, and leave a net deficit of $378 billion in place of the $5.6 trillion surplus for the ten years from 2002 to 2011. (See *Federal Budget Surplus* table.)

Figure I: Federal Budget Surplus (or Deficit) in Trillions of Dollars*

	FY 2002–2011
January 2001 CBO Projection	5.644
January 2003 CBO Projection	0.020
March 2003 CBO Projection	−0.378
March 2003 CBO Projection with FY2004 Presidents Budget	−2.122

Sources: Congressional Budget Office, Jan. 2001, Jan. 2003, March 2003.

* The federal budget surpluses and deficits in the table are for the unified budget which combines on-budget and off-budget (principally Social Security) federal government surpluses and deficits.

A $6 trillion reversal of fiscal fortune is a stunning accomplishment, even for a president with a proven knack for losing money in the private sector. Did the Bush administration—full of remorse over the tax giveaways to the rich of its first year in office—spend this past year bolstering the budget for social programs? Did the president decide that government borrowing is reasonable if the money is invested in meeting important human and infrastructure needs?

Not a chance.

The CBO report is clear about where the rest of that projected surplus did go. First off, the recession and worsening economic prospects made mincemeat of the CBO projections. A deeper than anticipated economic slump in 2001, slow growth since then, and a collapsing stock market made the CBO revenue estimates far too optimistic. When combined with unanticipated cost increases, especially escalating health care costs, these "technical changes" ate about 45% of the projected ten-year surplus.

These factors—arguably beyond the control of the Bush administration—aside, there was still $3 trillion in projected surpluses that the Bush budgets have entirely depleted. The major culprit in pushing the Bush budget into the red? That's easy: tax cuts, targeted to the wealthy. Tax cuts in the past two years accounted for nearly three-fifths of the lost surplus due to legislative changes (in other words, the remaining 55% of the lost surplus). That $1.757 trillion went to finance the Bush tax cuts enacted in 2001, including the phase-out of the estate tax and an across-the-board cut in income tax rates, and a far smaller rebate for income taxpayers in 2002. Over one-third of the benefits of those tax cuts, according to Citizens for Tax Justice, will go to the richest 1% of taxpayers, all with incomes greater than $384,000.

Increased government spending, the great bulk of which went to military appropriations, explains the remaining deterioration in the Bush budget picture. Additional military appropriations are more than double the new spending for discretionary nonmilitary domestic spending—programs such as public housing, supports for low income families, education *and* homeland security! (See Figure 2. Note that the breakdown in the figure is based on the CBO's January 2003 projection rather than on the most recent [March 2003] projection cited above.) Together with the Bush tax cuts, new military spending accounts for 83% of the ten-year costs of legislation enacted under the Bush administration. The remaining additional civilian spending went to new entitlement spending, primarily to a farm bill, compensation for 9/11 victims, an airline bailout and educational and other benefits for veterans and military retirees.

And all of that was before the Bush administration's guns 'n tax-cuts budget for FY 2004 reached Congress. If the Republican-controlled Congress enacts the current Bush budget proposal, loaded with more tax cuts for the well-to-do and a continued military buildup, budget deficits would grow to a whopping $2.1 trillion over the FY2002 to FY2011 period, says the CBO. Worse yet, the CBO's estimates (like the president's budget proposal) make no mention of the cost of the war in Iraq.

Figure 2: The Projected Surplus: Where it Went

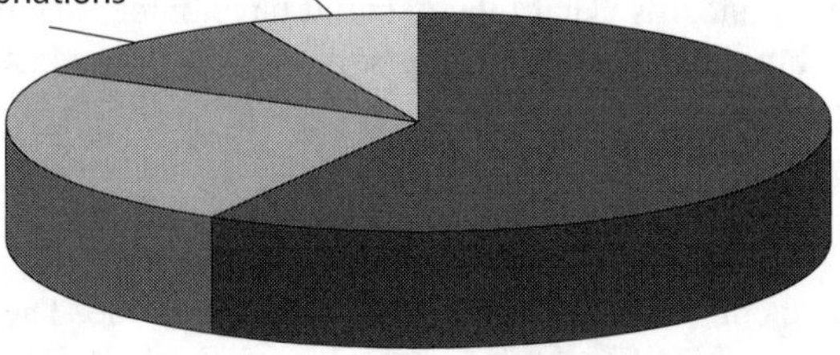

Entitlement Legislation[3]
7%

Non-Defense Appropriations[2]
11%

Military Appropriations
24%

Tax Cuts
58%

Source: Richard Kogan, "Are Tax Cuts a Minor or Major Factor in the Return of Deficits? What the CBO Data Show," Center on Budget and Policy Priorities, Feb. 12, 2003.

[1]Based on January 2001 CBO projection of the ten-year surplus FY 2001–2011, corrected for $2,577 billion due to overoptimistic revenue and cost estimates.

[2]Including Homeland Security.

[3]Entitlement legislation includes the farm bill, extended unemployment compensation, 9/11 victims compensation, the airline bailout, student loan changes, veterans education benefits, and dual benefits for military retirees and veterans, among others.

Big Deficits—Who Cares?

The Bush administration does not dispute that we have returned to an "era of large deficits." But Office of Management and Budget director Mitch Daniels says, "We ought not hyperventilate about this issue." Congressional Democrats are in fact having a hard time catching their breath as they beat the drum of fiscal responsibility. Kent Conrad, the ranking Democratic member of the Senate Budget Committee, warns that the Bush budget would post "the worst deficits in our nation's history." Federal Reserve chair Alan Greenspan, the Democrats' new patron saint, warned Congress that "If we do not ... reaffirm our commitment to fiscal discipline, years of hard effort could be squandered."

The real charge against the Bush administration and its wealthy patrons, however, is not that they squandered a surplus built of our hard-earned fiscal discipline, but that they squandered it on themselves. Turning surpluses into deficits, even deficits as large as the 3% to 4% of Gross Domestic Product (GDP) that the Bush administration is likely to ring up this year and next, would not be a problem had the surplus been put to good use.

Consider just two examples. For $350 billion over ten years, no more than the tax cut that the Bush budgets lavished on the richest 1% of taxpayers, the administration could have covered 25% of the prescription drug costs of the entire

Medicare population, according to budget analyst Richard Kogan with the Center on Budget and Policy Priorities. Likewise, $1.3 trillion, the cost of the 2001 Bush tax cut, is the amount of new spending the American Society of Civil Engineers recently found was necessary to bring U.S. infrastructure up to what it calls acceptable standards. That money could have made much-needed improvements in school buildings, sewers, airports, mass transit systems, roads, and other vital infrastructure.

The Next Budget

But precious little new social spending made its way into the Bush budgets, which have consistently turned butter into margarine. The Bush budget proposal for FY2004 is no different. It limits the growth of total discretionary spending to 4%, but that average masks large, damaging cuts to a whole host of domestic programs. To begin with, non-military discretionary spending (more or less everything outside of Social Security, Medicare, and the military) will increase at only a 2.3% annual rate through 2008, according to the CBO, barely keeping up with the expected rate of inflation. This does nothing to reverse the decline in non-military domestic discretionary spending from 4.7% of GDP in 1980 to 3.5% of GDP in 2002.

Key domestic spending programs are on the chopping block in the Bush budget proposal for FY2004, including funding for public housing, rural health programs, and community policing. Also singled out for cuts are infrastructure items such as roads and wastewater treatment facilities. The administration slashes employment and training programs by 11% even though the U.S. economy shed 2.3 million private sector jobs between January 2001 and January 2003. Even the Bush education budget would increase by less than the rate of inflation, while cutting spending on after-school programs and vocational training and eliminating four student aid programs. While the budget promises $400 billion for a Medicare prescription drug benefit, cuts in general Medicare funding in the Republican House budget would actually leave the program with a net increase of only $186 billion over the next ten years, far less than the amount necessary to fund any meaningful prescription drug benefit.

These budget cuts have already jeopardized the social safety net. But the long-term effects of the Bush policies are even more alarming. A recent study by the Center on Budget and Policy Priorities argued that the administration's tax-cutting agenda will endanger even our most basic entitlement programs. For example, over the next 75 years the Bush tax cuts would cost more than three times as much as the Social Security Administration's most recent estimate of the deficit in Social Security over the same time period!

The Bush budget does far better by military spending. After a 15% jump last year, military spending is still slated to increase by 4.7% a year through 2008. Military-related spending consumes the majority of the $782 billion in discretionary spending in the Bush FY2004 budget. Some $399 billion would go to the Pentagon (the Defense Department plus nuclear weapons programs in the Department of Energy). Homeland security gobbles up another $41.3 billion.

The Bush administration has requested an additional $75 billion in supplemental funding for this fiscal year to pay for its war with Iraq. But initial estimates of the cost of wars are notoriously low. The CBO puts the cost of a three-month ground war with a five-year occupation, its worst case scenario, at $272 billion. If the United States actually reconstructs Iraq, as the Bush administration promises, the costs run far higher. One estimate, by economist William Nordhaus of Yale, puts the cost of the war plus reconstruction as high as $755 billion; his worst-case estimate rises to nearly $2 trillion when negative impacts on the oil market and the macroeconomy are included. And alienated allies who picked up much of the tab for the Gulf War seem unlikely to bail the United States out this time around.

Despite earlier tax cuts and a slumping economy eating away at government revenues and the war with Iraq driving up expenditures, new tax cuts continue to be the signature of the Bush budget plan. This time, the Bush team wants $1.6 trillion in additional tax cuts over the coming decade. Some $624 billion would go to make permanent the $1.3 trillion tax giveaway to the wealthy Bush pushed through Congress in 2001. Another $726 billion would finance the Bush growth package proposed this January. Its centerpiece, the exclusion of dividends from taxation, would bestow 42% of its benefits on the richest 1% of taxpayers. Should his budget be adopted, the total cost of the Bush tax cuts, including those already enacted, would rise to $3.0 trillion over the years 2001 to 2013. Adding in the higher interest costs on the borrowing the government will have to do to make up for the revenue lost to those tax cuts, that cost reaches $3.7 trillion.

Tax cuts for the rich and military spending are the means that the Bush administration is using to constrict the flow of monies to programs that benefit working and low-income families. Giving to the rich, taking from the poor, and racking up large deficits is a policy combo straight out of the Reagan playbook.

But Bush's class-warfare budget is actually out of sync with how the United States has financed past wars. Large federal deficits have been a constant. But so too have been taxes levied against those most able to pay. For instance, in 1919, following World War I, the top tax bracket of the federal individual income tax jumped from 15% to 77%. During World War II, policy makers extended the income tax downward to apply to middle-income earners but also raised the top tax bracket. Even the President's father passed a tax increase during the first Persian Gulf War.

Not this time. Today we ask not one ounce of sacrifice from those best off in our society. Instead we spill red ink to pay for tax cuts for blue bloods and to finance an internationally-condemned war that spills the red blood of the people of a poor developing country who have already suffered through two decades of wars, political repression, and economic sanctions. That stain will remain with the Bush administration forever more.

Resources: Congressional Budget Office, "The Budget and Economic Outlook: Fiscal Years 2004–2013," January 2003; Congressional Budget Office, "An Analysis of the President's Budgetary Proposals for Fiscal Year 2004: An Interim Report," March 2003; Democratic Caucus of the Budget Committee, "Big Tax Cuts, Harmful Program Cuts, and Record Deficits: Summary and Analysis of President Bush's 2004 Budget," Feb. 7, 2003; Democratic Staff of the Senate Budget Committee, "Review & Analysis of the President's FY2004 Budget," February 27, 2003; Richard Kogan, "Are Tax Cuts A Minor or Major Factor in the Return of Deficits? What the CBO Data Show," (Center on Budget and Policy Priorities, February 12, 2003); Center on Budget and Policy Priorities, "House Republican Budget Contains large Cuts in Medicare, Medicaid, and Other Domestic Programs," March 17, 2003; Richard Kogan, "Costs of the Tax Cuts and of a Medicare Prescription Drug Benefit," (Center on Budget and Policy Priorities, June 14, 2002); Citizens For Tax Justice, "Revised Estimate Pegs Latest Bush Tax Cut Plan at $2.0 Trillion Over Decade," March 18, 2003.

Chapter 7

RHETORIC AND REALITY OF "GLOBALIZATION"

INTRODUCTION

Since NAFTA went into effect in 1994, business writers have been singing the praises of "free trade" agreements. Taking their cues from U.S. trade representatives and officials at global trade and financial institutions, journalists have largely accepted the premise that "more trade" would be the rising tide that lifted all boats. "More trade" would bring increased economic growth, which would in turn mean rising incomes for all—even, perhaps especially, the poor of the world.

In fact, "free trade" pacts were never about *how much* trade there should be, but *how* it should be conducted and *whom* it should serve. Agreements like NAFTA and the proposed Free Trade Area of the Americas (FTAA) were new constitutions covering vast areas of economic life—not only trade in goods, but also international capital flows and government regulation. Would these constitutions respect or trample labor standards, especially the rights of workers to organize and bargain collectively? Would they ensure or obliterate communities' rights to refuse investment that endangered public health or the natural environment?

As Lisa Climan explains in this chapter, "free trade" agreements have served the interests of corporations at the expense of workers and the environment. NAFTA, for instance, gave corporations the right to sue governments for "losses" they claim environmental and labor regulations impose on them—threatening to make laws in the public interest too costly to maintain. Today, with negotiations underway to expand NAFTA to the entire western hemisphere in the form of the FTAA, the threat of uncontrolled corporate power grows even greater ("On a Fast Track to 'Free Trade' Hell").

When the business press has printed critiques of "free trade," it has often suggested that workers in some countries are gaining at the expense of those elsewhere (à la Ross Perot's "giant sucking sound"—the noise he said Americans would hear as their jobs moved to Mexico). But Ellen Frank shows that "free trade" agreements have undermined the bargaining power of labor against capital in *all* the countries involved. NAFTA, she reports, has not only accelerated job loss in the U.S. manufacturing sector, but has contributed to plummeting wages and rising poverty in Mexico ("How Has NAFTA Affected Trade and Employment?").

"Free trade" has been just one of the neoliberal policy prescriptions promoted by institutions like the World Trade Organization, International Monetary Fund (IMF), and World Bank. The results in country after country have been disastrous. While the U.S. press spent the late 1990s high on fumes from an overheated stock market, crushing economic crises hit Mexico, Russia, Brazil, and East Asia. In each case, economic collapse was provoked or exacerbated by neoliberal policies, especially financial-market liberalization. These crises registered briefly in the mainstream press, but they were typically blamed on the countries themselves: the story went that the economies of East Asia collapsed because they practiced "crony capitalism" and had never really implemented neoliberal policies correctly. Arthur MacEwan challenges such stories by taking a close look at Argentina's 2001 meltdown—a disaster for the country and an embarrassment for the IMF. As MacEwan explains, the country had been a neoliberal poster child, and its collapse was the predictable result of IMF prescriptions ("Economic Debacle in Argentina").

Discredited by world-wide economic crises, and under pressure from the global economic justice movement, mainstream economic institutions have had to recast themselves as "antipoverty" organizations. Sarah Anderson shows how the World Bank and IMF have led the charge, hypocritically declaring themselves reformed even as they continue to push the same policies as ever ("The World Bank and IMF's Cosmetic Makeover"). Meanwhile, commentators like Paul Krugman have actually gone so far as to argue that sweatshops are a solution to—rather than part of—the problem of global poverty. This view depends in part on commentators' willingness to accept companies' self-serving reports on their factory conditions—reports that Dara O'Rourke exposes as dishonest whitewashes ("Sweatshops 101").

Today we often hear about the need for more trade to create economic growth and more economic growth to create prosperity. But the history of economic development shows that it's possible to achieve, by redistribution of resources and a public commitment to providing basic needs, much greater well-being for most people without much economic growth. It's possible to achieve substantial economic growth without high levels of international trade. And it's possible to have high levels of international trade without adopting "free trade" policies. These are ideas that have found no place in the business press. If they had, the rhetoric about "globalization" and "free trade" might not have masqueraded so long as a serious plan for global economic development.

THE IMF AND WORLD BANK'S COSMETIC MAKEOVER
By Sarah Anderson
January/February 2001

Medieval doctors always prescribed the same "cure"; no matter what the ailment, they applied leeches to patients and bled them. For the past decade and a half, critics have likened the World Bank and the International Monetary Fund (IMF) to these doctors. The two institutions have thrown millions of people deeper into poverty by promoting the same harsh economic reforms—including privatization, budget cuts, and labor "flexibility"—regardless of local culture, resources, or economic context. Strapped with heavy debts, most developing countries have reluctantly accepted these reforms, known as structural adjustment programs (SAPs), as a condition for receiving IMF or World Bank loans.

In recent years, the doctors' harsh medicine has been exposed in dozens of studies and in increasingly vocal street protests. In response, the World Bank and the IMF have been attempting to revamp their public image into that of anti-poverty crusaders. While the World Bank has long claimed a commitment to helping the poor, this is a real departure for the IMF, which has unrepentantly elevated financial and monetary stability above any other concern. Considering the two institutions' records, it is not surprising that the sudden conversion from crude medieval doctors to institutional Mother Theresas has provoked considerable skepticism.

Main elements of the SAP Formula
Reducing the size of the state: The IMF requires that countries privatize public companies and services and fire public sector workers. While this may free up more funds to pay off loans, domestic capacity is crippled as a result. In Haiti, for example, the IMF admits that privatization of schools has seen extreme deterioration in school quality and attendance that will likely hamper the country's human capacity for many years to come. For example, only 8% of teachers in private schools (now 89% of all schools) have professional qualifications, compared to 47% in public schools. Secondary school enrollment dropped from 28% to 15% between 1985 and 1997. Nevertheless, the IMF recommends further privatization in Haiti.

Balancing the government budget: Even though rich country governments commonly engage in deficit spending, the IMF and World Bank believe this is a big no-no for poor countries. Faced with tough choices, governments often must cut spending on health, education, and environmental protection, since these don't generate income for the federal budget. According to Friends of the Earth, Brazil was pressured to slash funding for environmental enforcement by over 50% after accepting an IMF bailout agreement in 1999.

Deregulating the economy: The World Bank and IMF continue to push for the elimination of trade and investment barriers, and for the export-orientation of poor countries' economies. Again, if poor countries increase their foreign currency earnings by boosting exports, they may be more able to repay international creditors. The people, however, will not necessarily benefit. The World Bank's own statistics show that, in many regions of the world, increased exports are not associated with increased personal consumption. For example, while export volume increased by 4.3% in Sub-Saharan Africa between 1989 and 1998, per capita consumption declined by 0.5%.

Weakening labor: The institutions have also ardently promoted so-called "labor market flexibility" through measures that make it easier to fire workers or undermine the ability of unions to represent their members. In the spring of 2000, Argentine legislators passed the harsher of two labor law reform proposals after IMF officials spoke out strongly in support of it. The IMF, backed up by the might of the global financial community, appears to have carried more weight than the tens of thousands of Argentines who carried out general strikes against the reform. Even though a recently released World Bank study shows a correlation between high rates of unionization and lower levels of inequality, the Bank and Fund maintain that they cannot engage in promoting labor rights because this would constitute interference in domestic politics.

Although the Bank and Fund have promoted SAPs as a virtual religion for nearly 20 years, they cannot even claim that they have achieved a reduction in the developing world's debt burden. Between 1980 and 1997, the debt of low-income countries grew by 544%, and that of middle-income countries by 481%.

The IMF Gets a Facelift

In 1999, in response to increasing opposition, the IMF gave its Enhanced Structural Adjustment Facility (through which it made SAP loans) the new moniker of Poverty Reduction and Growth Facility. Both the IMF and World Bank announced that under their new approach, they would require governments seeking loans and debt relief to consult with civil society to develop strategies for poverty reduction. In addition, the institutions vowed an increased commitment to debt relief for the poorest countries. World Bank President James Wolfensohn expressed his pride in these efforts by commenting that he comes in to work every day "thinking I'm doing God's work."

Although most of the new poverty reduction initiatives are in an early stage, the World Bank and IMF have given plenty of evidence to support the skeptics:

Anti-poverty PR stunts: Nonfovernmental organizations (NGOs) have raised strong criticism of the civil-society consultation processes that are supposed to take place as governments develop the required Poverty Reduction Strategy Papers. Sara Grusky of the Washington-based Globalization Challenge Initiative (GCI) doubts the value of "consultation" if countries will still have to accept the standard policies to get the IMF's "seal of approval." Carlos Pacheco Alizaga of

Nicaragua's Center for International Studies says that civil-society consultation is restricted to narrow discussions of social policy. He argues that the process "tries to dilute the central discussion which is the lack of a new model of development for the impoverished countries and the creation of a new world trade system that should not be controlled by the rich countries of the north and the transnational companies." As of October 2000, only two countries (Uganda and Burkina Faso) had completed a Poverty Reduction Strategy Paper. Another 13 had completed interim drafts, but in several cases civil-society groups have reported either a complete lack of public consultation or mere public relations stunts that excluded groups more critical of Bank and Fund policies.

Debt rhetoric: A year ago, the World Bank and IMF initiated a joint plan, called the "Heavily Indebted Poor Country" (HIPC) initiative, to provide a measure of debt relief to certain countries that agree to structural adjustment conditions. The World Bank touts HIPC as an example of its "leadership to relieve the unsustainable debt burdens that stand in the way of development and poverty reduction." The IMF may be more candid about HIPC's true goals. A statement on its web site identifies the main objective not as poverty reduction but rather the reduction of poor countries' debt burdens to levels that will "comfortably enable them to service their debt" and "broaden domestic support for policy reforms." As Soren Ambrose of the Alliance for Global Justice puts it, "HIPC is just a cruel hoax designed to trick developing countries into accepting more structural adjustment."

The World Bank and IMF have tried to tout the HIPC initiative as a permanent solution to the debt crisis by concocting wildly unrealistic predictions of the eligible countries' future economic performance. (As of October 2000, only 10 of the 41 countries had met the rigid HIPC criteria.) They estimate that export, GDP, and government revenue growth will average 7–12% in nominal dollar terms for the next 20 years—optimism that is completely unjustified by the countries' past performance.

Ecuador eruption: There is perhaps no stronger evidence of the continued havoc wreaked by IMF/World Bank orthodoxy than Ecuador. During the past year, indigenous groups, trade unions, and others have organized mass protests against a harsh IMF reform program that shifts the country's economic crisis onto the backs of the poor. In the midst of a general strike against the program in June 2000, a delegation of Ecuadoran human rights, women's, and trade union groups came to Washington, D.C., to ask the World Bank to postpone consideration of a new loan agreement conditioned on further implementation of IMF reforms. The NGOs argued that there had been a total lack of public consultation on the deal, which required low levels of social spending and removal of subsidies for basic goods, while ignoring the country's need for debt relief. Despite their pleas, the World Bank approved the loan package the following week.

Censorship: The dramatic resignations in the spring of 2000 of two high-level World Bank employees raised further doubts about the institutions' commitment to poverty reduction and civil-society participation. Former Chief Economist

Joseph Stiglitz claims that U.S. Treasury Secretary Lawrence Summers and IMF bigwigs succeeded in pushing him out of the Bank in retaliation for his charges that the Fund's policies helped precipitate and worsen the global financial crises that erupted in mid-1997. Stiglitz pointed out that while reckless international investors and domestic banks caused the crises, the costs were borne by the workers.

Then in June, the editor of the World Bank's *World Development Report*, Ravi Kanbur, broke his contract, reportedly in protest over demands that he water down content that had been developed through extensive civil-society participation. Once again, Summers and other supporters of "free market" orthodoxy had allegedly intervened to quash the report's calls for economic redistribution, claiming that economic growth was the ultimate solution for poverty.

Although the final report released in September 2000 contains some strong language about the need to empower the poor, there is no indication that the institutions are willing to consider a substantial reform of their policies. One chapter, "Making Markets Work Better for Poor People," attributes all problems of economic collapse and poverty growth to deficiencies in "market access." The report implies that those former Communist countries that have been mired in economic collapse and stagnation should have followed the examples of the countries that implemented reforms "forcefully and early." This contrasts sharply with the findings of many researchers that the most successful former Communist countries were those that adopted a more gradual and cautious approach.

Old Leeches, New Jars

So far there is little evidence of a genuine conversion on the part of the IMF and World Bank. They have not fundamentally rethought their formula of "structural adjustment," nor their overall commitment to the "free market" model. The medieval doctors have just repackaged their cruel ministrations with warm and fuzzy labels. The challenge for critics is to keep up the pressure, exposing this façade and unifying around a concrete set of meaningful alternative goals and policies—real transparency, real democracy, and a real commitment to fight poverty.

HOW HAS NAFTA AFFECTED TRADE AND EMPLOYMENT?
By Ellen Frank
January/February 2003

Dear Dr. Dollar:

Free-traders claim that free trade will increase U.S. exports, providing more jobs for Americans. So I would expect that NAFTA increased U.S. exports and reduced our trade deficit. I would also expect to see employment increase both in our country and in our trading partners. Has that in fact happened?

—*Lane Smith, Ronkonkoma, New York*

Since the North American Free Trade Agreement (NAFTA) between the United States, Mexico, and Canada went into effect, trade within North America has increased dramatically. Exports from the United States to Mexico have risen 150% and exports to Canada are up 66%. This much is beyond dispute.

NAFTA's effects on employment, on the other hand, are hotly debated. Clinton administration officials estimated in the late 1990s that expanded trade in North America had created over 300,000 new U.S. jobs. Economic Policy Institute (EPI) economists Robert Scott and Jesse Rothstein contend, however, that such claims amount to "trying to balance a checkbook by counting the deposits and not the withdrawals."

This is because NAFTA and other trade agreements have also increased U.S. imports from Canada and Mexico—and by quite a lot more than exports. Since 1993, America's trade deficit with its North American trading partners (exports minus imports) has ballooned from $16 billion to $82 billion annually. As Scott points out, "increases in U.S. exports create jobs in this country, but increases in imports destroy jobs because the imports displace goods that otherwise would have been made in the U.S. by domestic workers."

Employment in virtually all U.S. manufacturing industries has declined since NAFTA went into effect. Counting jobs that actually left the United States plus those that would have been created if not for rising imports, EPI estimates that NAFTA caused a net loss of 440,000 U.S. jobs. In fact, during the 1990s, the overall U.S. trade deficit quadrupled, resulting in a net loss of 3 million jobs, according to EPI president Jeff Faux.

Of course, in a large and complex economy, trade is only one of many factors that affect job creation, and its influence is difficult to isolate. As trade expanded during the 1990s, for example, the United States also experienced an investment boom that created jobs faster than rising imports destroyed them; overall, the number of jobs in the United States has risen by 28 million since 1994.

Any free-trade booster worth her lobbying fees would argue that the boom itself resulted from liberalized trade. Lower trade and investment barriers, the story goes, unleash entrepreneurial talents, spurring innovation and productivity gains. Old jobs lost are offset by new jobs gained, and falling wages by cheaper prices on imported goods. Moreover, free-traders contend, any reckoning of NAFTA's impact should tote up new jobs and factories in Mexico against shuttered plants in the United States.

So what about NAFTA's effect on Mexico? In a study for the Interhemispheric Resource Center, analysts Timothy Wise and Kevin Gallagher conclude that NAFTA has given Mexico "trade without development." Since NAFTA weakened barriers to U.S. investment in Mexico, foreign investment into the country tripled and exports grew rapidly. But the development promised by free-trade advocates never materialized. Mexican employment did grow during the early years of NAFTA, but in recent years, it has declined as mobile manufacturers have sought even cheaper labor in Asia. Mexican manufacturing wages fell 21% during the 1990s and poverty worsened.

Wise's and Gallagher's findings echo the conclusions of Harvard development specialist Dani Rodrik. Poor countries that turn to trade as a cure for poverty find themselves ensnared in the "mercantilist fallacy": they can't all export their way to riches, since one country's exports are another's imports. Someone has to buy all this stuff. The United States, with its annual trade deficit approaching $500 billion, is the world's buyer and its manufacturing industries suffer as a result. But poor countries don't fare much better. They face increasing competition from low-wage manufacturers in other poor countries, and world markets are now saturated with cheap apparel and electronics, driving prices and wages down.

The result is one thing that almost everybody who studies trade now agrees upon. Whatever else they have wrought—more jobs, fewer jobs, more or less poverty—globalized trade and production coincide with greater inequality both within and between countries. The reasons for this are complex—globalization weakens unions, strengthens multinationals, and increases competition and insecurity all around—but the data are clear. Markets do not distribute wealth equitably.

Resources: Robert Scott and Jesse Rothstein, "NAFTA and the States: Job Destruction is Widespread," <www.epinet.org>; Jeff Faux, "Why U.S. Manufacturing Needs a 'Strategic Pause in Trade Policy,'" Testimony before the Senate Committee on Commerce, Sciences and Transportation, June 21, 2001; Timothy Wise and Kevin Gallagher, "NAFTA: A Cautionary Tale," *FPIF Global Affairs Commentary*, 2002; Dani Rodrik, *The New Global Economy and Developing Countries: Making Openness Work* (Overseas Development Council, 1999).

ON A FAST TRACK TO "FREE TRADE" HELL
By Lisa Climan
January/February 2002, updated May 2003

What's the solution to the problem of terrorism? According to U.S. Trade Representative Robert Zoellick, more "free trade" agreements and more executive power to negotiate them. Congress "needs to send an unmistakable signal to the world," Zoellick wrote in the *Washington Post* shortly after September 11, "that the United States is committed to global leadership of openness and understands that the staying power of our new coalition depends on economic growth and hope." The signal he had in mind? Trade negotiating authority, better known as "fast track," for President Bush on the proposed Free Trade Area of the Americas (FTAA). Since Zoellick put this argument forward, Congress passed fast-track legislation—against protest from environmental, labor, and human rights activists. Under fast track, the President can negotiate multilateral trade agreements that Congress can approve or reject, but not amend. This authority boosts the administration's push for the hemisphere-wide "free-trade" zone, which critics have called "NAFTA on steroids."

When NAFTA passed in 1993, some legislators who voted for it pushed for "side agreements" protecting labor and environmental standards, they got a lot less than they would have liked. In fact, NAFTA's "Chapter 11" courts, where companies can bring complaints against member governments for violating the agreement's provisions, impose penalties on countries whose regulations interfere with investors' sacred right to make a profit.

In the 1980s, Richard Epstein, a law professor at the University of Chicago, came up with the theory of "regulatory takings." This theory states that investors are entitled to compensation if a government regulation deprives them of any profits they would have otherwise made—including profits they could theoretically make in the future. Regulatory takings, a few years ago widely considered nothing more than a crackpot right-wing theory, is now law thanks to Chapter 11—and could become the governing economic model for the entire Western hemisphere if the FTAA goes through.

Under the FTAA, NAFTA's rules would spread to an additional 31 Latin American and Caribbean nations by 2005. The effects on government regulation would be chilling, as governments would be "paying to regulate," according to Professor William Warren of Georgetown Law School. Already, companies have filed claims under Chapter 11 totaling over $13 billion. The September 2001 Public Citizen report *NAFTA Chapter 11 Investor-to-State Cases: Bankrupting Democracy* describes some of the most disturbing cases:

- *Metalclad v. the Municipality of Guadalcazar, Mexico*: The California-based Metalclad Corporation sued the Municipality of Guadalcazar for refusing it a toxic-waste-dumping permit, and the state of San Luis Potosí for declaring the proposed dumping site part of an "ecological zone." The NAFTA court awarded Metalclad $16.7 million.

- *United Parcel Service (UPS) v. Canadian Postal Service*: The Atlanta-based UPS sued for $160 million, claiming that the publicly owned Canadian Postal Service unfairly subsidizes its parcel-shipping operations. The case is still pending.

- *Methanex v. California*: The State of California ordered the toxic additive MBTE, which had contaminated the drinking-water supply, phased out of gasoline sold in California. The Canadian-based Methanex sued the state for $970 million in compensation for the company's reduced market value. The case is still pending.

If the FTAA becomes a reality, we can expect more—*much* more—of the same.

SWEATSHOPS 101: LESSONS IN MONITORING APPAREL PRODUCTION AROUND THE WORLD

By Dara O'Rourke

September/October 2001

Navy blue sweatshirts bearing a single foreign word, Michigan, and a well-known logo, the Nike swoosh, were piled high in a small room off the main factory floor. After cutting, stitching, and embroidering by the 1,100 workers outside, the sweatshirts landed in the spot-cleaning room, where six young Indonesian women prepared the garments for shipment to student stores and NikeTowns across America. The women spent hour after hour using chemical solvents to rid the sweatshirts of smudges and stains. With poor ventilation, ill-fitting respiratory protection, no gloves, and no chemical hazard training, the women sprayed solvents and aerosol cleaners containing benzene, methylene chloride, and perchloroethylene, all carcinogens, on the garments.

It used to be that the only thing people wondered when you wore a Harvard or Michigan sweatshirt was whether you had actually gone there. More and more, though, people are wondering out loud where that sweatshirt was made, and whether any workers were exploited in making it. Students, labor activists, and human-rights groups have spearheaded a movement demanding to know what really lies beneath their university logos, and whether our public universities and private colleges are profiting from global sweatshop production.

Where Was That Sweatshirt Made?

So far, few universities have been able to answer these questions. Universities generally don't even know where their products are produced, let alone whether workers were endangered to produce them. Indeed, with global out-sourcing many brand name companies cannot trace the supply chains which lead to the student store, and are blissfully ignorant of conditions in these factories.

Under pressure from student activists across the country, a small group of university administrators decided it was time to find out more about the garments bearing their schools' names and logos. As part of a collaborative research project, called the "Independent University Initiative" (IUI), funded by Harvard University, the University of Notre Dame, Ohio State University, the University of California, and the University of Michigan, I joined a team investigating where and under what conditions university garments were being made. Its report is available at web.mit.edu/dorourke/www. The team included staff from the business association Business for Social Responsibility, the non-profit Investor Responsibility Research Center, and the accounting firm PricewaterhouseCoopers (PwC). PwC was responsible for auditing the labor conditions in each of the factories included in the study. At the request of student activists, I joined the team as an outside evaluator.

The IUI research team evaluated garment manufacturing for the top apparel companies licensing the logos of these five universities. It looked at factories subcontracted by nine companies, including adidas, Champion, and Nike. The nine alone outsource university apparel to over 180 factories in 26 countries. This may sound like a lot, but it is actually the tip of the global production iceberg. Americans bought about $2.5 billion worth of university-logo garments in 1999. Overall, however, U.S. apparel sales totaled over $180 billion. There are an estimated 80,000 factories around the world producing garments for the U.S. market. The university garment industry is important not so much for its size, but for the critical opening it provides onto the larger industry.

The research team visited factories in the top seven countries producing apparel for the nine companies: China, El Salvador, Korea, Mexico, Pakistan, Thailand, and the United States. It inspected 13 work sites in all. I personally inspected factories for the project in China and Korea, and then inspected factories in Indonesia on my own to see what things looked like outside the official process. Through this research I discovered not only exploitative and hazardous working conditions, but also an official monitoring process designed to gloss over the biggest problems of the apparel industry. PwC auditors found minor violations of labor laws and codes of conduct, but missed major labor problems including serious health and safety hazards, barriers to freedom of association, and violations of overtime and wage laws. This was a learning experience I call "Sweatshops 101."

Lesson #1: Global Outsourcing

The garment industry is extremely complicated and highly disaggregated. The industry has multiple layers of licensees, brokers, jobbers, importer-exporters, component suppliers, and subcontractors on top of subcontractors.

The University of Michigan does not manufacture any of the products bearing its name. Nor does Notre Dame nor Harvard nor any other university. These schools simply license their names to apparel makers and other companies for a percentage of the sale—generally around 7% of the retail price for each T-shirt, sweatshirt, or key chain. Until recently, the universities had little interest in even knowing who produced their goods. If they tracked this at all, it was to catch companies using their logos without paying the licensing fee.

Sometimes the companies that license university names and logos own the factories where the apparel is produced. But more often the licensees simply contract production out to factories in developing countries. Nike owns none of the hundreds of factories that produce its garments and athletic shoes.

A sweatshirt factory itself may have multiple subcontractors who produce the fabric, embroider the logo, or stitch sub-components. This global supply chain stretches from the university administration building, to the corporate office of the licensee companies, to large-scale factories in China and Mexico, to small scale sub-contractor factories everywhere in between, and in some cases, all the way to women stitching garments in their living rooms.

Lesson #2: The Global Shell Game

The global garment industry is highly mobile, with contracts continuously shifting from subcontractor to subcontractor within and between countries. Licensees can move production between subcontractors after one year, one month, or even as little as one week.

It took the university research team three months to get from the licensee companies a list of the factories producing university-logo garments. However, because the actual factories producing university goods at any one time change so fast, by the time I had planned a trip to China and Korea to visit factories, the lists were essentially obsolete. One licensee in Korea had replaced eight of its eleven factories with new factories by the time I arrived in town. Over a four month period, the company had contracted with twenty one different factories. A range of factors—including price competition between contractors, changes in fashions (and factories capable of filling orders), fluctuations in exchange rates, and changing import quotas for different countries—is responsible for this constant state of flux.

Even after double-checking with a licensee, in almost every country the project team would arrive at the factory gates only to be told that the factories we planned to inspect were no longer producing university goods. Of course, some of this may have been the licensees playing games. Faced with inspections, some may have decided to shift production out of the chosen factory, or at least to tell us that it had been shifted.

Some of the largest, most profitable apparel firms in the world, known for their management prowess, however, simply did not know where their products were being produced. When asked how many factories Disney had around the world, company execs guessed there were 1,500 to 1,800 factories producing their garments, toys, videos, and other goods. As it turns out, they were only off by an order of magnitude. So far the company has counted over 20,000 factories around the world producing Disney-branded goods. Only recent exposés by labor, human rights, and environmental activists have convinced these companies that they need better control over their supply chains.

Lesson #3: Normal Operating Conditions

The day an inspector visits a factory is not a normal day. Any factory that has prior knowledge of an inspection is very likely to make changes on the day of the visit.

In a Nike-contracted shoe factory in Indonesia I visited in June 2000, all of the workers in the hot press section of the plant (a particularly dangerous area) were wearing brand new black dress shoes on the day of our inspection. One of the workers explained they had been given the shoes that morning and were expected to return them at the end of the shift. Managers often give workers new protective equipment—such as gloves, respirators, and even shoes—on the day of an inspection. However, as the workers have no training in how to even use this equipment, it is common to see brand-new respirators being worn below workers' noses, around their necks, or even upside down.

At one factory the university team visited in Mexico, the factory manager wanted to guarantee that the inspectors would find his factory spotless. So he locked all of the bathrooms on the day of the inspection. Workers were not allowed to use the bathrooms until the project team showed up, hours into the work day.

Licensees and subcontractors often try to subvert monitoring. They block auditors from inspecting on certain days or from visiting certain parts of a plant, claim production has moved, feign ignorance of factory locations, keep multiple sets of books on wages and hours, coach workers on responses to interviews, and threaten workers against complaining to inspectors. The university research team was unable to get around many of these obstructions.

Lesson #4: Conditions in University Factories

Factories producing university apparel often violate local laws and university codes of conduct on maximum hours of work, minimum and overtime wages, freedom of association, and health and safety protections.

In a 300-worker apparel plant in Shanghai, the university team found that many of the workers were working far in excess of maximum overtime laws. A quick review of timecards found women working over 315 hours in a month and 20 consecutive days without a day off. The legal maximum in China is only 204 hours per month, with at least one day off in seven. A sample of 25 workers showed that the average overtime worked was 101 hours, while the legal limit is 36 hours per month. One manager explained these gross violations with a shrug, saying, "Timecards are just used to make sure workers show up on time. Workers are actually paid based on a piece rate system."

The factory also had a wide range of health and safety problems, including a lack of guarding on sewing and cutting machines, high levels of cotton dust in one section of the plant, several blocked aisles and fire exits, no running water in certain toilets, no information for workers on the hazardous chemicals they were using, and a lack of protective equipment for the workers.

Living conditions for the workers who lived in a dormitory on site were also poor. The dormitory had 12 women packed into each room on six bunk beds. Each floor had four rooms (48 women) and only one bathroom. These bathrooms had only two shower heads and four toilet stalls each, and no dividers between them.

And what of workers' rights to complain or demand better conditions? The union in this factory was openly being run by the management. While 70% of workers were "members" of the union, one manager explained, "We don't have

U.S.-style unions here." No workers had ever tried to take control of this group or to form an independent union.

Lesson #5: The Challenges of Monitoring

Finding a dozen factories is relatively easy compared to the job of tracking the thousands of rapidly changing factories that produce university goods each year. Systematically monitoring and evaluating their practices on wages, hours, discrimination, and health and safety issues is an even bigger challenge.

Most universities don't have the capacity to individually monitor the conditions in "their" factories, so some are joining together to create cooperative monitoring programs. The concept behind "independent monitoring" is to have a consulting firm or non-governmental organization inspect and evaluate a factory's compliance with a code of conduct. There are now two major university monitoring systems. The Fair Labor Association (FLA) now has over 157 universities as members, and the Worker Rights Consortium (WRC) has over 80 affiliated universities. (The four smaller monitoring initiatives are Social Accountability International (SA8000), the Ethical Trading Initiative, the Clean Clothes Campaign, and the Worldwide Responsible Apparel Production (WRAP) program.)

The FLA emerged from the Clinton-convened "White House Apparel Industry Partnership" in 1998. It is supported by a small group of apparel companies including Nike, Reebok, adidas, Levi-Strauss, Liz Claiborne, and Philips Van Heusen. Students and labor-rights advocates have criticized the group for being industry-dominated and for allowing companies to monitor only 10% of their factories each year, to use monitors that the companies pay directly, to control when and where monitors inspect, and to restrict the information released to the public after the audits.

The United Students Against Sweatshops (USAS) and UNITE (the largest garment-workers' union in the United States) founded the WRC in 1999 as an alternative to the FLA. The WRC promotes systems for verifying factory conditions after workers have complained or after inspections have occurred, and to create greater public disclosure of conditions. The WRC differs from the FLA in that it refuses to certify that any company meets a code of conduct. The group argues that because of the problems of monitoring, it is simply not possible to systematically monitor or certify a company's compliance. Some universities and companies have criticized the WRC as being a haphazard "gotcha" monitoring system whose governing body excludes the very companies that must be part of solving these problems.

Both groups profess to support the International Labour Organization's core labor standards, including upholding workers' rights to freedom of association and collective bargaining, and prohibiting forced labor, child labor, and discrimination in the workplace. The WRC, however, goes further in advocating that workers be paid a "living wage," and that women's rights receive particular attention. Both programs assert a strong role for local NGOs, unions, and workers. However, the two have widely varying levels of transparency and public disclosure, and very different systems of sanctions and penalties.

Lesson #6: How Not To Monitor

Corporate-sponsored monitoring systems seem almost designed to miss the most critical issues in the factories they inspect. Auditors often act as if they are on the side of management rather than the workers.

PricewaterhouseCoopers (PwC) is the largest private monitor of codes of conduct and corporate labor practices in the world. The company performed over 6,000 factory audits in the year 2000, including monitoring for Nike, Disney, Walmart, and the Gap. (PwC recently announced that they were spinning off their labor monitoring services into a firm called Global Social Compliance.) PwC monitors for many of the top university licensees, and was hired as the monitor for the university project. Like other corporate monitors, the company has been criticized for covering up problems and assuaging the public conscience about sweatshop conditions that have not really been resolved.

PwC's monitoring systems epitomize current corporate monitoring efforts. The firm sends two auditors—who are actually financial accountants with minimal training on labor issues—into each factory for eight hours. The auditors use a checklist and a standard interview form to evaluate legal compliance, wages and benefits, working hours, freedom of association and collective bargaining, child labor, forced labor, disciplinary practices, and health and safety.

On the university project, PwC auditors failed to adequately examine any major issue in the factories I saw them inspect. In factories in Korea and Indonesia, PwC auditors completely missed exposure to toxic chemicals, something which could eventually cost workers their lives from cancer. In Korea, the auditors saw no problem in managers violating overtime wage laws. In China, the auditors went so far as to recommend ways for the managers to circumvent local laws on overtime hours, essentially providing advice on how to break university codes of conduct. And the auditors in Korea simply skipped the questions on workers' right to organize in their worker interviews, explaining, "They don't have a union in this factory, so those questions aren't relevant."

The PwC auditing method is biased towards managers. Before an inspection, PwC auditors send managers a questionnaire explaining what will be inspected. They prepare managers at an opening meeting before each inspection. In the Chinese factory, they asked managers to enter wages and hours data into the PwC spreadsheet. Even the worker interviews were biased towards the managers. PwC auditors asked the managers to help them select workers to be interviewed, had the managers bring their personnel files, and then had the managers bring the workers into the office used for the interviews. The managers knew who was being interviewed, for how long, and on what issues. Workers knew this as well, and answered questions accordingly.

The final reports that PwC delivered to its clients gave a largely sanitized picture of the factories inspected. This is unsurprising, considering PwC's business interest in providing companies with "acceptable" audits.

Where to Begin?

Universities face increasing public pressure to guarantee that workers are not being injured or exploited to produce their insignia products. They have no system, however, to track apparel production around the world, and often no idea where their production is occurring. Monitoring systems are still in their fledgling stages, so universities are starting from a difficult position, albeit one they have profited from for years.

What can universities do about this? They should do what they are best at: produce information. They should take the lead in demanding that corporations— beginning with those they do business with—open themselves up to public inspection and evaluation. Universities have done this before, such as during the anti-apartheid campaign for South Africa. By doing this on the sweatshop issue, universities could spur a critical dialogue on labor issues around the world.

To start, the universities could establish a central coordinating office to collect and compare information on factory performance for member universities' licensees. (The WRC has proposed such a model.) This new office would be responsible for keeping records on licensee compliance, for making this information available over the internet, for registering local NGOs and worker organizations to conduct independent verifications of factory conditions, and for assessing sanctions.

Such a program would allow universities to evaluate different strategies for improving conditions in different parts of the world. This would avoid the danger of locking in one code of conduct or one certification system. In place of sporadic media exposés embarrassing one company at a time, we would have an international system of disclosure and learning—benchmarking good performers, identifying and targeting the worst performers, and motivating improvement.

It is clearly not enough to expose one company at a time, nor to count on industry-paid consulting firms to monitor labor conditions. The building blocks of a new system depend on information. This fits the mission of universities. Universities should focus on information gathering and dissemination, and most importantly, on learning. If the universities learn nothing else from "Sweatshops 101," it is that they still have a lot of homework do to—and their next test will be coming soon.

ECONOMIC DEBACLE IN ARGENTINA: THE IMF STRIKES AGAIN

By Arthur MacEwan

March/April 2002

In the days just before Christmas, with increasing cutbacks in social programs and an official unemployment rate approaching 20%, Argentinians took to the streets in protest. At the time, Argentina was in the midst of its fourth year of recession. The immediate spark for the unrest was the government's latest economic policies, which restricted the amount of money people could withdraw from their bank accounts. Political demonstrations and the looting of grocery stores quickly spread across the country.

The government declared a state of siege, but police often stood by and watched the looting "with their hands behind their backs." There was little the government could do. Within a day after the demonstrations began, principal economic minister Domingo Cavallo had resigned; a few days later, President Fernando de la Rúa stepped down.

In the wake of the resignations, a hastily assembled interim government immediately defaulted on $155 billion of Argentina's foreign debt, the largest debt default in history. The new government also promised a public works jobs program and announced plans to issue a new currency, the argentino, that would circulate alongside the Argentine peso and the U.S. dollar. As economic instability deepened, however, the argentino plan was abandoned. And the new public works program did little to address the fact that per capita income had dropped by 14% since 1998. Unable to win the popular support it needed, the new government quickly dissolved. The current president, Eduardo Duhalde, was sworn in on January 1; he was the fifth president to serve in two weeks.

As of this writing (mid-February), Argentina still faces widespread political and economic uncertainty. In the short run, many anticipate more unemployment, severe inflation, or both. Also, Argentina's currency remains highly unstable. After experimenting with several different exchange rates, the Duhalde government is now permitting the peso to "float." The peso has already dropped from its previous value (one to the dollar) down to two to the dollar on the open market, and further devaluation is widely anticipated.

Argentina's experience leading into the current debacle provides one more lesson regarding the perils of "free market" ideology, and specifically the economic policies that the International Monetary Fund (IMF) pushes on governments around the globe. In Argentina, as in other places, these policies have been embraced by local elites, who see their fortunes (both real and metaphoric) as tied to the deregulation of commerce and the curtailment of social programs. Yet the claims that these policies bring economic growth and widespread well-being have been thoroughly discredited, as events in Argentina have shown.

From Good to Bad to Ugly

Not long ago, Argentina was the poster child for the conservative economic policies of the IMF. From the late 1980s onward, a series of loans gave the IMF the leverage to guide Argentine policymakers in privatizing state enterprises, liberalizing foreign trade and investment, and tightening government fiscal and monetary policy. During the 1990s, the country's economy seemed to do well, with real per capita income growing at the very rapid annual rate of about 4.5%.

The rapid economic growth through most of the 1990s, however, was built on weak foundations. That growth, while substantial, appears to have resulted largely from an increasing accumulation of international obligations (debt to private banks, the IMF, and foreign governments, as well as direct foreign investment), fortuitous expansion of foreign markets for Argentine exports, and short-term injections of government revenues from the sale of state enterprises. Before the end of the decade, things began to fall apart.

Argentina's current problems are all the more severe because in the early 1990s, in the name of fighting inflation, the government created a "currency board." The board was charged with regulating the country's currency so that the Argentine peso would exchange one-to-one with the U.S. dollar. To assure this fixed exchange rate, the board kept a supply of dollars on reserve, and could not expand the supply of pesos without an equivalent increase in the dollars that it held. The currency board system appeared attractive because of absurd rates of inflation in the 1980s, with price increases of up to 200% a month. By restricting the growth of the money supply, the system brought inflation rates to heel.

Although the currency board system had virtually eliminated inflation in Argentina by the mid-1990s, it had also eliminated flexibility in monetary policy. When the current recession began to develop in the late 1990s, the government could not stimulate economic activity by expanding the money supply.

Worse yet, as the economy continued to spiral downward, the inflow of dollars slowed, forcing the currency board to restrict the country's money supply even further. And still worse, in the late 1990s, the U.S. dollar appreciated against other currencies, which meant (because of the one-to-one rule) that the peso also increased in value. As a result, the price of Argentine exports rose, further weakening world demand for Argentina's goods.

As Argentina entered into the lasting downturn of the period since 1998, the IMF continued, unwavering, in its financial support. The IMF provided "small" loans, such as $3 billion in early 1998 when the country's economic difficulties began to appear. As the crisis deepened, the IMF increased its support, supplying a loan of $13.7 billion and arranging $26 billion more from other sources at the end of 2000. As conditions worsened further in 2001, the IMF pledged another $8 billion.

However, the IMF coupled its largesse with the condition that the Argentine government maintain its severe monetary policy and continue to tighten its fiscal policy by eliminating its budget deficit. (The IMF considers deficit reduction to be the key to macroeconomic stability and, in turn, the key to economic growth.)

The Argentine government undertook deficit reduction with a vengeance. With the economy in a nosedive and tax revenues plummeting, the only way to balance the budget was to drastically cut government spending. In early July 2001, just before making a major government bond offering, Argentine officials announced budget cuts totaling $1.6 billion (about 3% of the federal budget), which they hoped would reassure investors and allow interest rates to fall. Apparently, however, investors saw the cuts as another sign of worsening crisis, and the bonds could only be sold at high interest rates (14%, as compared to 9% on similar bonds sold just a few weeks before the announcement of budget cuts). By December, the effort to balance the budget required cuts that were far more severe; the government announced a drastic reduction of $9.2 billion in spending, or about 18% of its entire budget.

With these cutbacks, the government both eviscerated social programs and reduced overall demand. In mid-December, the government announced that it would cut the salaries of public employees by 20% and reduce pension payments. At the same time, as the worsening crisis raised fears that Argentina would abandon the currency board system and devalue the peso, the government moved to prevent people from trading their pesos for dollars by limiting bank withdrawals. These steps were the final straws, and in the week before Christmas, all hell broke loose.

Who Benefits from IMF Policies?

Argentina is just the latest example of how IMF policies have failed to establish the basis for long-term economic growth in low-income countries. IMF policies usually do succeed in curtailing inflation, as they did in Argentina in the mid-1990s, because sharp cuts in government spending and restrictions on the money supply tend to yield reduced price increases. Also, as the Argentine case illustrates, adopting IMF programs can open the door to large influxes of foreign loans—from the Fund itself, the World Bank, the governments of the United States and other high-income countries, and (with the IMF's approval) internationally operating banks. But nowhere, including Argentina, has the IMF policy package led to stable, sustained economic expansion.

What IMF policies do often lead to, though, is growing inequality. Officially, the IMF laments that its policies—specifically reductions in government spending—have a severe negative impact on low-income groups (because they generate high rates of unemployment and lead to the gutting of social programs). Yet IMF officials rationalize their mania for spending cuts in times of crisis by claiming that balanced budgets are the foundation of long-term economic stability and growth.

Nonsense. In recessions, moderate government deficits, like those in Argentina in recent years, are a desirable policy because they boost spending, which counteracts the downturn; balanced budgets in such circumstances tend to exacerbate downturns. Also, curtailing social spending—on education, health care, infrastructure projects—cuts the legs out from under long-term economic progress.

Yet the IMF sticks to its policies, probably because those policies serve important and powerful interests in the U.S. and world economies. The IMF is controlled by the governments of the high-income countries that finance its operations. The U.S. government, with over 18% of the voting shares in the Fund, has by far the greatest influence. Indeed, over the years, the IMF has operated largely as a branch of the U.S. foreign policy apparatus, attempting to create a context that assures the well-being of U.S. interests—which is to say the interests of U.S.-based internationally operating firms. Since the same context serves the interests of firms based in Europe, Japan, and elsewhere, the U.S. government generally has the support of its allied governments in directing the IMF.

To serve those interests, the IMF tells governments that a key to economic growth lies in providing unrestricted access for imports and foreign investment. In fact, virtually all experience suggests the opposite. Britain, the United States, Japan, the countries of Western Europe, Taiwan, South Korea—all built the foundations for successful economic growth not on "free trade," but on government regulation of trade. The IMF gets around the inconvenient facts of history by conflating free trade with extensive engagement in the international economy. But the two are not the same. Yes, successful development has always been accompanied by extensive international engagement, but through regulated commerce, not free trade.

During the 1980s and 1990s, the IMF pushed governments in low-income countries to liberalize their capital markets, claiming that capital controls were anathema to development. Then came 1997, when the open capital markets of East Asian countries were instruments of disaster. In the aftermath of 1997, it seemed clear that the real winners from open capital markets were financial firms based in the United States and other high-income countries.

These same financial firms have also been the winners of another component in the IMF policy package. "Fiscal responsibility," according to the IMF, means that governments must give the highest priority to repaying their international debts. However, experience does not support the contention that, when governments fail to pay foreign debts, they bring on financial disaster. Instead, experience suggests that, at times, defaulting on foreign debt can be an effective, positive policy option. It is the banks operating out of New York and other financial centers, not people in low-income countries, that gain from giving first priority to debt repayment.

The IMF's advocacy of privatization offers one more way to open the world economy more fully to U.S.-based firms. When state enterprises in low-income countries are sold, they are often bought by large internationally operating firms, able to move in quickly with their huge supply of capital. Of course, in Argentina and elsewhere, local business groups have often benefited directly from privatization, sometimes on their own and sometimes as junior partners of firms based abroad. Either way, this enlargement of the private sphere works in favor of private firms. The problem here is not that privatization is always inappropriate, but simply that, contrary to IMF nostrums, it is not always appropriate. Privatization is especially problematic when it only replaces an inefficient government monopoly with a private monopoly yielding huge profits for its owners. Moreover, the record from Mexico City to Moscow demonstrates that privatization is often a hugely corrupt process.

Forging an Argentine Alternative?

The recent political upheaval in Argentina lends new strength to the argument that IMF policies not only fail to bolster economic development but also lead to social and political disintegration. It also provides new opportunities to call for alternative strategies that support democratic, egalitarian forms of economic development. Such strategies would promote investment in social programs and other public services, the expansion of government revenues (raising taxes), and regulations to keep the private sector from being guided simply by private profits. These strategies, unlike those of the IMF, would establish a foundation for long-run economic expansion—and economic equality.

Could such strategies succeed in Argentina? The demonstrations that brought down the de la Rúa government seem to have brought together unemployed people, workers, and large segments of the middle class, at least for a time. Sporadic rioting continues, and in Buenos Aires, scores of neighborhood-based assemblies, attracting thousands of participants, are calling for a more democratic political system as well as issuing demands for economic change.

Nonetheless, positive changes will be difficult to attain. Although the Argentine government did default on the debt (a key element in repudiating the policies of the IMF), it did so as an act of desperation, not in a controlled manner that might yield the greatest advantage. Also, while deputy economic minister Jorge Todesca has been harshly critical of the IMF, he is also trying to appease foreign investors, saying that the government is "not thinking of" nationalizing the banking system or establishing price controls.

Externally, there are substantial political barriers to an alternative model of economic growth. At the end of December, even as a new spate of rioting broke out in Buenos Aires, President Bush told the Argentine government to seek guidance from the IMF and "to work closely with" the Fund in developing its economic plans. In early February, the finance ministers of the G-7 (the world's seven wealthiest industrial nations) rejected Argentina's request for a $20 billion loan, saying that the IMF must be on board in order to bring about a "sustainable" plan. At this writing, Argentina's current economic minister, Jorge Remes Lenicov, is meeting with IMF officials in Washington, D.C.

And the IMF is unlikely to change its program in any significant way. Indeed, as Argentinians took to the streets in response to their long suffering under the aegis of the IMF, the IMF disclaimed all responsibility. "The economic program of Argentina was designed by the government of Argentina and the objective of eliminating the budget deficit was approved by the Congress of Argentina," declared the IMF's spokesperson on December 21. Continued pressure from the U.S. government, combined with the IMF's persistence in pursuing its discredited policies, will make progressive change difficult.

Also, powerful elites in Argentina will reinforce the barriers to change. In spite of the current difficulties, Argentina's economic policies of the past 15 years have delivered substantial benefits to the country's business elite, especially those whose incomes derive from the financial sector and primary product exports (grain and beef). Those policies have allowed the elite to strengthen their position in their own country and to secure their roles as junior partners with U.S.-based and other internationally operating firms. Changing policies will therefore require shifting the balance of power within Argentina, and that will be no easy task.

A version of this article appeared in Foreign Policy in Focus *<www.foreign-policyinfocus.org>, 2 January 2002.*

Chapter 8

THE PROFITS OF WAR

INTRODUCTION

"Imperialism" is back. While the reality of imperialism never went anywhere, for much of the 20th century the word itself was pushed off the pages of mainstream newspapers and books because of its association with Marxist theories of capitalist exploitation. Marxists didn't invent the term, however: before it became taboo, British imperialists like Cecil Rhodes frankly applied it to themselves. And today, in a sudden reversal, members of the U.S. ruling elite are likewise celebrating their "imperial power."

References to a "Pax Americana," an "American empire," "imperial America," and the like proliferate in the U.S. mass media, policy think tanks, and academia—from the *Christian Science Monitor*, to *U.S. News and World Report*, to publications of the conservative Cato Institute. For the most part, the mainstream media have embraced the "civilizing mission" of U.S. imperialism. They may doubt the wisdom of trying to "modernize" wide swaths of the world, or the likelihood of success in spreading "free markets and democracy," but they have shown little skepticism that the aims of the imperial project are noble.

Where most news outlets have parroted U.S. generals' Orwellian talk of "coalition forces," Alejandro Reuss argues that U.S. elites want anything but a balance of power among countries. Reuss provides hard numbers on U.S. military spending, and contends that U.S. elites—no longer able to dominate the world through economic power—are counting on a preponderance of military force to prevent the emergence of potential rivals ("Ruling the Empire"). Likewise, James M. Cypher looks at lucrative new arms contracts, and connects the military buildup to a U.S. power play in Central Asia. In the wake of its lightning war in Afghanistan, the U.S. military left an archipelago of bases and new client regimes ("Return of the Iron Triangle: The New Military Buildup").

Arthur MacEwan explains exactly how the U.S. war against Iraq was about oil. Even in progressive circles, there has been a great deal of confusion on this point. Many have described the war as a way to ensure a steady flow of oil for U.S. consumers. But MacEwan suggests that the U.S. government sought to ensure a steady flow of profits to major U.S. oil companies ("Is it Oil?").

Finally, the mainstream media have consistently whitewashed the harm done by U.S. imperialism. Infatuated by high-tech military gadgetry (when not actually dressing their reporters up in fatigues), most news outlets failed to report the enormous toll that U.S. sanctions took on Iraq during the last decade. Even long-time critics of Bush and his administration's unilateralism can learn from Richard Walton's chilling description of the disease and death brought down on Iraq, carried out by both Democratic and Republican administrations—and under United Nations auspices to boot ("The Deadliest Weapon: Sanctions and Public Health in Iraq"). Finally, Rodney Ward shows how, in a less extreme way, ordinary people in the United States have also been the targets and victims of the U.S. war machine. Whether it was reservists facing the loss of their jobs and homes when sent overseas, immigrants experiencing a new nativist crackdown, or government workers confronting union-busting in the guise of "national security," the U.S. working class has paid a high price for U.S. imperialism ("In Harm's Way: War and the Working Class").

RULING THE EMPIRE
By Alejandro Reuss
January/February 2003

Every few years, the President issues a document called the "National Security Strategy of the United States." Always eagerly awaited, the document is often described as the administration's "blueprint" for U.S. foreign policy. But it's really more like a press release, designed to give the U.S. government's global aims a noble-sounding spin.

The Bush administration's new "National Security Strategy," issued September 2002, abounds with pious lip service: On the subject of democracy, it applauds the "elected leaders replac[ing] generals in Latin America" without mentioning who put the generals in power in the first place. On the environment, it calls for "global efforts to stabilize greenhouse gas concentrations" without mentioning that the U.S. government had scuttled the Kyoto Protocol. On the global economy, it decries as "neither just nor stable" a state of affairs "where some live in comfort and plenty, while half of the human race lives on less than $2 a day," yet it offers no solution other than more "free markets and free trade."

The document's crowning hypocrisy, however, is its repeated use of the buzz-phrase "a balance of power that favors freedom," as if that were what the U.S. government was really after. You get the distinct feeling that the drafters don't believe in it for a minute. By its final and most important section, on the country's "National Security Institutions," the document abandons all pretext. The "unparalleled strength of the United States armed forces, and their forward presence, have maintained the peace," it declares. The United States must "reaffirm the essential role of American military strength" and "build and maintain our defenses beyond challenge." It must maintain forces "strong enough to dissuade potential adversaries" from the dream of ever "surpassing, or equaling, the power of the United States."

Well, if those are the real aims of U.S. ruling elites, they're off to a good start. In 2001, U.S. military spending—the highest, by far, of any country in the world—exceeded the combined spending of the next eight countries—Russia, France, Japan, the United Kingdom, Germany, China, Saudi Arabia, and Italy (see Graph 1). In fact, U.S. military spending represented over one third of the total of the *entire world*. This grotesquely overgrown war machine comes at no little cost. In 2001, total federal military spending (including interest payments on past

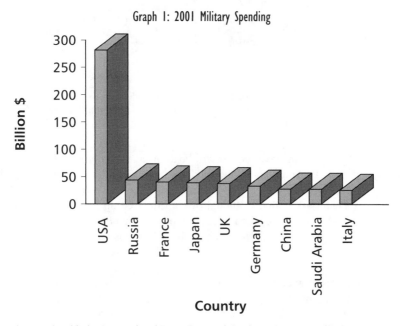

Graph 1: 2001 Military Spending

Source: Stockholm International Peace Research Institute, SIPRI Yearbook 2002.

military spending and benefits for former military personnel) devoured about one third of the federal funds portion of the budget (not including trust fund items like Social Security), as much as spending on health, income security, education, nutrition, and housing *combined* (see Graph 2).

In light of these realities, the "balance of power" rhetoric isn't really fooling anybody. Writing in the mainstream *Christian Science Monitor*, Gail Russell Chaddock argues that the document "asserts American dominance as the lone

Graph 2: 2001 Federal Funds Budget (Excludes Social Security).

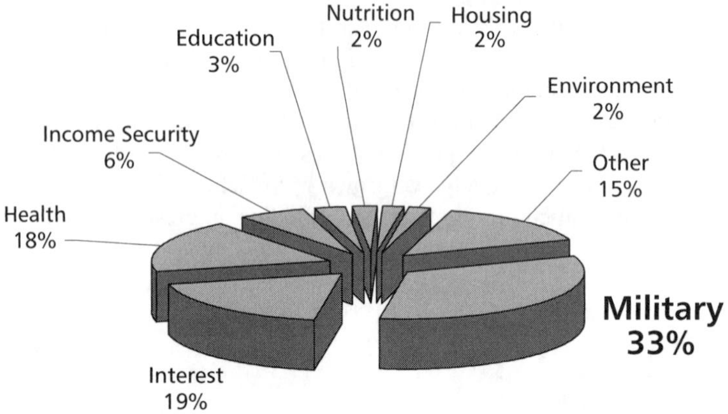

Education
3%

Nutrition
2%

Housing
2%

Environment
2%

Income Security
6%

Other
15%

Health
18%

Military
33%

Interest
19%

Source: National Priorities Project. Includes only the federal funds portion of the federal budget. Military includes veterans' benefits and the military share of interest on the national debt.

superpower—a status no rival power will be allowed to challenge." It is a vision, she says, of a "Pax Americana" (the modern-day equivalent of Roman imperial power). Even the senior defense policy analyst at the right-wing Cato Institute, Charles V. Peña, writes that "although it's all dressed up with the rationale of extending liberty, democracy, and freedom around the globe (except, of course, in Saudi Arabia and Pakistan)" the document really envisions a "Pax Americana enforced by dominant military power and … U.S. forces deployed around the globe."

None of this is exactly news. The United States, after all, has been a major imperial power in the Western Hemisphere for over a century. And it has been the single dominant capitalist power for more than half that period. The truth, however, should be clearer than ever. As the title of Peña's article puts it: "The New National Security Strategy Is American Empire."

RETURN OF THE IRON TRIANGLE: THE NEW MILITARY BUILDUP
By James M. Cypher
January/February 2002

The U.S. government's Commission on National Security/21st Century, convened in October 1998, was a who's who of industry, government, and military—that is, of the country's power elite. Former Senators Gary Hart and Warren Rudman chaired the Commission. Its commissioners included Martin Marietta CEO Norm Augustine and former House Speaker Newt Gingrich. Its 29 "study group members" came from top universities like MIT and Princeton, and think tanks including the RAND Corporation, the Cato Institute, and the Brookings Institution. The Commission also enjoyed the cooperation of the Departments of Defense and State, as well as top intelligence agencies like the CIA and the National Security Agency (NSA). In 1998, the Commission began a major review of U.S. military strategy. Its aim? To redesign the institutional structure of the military for the post-Cold War era.

The Commission's 1999 report *New World Coming: American Security in the 21st Century*, outlined a strategy for the United States to "remain the principal military power in the world." In the coming century, the report argued, the United States will become increasingly vulnerable to direct "nontraditional" attacks—against its information-technology infrastructure, for example. It will have to intervene abroad more frequently to deal with state fragmentation or to ensure an "uninterrupted" supply of oil from the Persian Gulf region or elsewhere. And it will face rivals in its drive to dominate space. The report concluded that to ensure continued U.S. dominance, U.S. military spending will have to rise dramatically.

Big and Heavy, Fast and Light
The Clinton administration, which had overseen a dramatic decline in military spending over the course of the 1990s, basically ignored the Commission's conclusions. It now looks, however, like U.S. military doctrine will follow many of the recommendations in *New World Coming*.

The Department of Defense's latest big picture document, the October 2001 *Quadrennial Defense Review*, aims both to "restore the defense of the U.S. as the department's primary mission" and to build forces capable of moving rapidly overseas. Not to be outdone, the Army has produced two major documents outlining plans to retain the military's heavy aircraft and tank forces while developing lighter, faster units that it can deploy virtually anywhere in the world within 96 hours.

The post-September 11 era of military spending will allow the Pentagon to have its cake and eat it too—continuing major Cold War-era weapons systems and funding the cyber-age "Revolution in Military Affairs" (RMA). The RMA emphasizes high-tech warfare—communications networks, satellites, robot observation planes, smart bombs, night-vision instruments, highly mobile "light" armor, and global positioning system (GPS)-equipped soldiers—over old-fashioned heavy-weapons systems. Many Pentagon officials and major weapons contractors feared the RMA because it could disrupt the method of military contracting going back to the beginning of the Cold War—building a huge arsenal of ships, planes, tanks, and missiles to confront the Soviet "threat." Military officials had built their careers on that approach, and weapons contractors had made many fortunes from the resulting arms contracts. They feared that the RMA would marginalize them. The novelty of the Army's approach is to spend enough money to keep everyone happy, funding the "old military" and the "new military" alike.

Balancing the Iron Triangle

The "Iron Triangle" forms the U.S. military establishment's decision-making structure and includes its major interest groups. One side of the triangle includes the "civilian" agencies that shape U.S. military policy—the Office of the President, the National Security Council, the Senate and House Armed Services Committees, and civilian intelligence agencies like the CIA and NSA. A second side includes the military institutions—the Joint Chiefs of Staff, the top brass of the Air Force, Army, Marines, and Navy, the powerful "proconsul" regional commands (known as "CINCs"), and, in a supporting role, veterans' organizations like the American Legion and the Veterans of Foreign Wars. At the *base* of the triangle are the 85,000 private firms that profit from the military contracting system, and that use their sway over millions of defense workers to push for ever-higher military budgets.

Everyone in the Iron Triangle knew that the Bush Administration would increase military spending. The question was whether the increase would be vast enough to fund the old weapons systems, the "Star Wars" National Missile Defense scheme, and the RMA. And if not, who would pay the price? On February 13, 2001, President Bush announced that the United States would be moving beyond the Cold War model and into the RMA. In March 2001, he submitted a 2002 budget that upped military spending by only $14 billion over Clinton's 2001 budget. Many powerful members of the Iron Triangle, who had staked their careers on the old system, could now foresee their marginalization.

They were not about to go without a fight. Between March and August 2001, they struggled to save outmoded weapons systems like the F-22, the most expensive fighter plane in history, and the plan to build the unreliable V-22 Osprey aircraft, a project that then-Secretary of Defense Dick Cheney nearly killed eleven years before. It was, according to *The New York Times*, a battle "as intense and intemperate as any in recent memory" within the Iron Triangle.

Even before September 11, Secretary of Defense Donald Rumsfeld advocated a revised military budget with a total spending increase of $52 billion. He still favored, however, reconfiguring the military along RMA lines, reducing military units, cutting bases, and retiring unneeded weapons systems. Even while he proposed the larger spending increase, Rumsfeld's opponents in the Pentagon succeeded in portraying him as weak, unfocused, and "spiraling down." Legislators fought him on base closures, contractors resisted any reduction in lucrative weapons contracts, the Armed Services fought him on manpower reductions, and Democrats resisted the National Missile Defense program—which Rumsfeld had spearheaded. Post-September 11 emergency spending allocated an additional $25.5 billion to military objectives. In all, military spending will rise by at least $58.6 billion over 2001 levels, a 19% increase—just exceeding Rumsfeld's goal. ("Special Appropriations" will probably push the basic military budget even higher during the current fiscal year.) Now, Rumsfeld will be able to make a down payment on the RMA, while the vested interests will see plenty of funds for the old-style "legacy system" military.

Fighter-plane programs will get an incredible $400 billion in new multi-year contracts. Lockheed Martin will get $225 billion over 12 years to build nearly 3,000 Joint Strike Fighter planes for the Air Force, Marines, and Navy. According to *Business Week,* Lockheed also stands to make $175 billion in sales to foreign buyers over the next 25 years. Drowning in its record trade deficit, the United States desperately needs the boost to the trade balance provided by arms exports. The Joint Strike Fighter, if it brings in the expected $175 billion in export sales, may go down in history as the largest single boost to the balance of payments ever. Currently the United States controls 50% of the global arms market, with foreign military sales running at $16.5 billion in 1999. That figure will be on the rise as new weapons are delivered to Pakistan, Uzbekistan, Tajikistan, Oman, the United Arab Emirates, and Egypt.

Looking ahead, the RMA's fantastic weaponry—and its enormous costs—are only just beginning to emerge. Northrup Grumman, General Atomics, and Boeing are speeding robot airplanes into production. Other contractors are developing thermal imaging sensors to "see" targets through night, distance, fog, and even rock formations. The Navy is promoting a new destroyer-class warship, the DD-21, loaded with cruise missiles and guns capable of hitting targets 100 miles inland. Known as the "stealth bomber for the ocean," the DD-21 is estimated to cost $24 billion. Cost overruns of 300% are common, however, so there's no telling what taxpayers will ultimately pay.

The Economic Impact

Bush justified his mammoth June 2001 tax cut partially as a measure to reverse the economic downturn that began the previous March. In October 2001, he proposed further tax cuts as an "economic stimulus" package. The two tax cuts combined, however, will likely provide less of a short-term boost than the nearly $60 billion increase in military spending. Most of the June tax cut will go to people with high incomes, who tend to spend a smaller proportion of the additional income they receive from a tax cut. And a large portion of what they do spend, they tend to spend on imported luxury goods, rather than domestic goods.

Most of the proposed "stimulus" program suffers from the same problems, plus a few more. The new proposal also includes a clause allowing businesses a bigger write-off for equipment as it decreases in value. But a corporation can take the write-off while spending on capital depreciation that they would have done anyway. The same is true of the elimination of the corporate "alternative minimum tax," which had set a tax "floor" for corporations no matter how many deductions they could claim. Corporations will use these windfalls to pay off debt or to invest outside of the United States.

Compare this to the $60 billion in new military outlays. Most of this money will go to civilian suppliers who will use it to pay for domestic labor, materials, and equipment. Only a modest portion, 5-10%, will leak out of the United States to military base operations. (Even that may not be as large a "leak" as it might seem, since base employees stationed overseas often buy U.S. exports.) Moreover, because of the new emphasis on the RMA, the military will be buying more newly designed weapons than it has in a long time, and this will have a strong impact on the economy (see box).

Military Purchases and Linked Investment Effects

To deliver the brand-new weapons the Pentagon wants, military contractors will have to either create or drastically alter their production systems. This means that in addition to the nearly $60 billion worth of goods and services bought, military contractors will have to invest in new capital goods needed for new production lines. Through these "linked investment" effects, the $60 billion could end up translating into nearly $132 in total spending (public and private).

How?

$24 billion (40% of the $60 billion) will likely be spent on research, development, testing, and production of new systems. But contractors will need new production lines to build these new systems. Economists estimate that the companies will have to invest three dollars in capital for each dollar of new output. So contractors will have to invest $72 billion (3 x $24 billion) in new structures, machines, and equipment. This means that current military orders could put into motion $96 billion ($24 billion + $72 billion) in new spending, plus the remaining 60% of the original $60 billion ($36 billion). The total impact, then, would be an economic stimulus of $132 billion ($96 billion + $36 billion).

This estimate is probably too high, because contractors will use some old capital to produce the new weapons and because some of the new military spending will be spent on imports. Still, much of the new spending will go to new technologies. The information technology sector will probably gain the most, since the RMA and the next "generation" of weapons will be loaded with far more information technology than hardware. Already in 2000, according to Business Week, electronics and communications components accounted for 40% of weapons purchases. So the jump in military spending will function as an industrial policy for the information technology and communications industries, boosting these hard-hit sectors of the U.S. economy.

But will this counter the current recession? University of Texas economist James K. Galbraith has argued that the United States will need $600 billion in new spending in 2002 to pull out of the recession. However, only about $214 billion will come from increases in emergency and military spending plus the two tax cuts. Reduced interest rates will also stimulate new spending, but probably not on the scale required. If Galbraith is correct, even the massive outlays for the military will fall far short of the sum needed to turn the U.S. economy around.

What about its long-term effects? Some claim that increased military spending will drain U.S. productivity and slow long-term growth. But much of the United States' growth during the post-WWII period was stimulated by military spending. As *Business Week* noted in October 2001:

> Defense spending on research and development has sparked much innovation. Microchips, radar, lasers, satellite communications, cell phones, GPS, and the Internet all came out of Defense Dept. funding for basic research at the Massachusetts Institute of Technology, Stanford University and national laboratories. There were breakthroughs at IBM and Bell Laboratories, and all were commercialized by Intel Corp., Motorola Inc., and other corporations.

The same is true of artificial intelligence, supercomputers, high-speed fiber optics, and many other breakthroughs. The bulk of information technologies, in fact, were developed through massive R&D investments in military technology.

The argument that military spending undercuts productivity must be seen in a broader context: Conservative economists have long argued that government spending does not increase investment because it causes an offsetting reduction in private investment—known as "crowding out." Some liberal economists have appropriated this argument to oppose military spending as a drain on the economy. That argument underestimates the structural importance of military spending and the arms industry to capitalism. The new military buildup is not likely to "crowd out" private investment, but to stimulate investment and technical innovation. The military buildup will definitely "crowd out," however, spending on public needs, such as a viable rapid rail system, public education, and a national health care system—all of which could greatly enhance productivity. More military spending will focus inordinately on information technology and other high-tech systems. More artificial intelligence technologies, global positioning systems, robot planes, and thermal imaging sensors, however, are not going to house, educate, or heal people who lack housing, education, or health care.

Big Visions, Big Plans

The current military buildup is about much more than countering the slide in the high-tech sector, or countering the current economic recession. It is about consolidating the United States' position as the only superpower. Continued U.S. dominance requires continued control of the world's most important traded commodity—energy. The United States imports 52% of the oil, and a growing share of the natural gas, that it consumes. The profits of oil giants like Shell,

Exxon/Mobil, and Chevron/Texaco come from their global control of oil and gas resources. Securing this control is one of the major functions of the U.S. military.

RUSSIA
14.0

KAZAKHSTAN
106.1

AZERBAIJAN
37.6

UZBEKISTAN
7.6

KYRGYZSTAN

CASPIAN
SEA

TURKMENISTAN
105.5

TAJIKISTAN

CHINA

16.8
IRAN

AFGHANISTAN

Total possible oil and gas reserves
(in billions of barrels of oil).

= 5 billion barrels

= 50 billion barrels

PAKISTAN

INDIA

Source: U.S. Department of Energy, Energy Information Administration, "Caspian Sea Region," June 2000. Russia figure for area bordering Caspian Sea only.

U.S. foreign policy will focus increasingly on securing global resources, longtime observer and critic of U.S. military affairs Michael Klare argues in his new book *Resource Wars*. (This stands in contrast to the Cold War era, when directly economic motives were less important to U.S. foreign policy than the superpower rivalry with the USSR.) The Pentagon and other centers of U.S. power clearly view Middle East energy resources as a "vital interest," warranting massive military outlays and the export of the top-level weapons to client regimes in the region. Between 1990 and 1997, the United States exported $42 billion in arms to the Persian Gulf states, of which $36 billion went to Saudi Arabia.

This focus on the oil-exporting regions will only rise under the Bush administration. Even though the Bushes never really established themselves in the oil industry, their tilt toward "big energy" is unmistakable. George W. Bush's number-one corporate donor was Houston's Enron Corporation, the ill-fated energy trader; Vice President Dick Cheney comes fresh from his job as CEO of Dallas' Halliburton Corporation, the world's largest oil-well service company; and Condoleezza Rice served as a director of the Chevron Corporation before becoming National Security Advisor.

"Oil runs the world and the Saudis are the linchpin of oil production," a unnamed senior administration official told the *New York Times* in October 2001. The United States has struggled in the past to reduce its reliance on Middle East oil supplies—pressuring Mexico and Venezuela to increase production, hoping for big increases from Colombia's rich oilfields, and so on. Since 1990, the United States has reduced OPEC oil from approximately 61% of its total oil imports to 52%—so only about 27% of the oil consumed in the United States now comes from OPEC (including Venezuela). But this is not the whole story: The United States has also assumed the role of military guarantor of oil stability for Europe and Japan. The growing instability of the Persian Gulf states, in spite of the huge sums that they and the United States have committed to military defense, portends even greater U.S. military involvement in the region for the foreseeable future.

Meanwhile, near the Gulf, two alternative sources of oil are becoming increasingly attractive—the Caspian Sea region and the rest of the former USSR. U.S. oil companies are now plunging into Russia. Halliburton has 300 specialists in Western Siberia struggling to revive the Samatlor oilfield, while Shell and Exxon/Mobil are investing in a new field off Shakalin Island. Exxon has committed $5 billion to the effort over the next five years. Russia is now exporting about 3.3 million barrels a day, nearly half what Saudi Arabia exports. But if the oil giants invest in new pipelines, Russian exports could leap to 5.3 million barrels a day by 2004, according to *Business Week*. Much of this new oil, and huge quantities of natural gas—one third of the world's gas reserves are located in the former Soviet Union—would come from the Caspian Sea region of Central Asia, the biggest economic prize since the United States took effective control of Saudi oil in February 1945.

This makes Afghanistan, through which a major Caspian pipeline would likely run, a strategic linchpin of the global energy industry and the world economy. U.S., European, and Russian gas and oil firms have taken a major interest in the Caspian region's vast oil and gas reserves since the early 1990s. Major pipelines now carry these resources to Turkey, from which they can be shipped to Western Europe, the United States, and the rest of the world. Unocal, Pennzoil, British Petroleum, and Amoco were major participants in the Azerbaijan International Operating Company (AIOC), a large-scale project to build pipelines from the Caspian Basin to Turkey and the Black Sea. Unocal has also proposed a pipeline from Turkmenistan, Uzbekistan, and Kazakhstan through Afghanistan to India and Pakistan, and to the Pakistan coast for export to China—though the company now says it has shelved the project.

The U.S. military is now developing a long-term presence in Central Asia, which it will undoubtedly use to secure the rich supply of Caspian oil and gas. The

Pentagon has been courting the government of Uzbekistan for years, giving its officers military training in the United States since 1995, and conducting military exercises in Uzbekistan since 1999. In November 2001, the U.S. military began negotiating with the government of Tajikistan to use former Soviet military bases there during the U.S. war in Afghanistan. Considering that a U.S. garrison has been permanently stationed in Saudi Arabia since the Gulf War, it seems unlikely that the U.S. military will leave either Uzbekistan or Tajikistan after the Afghanistan war.

The outcome of this high-stakes struggle remains to be seen. Russia and the Caspian region resemble the Persian Gulf region in their fragile social foundations. So shifting to the former for imported oil and gas will not eliminate the United States' reliance for energy on states with huge potential for instability. If an Afghanistan pipeline is ever built, however, it will help give U.S. and Russian oil interests leverage they have not had in decades over the Persian Gulf region, just by making the Gulf's oil supplies a much smaller part of global production. Moreover, with energy demand in developing Asia predicted to surpass that of North America by 2020, it will give the United States added leverage over these economies. The current U.S. power play in Central Asia, in short, dramatically increases the likelihood that the U.S. military will succeed in achieving the goals articulated by the Commission on National Security/21st Century— securing control of the global energy supply, and maintaining the United States' position as the world's only superpower.

Resources: U.S. Commission on National Security/21st Century, *New World Coming: American Security in the 21st Century*, 1999 <www.nssg.gov>. Michael Klare, *Resource Wars*, Metropolitan Books, 2001. James Galbraith, "The War Economy," Levy Economic Institute, 2001 <www.levy.org>.

THE DEADLIEST WEAPON: SANCTIONS AND PUBLIC HEALTH IN IRAQ
By Richard J. Walton
May/June 2001

Saddam Hussein is the enemy, three successive U.S. presidents—George Bush the Elder, Bill Clinton, and now Bush the Younger—have proclaimed. So what have ten years of UN sanctions (the most draconian in world history) accomplished? Well, the Iraqi dictator is more secure than he was a decade ago. And about a million Iraqi civilians, most of them young children, have perished from malnutrition and disease.

Step into the Children's Hospital in Baghdad. There are no enemies here, just dying kids who would not be sick, or who could easily be cured, if not for the sanctions. You blink back tears as you move from one shabby ward to the next, each crowded with family members, most of them stoic, some wailing in grief.

One scene I will always remember: One of our group, a woman from Massachusetts, standing at a bed silently stroking the head of an unconscious infant while the baby's black-robed mother looked on. Neither spoke. Even if they had a common language, what could they say?

During the Gulf War, the United Nations (largely the United States) unleashed one of the most ferocious aerial bombardments in the history of air warfare, much of it against civilian targets. Among those targets were water purification systems, sewage systems, and food production, processing, storage, and distribution facilities. Then came the economic sanctions, which embargoed any goods that could have a "dual use," that is, military or civilian. In a modern economy, that covers almost everything: For example, chlorine, which is used in water purification, is designated as a "dual use" commodity. The sanctions have made it difficult, often impossible, to restore potable water and public sanitation or to produce or buy sufficient food.

Over the last ten years, the ancient plagues of hunger and disease have been visited on the Iraqi people to a shocking degree. The following gives some idea of the progression. In 1989, just before the Gulf War began, there were 7,110 deaths of children under five from respiratory infection, diarrhea, gastroenteritis, and malnutrition. Within a year of the war and the imposition of sanctions, the number of deaths had risen to 27,473. By 1994, the figure stood at 52,905, and in the first 11 months of 1999, it soared to 73,572. That's a ten-fold increase over ten years.

Here is another measure. In 1990, only 4.5% of Iraqi children were born with low birth weight (less than 2.5 kilograms, or about five and a half pounds). By November 1999, the figure was 24.1%, or just under one in four. Many of these children will have underdeveloped organs, suffer from mental retardation, and be more prone to illness, malnutrition, and low life expectancy.

One nutrition-influenced disease, kwashiorkor (seen in children with horribly swollen bellies, who can suffer long-term organ damage, including brain damage, unless the condition is quickly arrested) was rare in Iraq before 1990. By 1998, it had increased by 61.4 times. Cases of marasmus, which causes children to waste away, increased more than 50-fold. Also in 1998, nearly two million Iraqis (out of a population of about 23 million) were suffering from severe and protracted malnutrition.

The war and the sanctions are directly responsible for these terrifying health problems. The galloping increases in grotesque birth defects and childhood leukemia are attributable to the widespread use of depleted uranium in U.S. ammunition. There has been a dramatic rise in cases of cholera (from zero in 1989 to 2,560 in 1998), amoebic dysentery (a 13-fold increase, up to 264,000 cases in 1998), and typhoid fever (a nearly 11-fold increase)—all rarely found in Iraq before the sanctions, all preventable with potable water and effective sewage treatment. Because of vaccine shortages, such diseases as whooping cough, measles, mumps, and even polio (which had been all but eradicated) have also increased.

In addition, hospital patients are dying because of a lack of antibiotics, anesthesia, oxygen, antiseptics, x-ray film, functioning medical equipment, and even aspirin. Major surgical operations have plummeted from a monthly average of 15,125 in 1989 to 3,823 in November 1999, a decline of 74%.

In short, the ongoing war against Iraq has reduced a resource-rich country with free, cradle-to-grave medical care to the level of an impoverished African nation, where illness and malnutrition are widespread.

There is a terrible irony here. The U.S. government claims that sanctions are necessary because the Iraqi regime *might* develop weapons of mass destruction, which it *might* use against its neighbors. So the United States (no other country on the UN Security Council, except for the United Kingdom, continues to support the present sanctions) deploys *actual* weapons of mass destruction—epidemic disease and hunger on a massive scale.

Resources: The data provided here are compiled from a variety of sources, primarily the UN and its various agencies, the World Health Organization, the Food and Agriculture Organization, the World Food Program, and UNICEF. Other sources include Iraqi ministries.

IS IT OIL?
By Arthur MacEwan
May/June 2003

Before U.S. forces invaded Iraq, the United Nations inspection team that had been searching the country for weapons of mass destruction was unable to find either such weapons or a capacity to produce them in the near future. As of mid-April, while the U.S. military is apparently wrapping up its invasion, it too has not found the alleged weapons. The U.S. government continues to claim that weapons of mass destruction exist in Iraq but provides scant evidence to substantiate its claim.

While weapons of mass destruction are hard to find in Iraq, there is one thing that is relatively easy to find: oil. Lots of oil. With 112.5 billion barrels of proven reserves, Iraq has greater stores of oil than any country except Saudi Arabia. This combination—lots of oil and no weapons of mass destruction—begs the question: *Is it oil* and not weapons of mass destruction that motivates the U.S. government's aggressive policy towards Iraq?

The U.S. "Need" for Oil?
Much of the discussion of the United States, oil, and Iraq focuses on the U.S. economy's overall dependence on oil. We are a country highly dependent on oil, consuming far more than we produce. We have a small share, about 3%, of the world's total proven oil reserves. By depleting our reserves at a much higher rate

than most other countries, the United States accounts for about 10% of world production. But, by importing from the rest of the world, we can consume oil at a still higher rate: U.S. oil consumption is over 25% of the world's total. (See the accompanying figures for these and related data.) Thus, the United States relies on the rest of the world's oil in order to keep its economy running—or at least running in its present oil-dependent form. Moreover, for the United States to operate as it does and maintain current standards of living, we need access to oil at low prices. Otherwise we would have to turn over a large share of U.S. GDP as payment to those who supply us with oil.

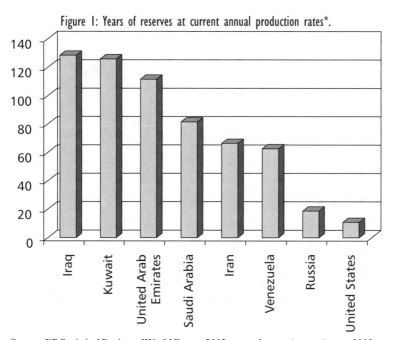

Figure I: Years of reserves at current annual production rates*.

Source: BP Statistical Review of World Energy 2002 <www.bp.com/centres/energy2002>

*The number of years it would take to use up existing reserves at current production rate. Past experience, however, suggests that more reserves will be found. In the 1980s, the world's proven reserves expanded by 47%, even as the consumption continued apace. With a more rapid rate of economic growth in the 1990s, and thus with the more rapid rate of oil consumption, the world's reserves rose by almost 5%.

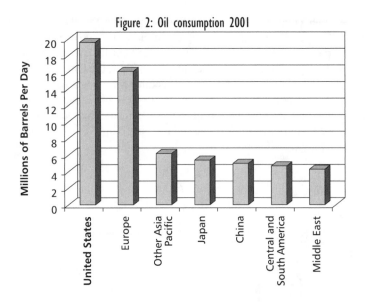

Figure 2: Oil consumption 2001

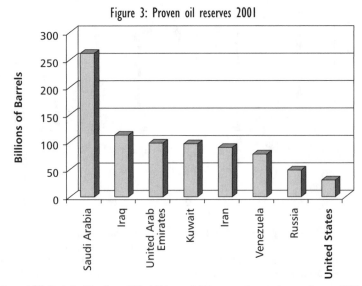

Figure 3: Proven oil reserves 2001

Source: BP Statistical Review of World Energy 2002 <www.bp.com/centres/energy2002>

Iraq could present the United States with supply problems. With a hostile government in Baghdad, the likelihood that the United States would be subject to some sort of boycott as in the early 1970s is greater than otherwise. Likewise, a government in Baghdad that does not cooperate with Washington could be a catalyst to a reinvigoration of the Organization of Petroleum Exporting Countries (OPEC) and the result could be higher oil prices.

Such threats, however, while real, are not as great as they might first appear. Boycotts are hard to maintain. The sellers of oil need to sell as much as the buyers need to buy; oil exporters depend on the U.S. market, just as U.S. consumers depend on those exporters. (An illustration of this mutual dependence is provided by the continuing oil trade between Iraq and the United States in recent years. During 2001, while the two countries were in a virtual state of war, the United States bought 284 million barrels of oil from Iraq, about 7% of U.S. imports and almost a third of Iraq's exports.) Also, U.S. oil imports come from diverse sources, with less than half from OPEC countries and less than one-quarter from Persian Gulf nations.

Most important, ever since the initial surge of OPEC in the 1970s, the organization has followed a policy of price restraint. While price restraint may in part be a strategy of political cooperation, resulting from the close U.S.-Saudi relationship in particular, it is also a policy adopted because high prices are counter-productive for OPEC itself; high prices lead consumers to switch sources of supply and conserve energy, undercutting the longer term profits for the oil suppliers. Furthermore, a sudden rise in prices can lead to general economic disruption, which is no more desirable for the oil exporters than for the oil importers. To be sure, the United States would prefer to have cooperative governments in oil producing countries, but the specter of another boycott as in the 1970s or somewhat higher prices for oil hardly provides a rationale, let alone a justification, for war.

The Profits Problem

There is, however, also the importance of oil in the profits of large U.S. firms: the oil companies themselves (with ExxonMobil at the head of the list) but also the numerous drilling, shipping, refining, and marketing firms that make up the rest of the oil industry. Perhaps the most famous of this latter group, because former CEO Dick Cheney is now vice president, is the Halliburton Company, which supplies a wide range of equipment and engineering services to the industry. Even while many governments—Saudi Arabia, Kuwait, and Venezuela, for example—have taken ownership of their countries' oil reserves, these companies have been able to maintain their profits because of their decisive roles at each stage in the long sequence from exploration through drilling to refining and marketing. Ultimately, however, as with any resource-based industry, the monopolistic position—and thus the large profits—of the firms that dominate the oil industry depends on their access to the supply of the resource. Their access, in turn, depends on the relations they are able to establish with the governments of oil-producing countries.

From the perspective of the major U.S. oil companies, a hostile Iraqi government presents a clear set of problems. To begin with, there is the obvious:

because Iraq has a lot of oil, access to that oil would represent an important profit-making opportunity. What's more, Iraqi oil can be easily extracted and thus produced at very low cost. With all oil selling at the same price on the world market, Iraqi oil thus presents opportunities for especially large profits per unit of production. According to the *Guardian* newspaper (London), Iraqi oil could cost as little as 97 cents a barrel to produce, compared to the UK's North Sea oil produced at $3 to $4 per barrel. As one oil executive told the *Guardian* last November, "Ninety cents a barrel for oil that sells for $30—that's the kind of business anyone would want to be in. A 97% profit margin—you can live with that." The *Guardian* continues: "The stakes are high. Iraq could be producing 8 million barrels a day within the decade. The math is impressive—8 million times 365 at $30 per barrel or $87.5 billion a year. Any share would be worth fighting for." The question for the oil companies is: what share will they be able to claim and what share will be claimed by the Iraqi government? The split would undoubtedly be more favorable for the oil companies with a compliant U.S.-installed government in Baghdad.

Furthermore, the conflict is not simply one between the private oil companies and the government of Iraq. The U.S.-based firms and their British (and British-Dutch) allies are vying with French, Russian, and Chinese firms for access to Iraqi oil. During recent years, firms from these other nations signed oil exploration and development contracts with the Hussein government in Iraq, and, if there were no "regime change," they would preempt the operations of the U.S. and British firms in that country. If, however, the U.S. government succeeds in replacing the government of Saddam Hussein with its preferred allies in the Iraqi opposition, the outlook will change dramatically. According to Ahmed Chalabi, head of the Iraqi National Congress and a figure in the Iraqi opposition who seems to be currently favored by Washington, "The future democratic government in Iraq will be grateful to the United States for helping the Iraqi people liberate themselves and getting rid of Saddam.... American companies, we expect, will play an important and leading role in the future oil situation." (In recent years, U.S. firms have not been fully frozen out of the oil business in Iraq. For example, according to a June 2001 report in the *Washington Post*, while Vice President Cheney was CEO at Halliburton Company during the late 1990s, the firm operated through subsidiaries to sell some $73 million of oil production equipment and spare parts to Iraq.)

The rivalry with French, Russian and Chinese oil companies is in part driven by the direct prize of the profits to be obtained from Iraqi operations. In addition, in order to maintain their dominant positions in the world oil industry, it is important for the U.S. and British-based firms to deprive their rivals of the growth potential that access to Iraq would afford. In any monopolistic industry, leading firms need to deny their potential competitors market position and control of new sources of supply; otherwise, those competitors will be in a better position to challenge the leaders. The British *Guardian* reports that the Hussein government is "believed to have offered the French company TotalFinaElf exclusive rights to the largest of

Iraq's oil fields, the Majoon, which would more than double the company's entire output at a single stroke." Such a development would catapult TotalFinaElf from the second ranks into the first ranks of the major oil firms. The basic structure of the world oil industry would not change, but the sharing of power and profits among the leaders would be altered. Thus for ExxonMobil, Chevron, Shell and the other traditional "majors" in the industry, access to Iraq is a defensive as well as an offensive goal. ("Regime change" in Iraq will not necessarily provide the legal basis for cancellation of contracts signed between the Hussein regime and various oil companies. International law would not allow a new regime simply to turn things over to the U.S. oil companies. "Should 'regime change' happen, one thing is guaranteed," according to the *Guardian*, "shortly afterwards there will be the mother of all legal battles.")

Oil companies are big and powerful. The biggest, ExxonMobil, had 2002 profits of $15 billion, more than any other corporation, in the United States or in the world. Chevron-Texaco came in with $3.3 billion in 2002 profits, and Phillips-Tosco garnered $1.7 billion. British Petroleum-Amoco-Arco pulled in $8 billion, while Royal Dutch/Shell Group registered almost $11 billion. Firms of this magnitude have a large role affecting the policies of their governments, and, for that matter, the governments of many other countries.

With the ascendancy of the Bush-Cheney team to the White House in 2000, perhaps the relationship between oil and the government became more personal, but it was not new. Big oil has been important in shaping U.S. foreign policy since the end of the 19th century (to say nothing of its role in shaping other policy realms, particularly environmental regulation). From 1914, when the Marines landed at Mexico's Tampico Bay to protect U.S. oil interests, to the CIA-engineered overthrow of the Mosadegh government in Iran in 1953, to the close relationship with the oppressive Saudi monarchy through the past 70 years, oil and the interests of the oil companies have been central factors in U.S. foreign policy. Iraq today is one more chapter in a long story.

The Larger Issue

Yet in Iraq today, as in many other instances of the U.S. government's international actions, oil is not the whole story. The international policies of the U.S. government are certainly shaped in significant part by the interests of U.S.-based firms, but not only the oil companies. ExxonMobil may have had the largest 2002 profits, but there are many additional large U.S. firms with international interests: Citbank and the other huge financial firms; IBM, Microsoft, and other information technology companies; General Motors and Ford; Merck, Pfizer and the other pharmaceutical corporations; large retailers like MacDonald's and Wal-Mart (and many more) depend on access to foreign markets and foreign sources of supply for large shares of their sales and profits.

The U.S. government (like other governments) has long defined its role in international affairs as protecting the interests of its nationals, and by far the largest interests of U.S. nationals abroad are the interests of these large U.S. companies. The day-to-day activities of U.S. embassies and consular offices around the world are dominated by efforts to further the interests of particular U.S. firms—for example, helping the firms establish local markets, negotiate a country's regulations, or develop relations with local businesses. When the issue is large, such as when governments in low-income countries have attempted to assure the availability of HIV-AIDS drugs in spite of patents held by U.S. firms, Washington steps directly into the fray. On the broadest level, the U.S. government tries to shape the rules and institutions of the world economy in ways that work well for U.S. firms. These rules are summed up under the heading of "free trade," which in practice means free access of U.S. firms to the markets and resources of the rest of the world.

In normal times, Washington uses diplomacy and institutions like the International Monetary Fund, the World Bank, and the World Trade Organization to shape the rules of the world economy. But times are not always "normal." When governments have attempted to remove their economies from the open system and break with the "rules of the game," the U.S. government has responded with overt or covert military interventions. Latin America has had a long history of such interventions, where Guatemala (1954), Cuba (1961), Chile (1973) and Nicaragua (1980s) provide fairly recent examples. The Middle East also provides several illustrations of this approach to foreign affairs, with U.S. interventions in Iran (1953), Lebanon (1958), Libya (1981), and now Iraq. These interventions are generally presented as efforts to preserve freedom and democracy, but, if freedom and democracy were actually the goals of U.S. interventions the record would be very different; both the Saudi monarchy and the Shah of Iran, in an earlier era, would then have been high on the U.S. hit list. (Also, as with maintaining the source of supply of oil, the U.S. government did not intervene in Guatemala in 1954 to maintain our supply of bananas; the profits of the United Fruit Company, however, did provide a powerful causal factor.)

The rhetorical rationale of U.S. foreign policy has seen many alterations and adjustments over the last century: at the end of the 19th century, U.S. officials spoke of the need to spread Christianity; Woodrow Wilson defined the mission as keeping the world safe for democracy; for most of the latter half of the 20th century, the fight against Communism was the paramount rationale; for a fleeting moment during the Carter administration, the protection of human rights entered the government's vocabulary; in recent years we have seen the war against drugs; and now we have the current administration's war against terrorism.

What distinguishes the current administration in Washington is neither its approach toward foreign affairs and U.S. business interests in general nor its policy in the Middle East and oil interests in particular. Even its rhetoric builds on well established traditions, albeit with new twists. What does distinguish the Bush administration is the clarity and aggressiveness with which it has put forth its goal of maintaining U.S. domination internationally. The "Bush Doctrine" that the administration has articulated claims legitimacy for pre-emptive action against those who might threaten U.S. interests, and it is clear from the statement of that doctrine in last September's issuance of *The National Security Strategy of the United States of America* that "U.S. interests" includes economic interests.

The economic story is never the whole story, and oil is never the whole economic story. In the particular application of U.S. power, numerous strategic and political considerations come into play. With the application of the Bush Doctrine in the case of Iraq, the especially heinous character of the Hussein regime is certainly a factor, as is the regime's history of conflict with other nations of the region (at times with U.S. support) and its apparent efforts at developing nuclear, chemical, and biological weapons; certainly the weakness of the Iraqi military also affects the U.S. government's willingness to go to war. Yet, as September's *Security Strategy* document makes clear, the U.S. government is concerned with domination and a major factor driving that goal of domination is economic. In the Middle East, Iraq and elsewhere, oil—or, more precisely, the profit from oil—looms large in the picture.

An earlier version of this article was prepared for the newsletter of the Joiner Center for War and Social Consequences at the University of Massachusetts-Boston.

IN HARM'S WAY: THE WORKING CLASS ON THE WAR FRONT AND THE HOME FRONT
By Rodney Ward
May/June 2003

> "Old man Bush wasn't half the president his son is. When the father was president, I only took a 15% pay cut. Now that his idiot son is president, I get to take a 40% pay cut. Way to go, George!"
> —a US Airways Fleet Services union activist

> "I've had enough of being fired at from all directions. I just want to go home."
> —a U.S. Marine, speaking to BBC News

First, the obvious: In Iraq, a U.S. and allied military made up of working-class soldiers has fought against a working-class Iraqi military. But the war tears at the lives of working people in the United States as well. As Martin Luther King observed about an earlier war, the bombs raining down on the "enemy" also jeopardize the futures and livelihoods of people in poor and working-class communities in the United States.

On any number of dimensions, the war in Iraq is hurting working people back home. The U.S. soldiers who return will find their benefits slashed by Congress and their prospects limited by continuing economic stagnation. The massive cost of the war and occupation robs resources from those who can least afford it and exacerbates federal and state budget crises. In turn, the social safety net is unraveling further just as wartime anxiety pushes the economy back toward recession.

The Bush administration is using wartime insecurity as a pretext to strip union rights from many federal workers and to intensify the criminalization of immigrant communities. In the private sector, entire industries—most notably, the airlines—are using the moment as an opportunity to bludgeon unions and savagely restructure their workplaces. As the shooting in Iraq winds down, an unwelcome occupation begins that will drain more resources away from meeting urgent human needs; just as important, it will prolong an atmosphere of crisis that gives cover for those whose agenda is to weaken the union movement and workers' rights.

Working Warriors

The modern U.S. military is vaunted as an all-volunteer force, but the truth is more complex. Conscription was ended in 1973 as a result of antiwar protest at home and, more important, among soldiers. Since then, the Department of Defense has built a voluntary military, primarily on a system of economic incentives. The military targets communities that have been devastated by disinvestment for recruitment, and military service has become a primary economic opportunity structure for working-class communities, disproportionately so for people of color.

Oskar Castro of the Youth and Militarism Project of the American Friends Service Committee (AFSC) points out that "most people didn't sign up because they were gung-ho warriors. Most people signed up for the college money and wonderful career opportunities, leadership skills and respect" that military recruiters offer—attractive promises to a young person whose alternatives are a dead-end job or unemployment. Researchers at the Rand Corporation found that low personal or family income and unemployment (particularly long term) increase the chances that someone will enlist. Not surprisingly, the military "seems to resemble the makeup of a two-year commuter or trade school outside Birmingham or Biloxi," note *New York Times* reporters David Halbfinger and Steven Holmes. As a result, close observers of military enlistment like the Central Committee for Conscientious Objectors refer to today's recruitment strategy as a "poverty draft."

Half of the 3.2 million soldiers in the U.S. military are reservists. In addition to the emotional trauma soldiers and their loved ones experience during a wartime mobilization, reservists also endure significant economic hardships. As they are activated from civilian jobs, many face dramatic pay cuts and disruption of health benefits. Tod Ensign of Citizen Soldier, an advocacy group for soldiers, explains, "Take an EMT making $42K driving an ambulance, enough to support a wife and two or three kids in a working-class suburb of New York City. They will earn $18K–22K once activated. Setting aside the risk of war, these people are taking heavy hits, often 30% to 50% cuts in pay!" Though some unionized workers have contractual pay protections in the event of reserve call-up, most reservists are out of luck. Civilian bills at best stay the same; with one parent absent, child care costs may go up. One New York City reservist explained that activation would mean his family would lose their home.

And when the war is over, the GIs will return home to find that politicians—many of whom used privilege to avoid military service themselves—are mouthing support while actually pulling the rug out from under soldiers' futures. On March 20, the Congress overwhelmingly passed a resolution to "express the gratitude of the Nation to all members of the United States Armed Forces." Then, early the next morning, the House of Representatives voted to cut funding for veterans' health care and benefit programs by nearly $25 billion over the next ten years. The cuts are designed to accommodate the massive tax cuts the Bush administration has been pursuing—while the war diverts the public's attention. The government track record on ignoring postwar problems like Agent Orange, post-traumatic stress disorder, and Gulf War Syndrome does not bode well for the soldiers fighting the current war. Says the AFSC's Castro, "Even the military doesn't support the troops. Families are not supported. When it comes to dollars and cents, the military doesn't put its money where its mouth is."

Speaking of money, Defense Secretary Donald Rumsfeld's strategy for the Iraq war was based on the cost-cutting lean, just-in-time production model favored by corporate restructuring consultants. Rumsfeld apparently quashed the logistics plans of experienced officers, pressuring them to stage far fewer personnel and much less hardware in the Gulf than they considered adequate. Observers of the impact of lean restructuring in the corporate world report that increased workplace injuries are a major result. One wonders what impact importing this model into the battlefield will have on soldiers and civilians.

Union Busting as Homeland Security

Meanwhile, on the home front, both public- and private-sector workers are suffering a savage assault. The fiscal crisis brought about by war spending, recession, and tax cuts for the wealthy is squeezing public workers at all levels, resulting in wage freezes and elimination of entire departments. Thousands of public-sector workers are losing their jobs. Treasury Department worker Renee Toback reports that her department was told their budget would be "taxed" to pay for the war in Iraq.

At the same time, the Bush administration has stripped thousands of federal workers in the hastily cobbled-together Department of Homeland Security of union rights in the name of national security. The Department of Defense is developing plans to do the same. Are fearful employees with no voice on the job in the best position to protect national security? No. But it's no surprise that the administration's agenda prioritizes union busting over public safety. AFL-CIO Organizing Director Stewart Acuff says, "The most outrageous thing they [the Bush administration] said was that they had to remove union rights from the

Department of Homeland Security when all of the people who answered the call on September 11, all of the firefighters and cops who died trying to save people, were union members! And 90% of the people who cleaned up in the aftermath were union members as well." Against this backdrop, the administration has also called for the privatization of as many as 800,000 non-postal federal jobs. If Bush succeeds, this move would replace large numbers of union jobs with non-union ones at lower pay and with less accountability; it would strike a huge blow at the strength of public-sector unions. (Naturally, Bush also plans to privatize Iraqi health care and education.)

Diane Witiak, an American Federation of Government Employees (AFGE) spokeswoman, describes the current atmosphere: "If you dare to oppose the administration, you're almost considered a traitor. We resent that the administration considers unionization and patriotism incompatible. In fact, [unionization is] essential. [The administration] will go back to the old cronyism and favoritism that the Civil Service Act corrected. It's only a matter of time before Bush starts with the private sector!"

Much as Witiak predicted, the administration is using the national-security pretext to erode the rights of some private-sector workers as well. Last year, Homeland Security director Tom Ridge called the president of the west coast longshore union. He claimed a strike would harm national security and threatened dockworkers with replacement by military personnel. Ultimately, it was management that locked out the dockworkers, but Bush invoked the Taft-Hartley Act and threatened to prosecute International Longshore and Warehouse Union members who engaged in any kind of work slowdown or other industrial action.

More broadly, efforts are under way in Congress to ban strikes by airline workers and to pass a number of other anti-worker measures. Among these are expansion of the restrictive Railway Labor Act's jurisdiction to include certain industries now under the umbrella of the National Labor Relations Act, making it harder for workers in these sectors to win union recognition and severely limiting their right to strike. Another legislative initiative would eliminate "card-check," the system of conducting a union recognition election once a certain number of representation petition cards have been signed by workers at a particular facility. In recent years, card-check has been the chief mechanism of successful union organizing drives. The AFL-CIO's Acuff points out that "the direction the government is moving in will indeed have a chilling effect on mobilizations, collective activity, demonstrations and direct action, all necessary parts of contract and bargaining campaigns and union strength. This administration, by law and by culture, is trying to stigmatize or make illegal the kinds of activity that are necessary to build union workplace strength."

What Does a Terrorist Look Like?

Wartime is always dangerous for immigrant communities. When the towers collapsed on September 11, they crushed the movement to give undocumented immigrants amnesty. Since then, immigrants have been subject to a dramatically stepped-up campaign by the federal government to find and deport them. Rachael Kamel, AFSC education director, points to "growing attempts to criminalize immigrant workers—all now justified in the name of security." As the next episode in the now-permanent war on terror, the war in Iraq only serves to extend the period in which such policies appear legitimate.

For example, the Social Security Administration (SSA) sends so-called no-match letters to employers when it finds that a worker's Social Security number does not match SSA records. These letters serve to intimidate workers, since employers can threaten to turn them in to the Immigration and Naturalization Service (INS). The number of no-match letters has increased 800% since 9/11. Similarly, special registration of immigrants from a select list of countries, mostly in the Middle East and Southern Asia, has snared thousands of people with minor visa infractions, many of whom face deportation. (Of bizarre note is the case of Iraqi exile Katrin Michael. She met with President Bush on March 14 to recount the gas attack she survived, and then found herself on the INS deportation list the next week, according to a *Washington Post* story.)

All of this has a powerful impact on worker organization because, for the past decade, immigrant workers have been the bedrock of aggressive labor organizing campaigns in economically strategic states like California, Texas and New York. Last year in Los Angeles, 60 workers active in organizing the Koreatown Assi Supermarket were placed on indefinite suspension after their names appeared on no-match letters. And the same Homeland Security rules that stripped newly-federalized airport screeners of union rights also banned immigrant workers in those positions. As a result, 7,000 immigrant airport security screeners—some of whom had just succeeded in winning union representation—have been fired.

Shock and Awe for Airline Workers?

Amid official and unofficial repression against public sector workers and immigrant communities, the economy appears stalled and is likely heading for a double-dip recession. The World Bank is already estimating that the Iraq war will reduce worldwide economic growth by one-half of a percentage point during the first six months of this year.

When the economy is weak, the industries most affected make cuts wherever they can, and workers bear the brunt of industry restructuring. The airline industry continues to be the crucible of this restructuring; as such, it provides an instructive case study. Before the war, the industry's Air Transport Association predicted 70,000 layoffs (100,000 if a terrorist attack accompanied the war) in addition to the thousands already cut since September 11, as well as $4 billion in additional losses. Editorials intoned about "Airline Apocalypse."

True to their word, airlines began shedding employees by the thousands as soon as the bombs started to fall on Baghdad. Continental laid off 1,200, with more to come, Northwest, 4,900, while United and American (possibly in Chapter 11 bankruptcy reorganization by the time you read this) plan to get rid of thousands more. Jeff Matthews, the Aircraft Mechanics Fraternal Association's national contract coordinator at Northwest, told Reuters: "Northwest is using the Iraq conflict as an excuse to justify mass layoffs planned before the conflict started. The number of planned layoffs is far larger than would be justified based on the number of planes Northwest is removing from service." One United employee and Marines veteran describes wartime layoffs as United's own campaign of "shock and awe."

All of these airlines have succeeded in, or are in the process of, extracting concessions on levels unheard of in the history of the industry. Of particular importance has been US Airways' use of the war as leverage to terminate the defined-benefit pension plan for its pilots. At a time when defined-benefit plans are underfunded by about $300 billion in the United States, this is alarming. Representative Bernie Sanders (I-Vt.) warned in the *Wall Street Journal* that "this could set a horrible precedent by making it easier for companies to renege on the retirement promises they made to their workers." Nomi Prins, author of the forthcoming book *Money for Nothing*, points out, "The poor stock market is offering a convenient excuse for companies that already desired to reduce future plan benefits."

The airlines cite the war as a major reason for the concessions they demand. United mechanic Jennifer Salazar-Biddle remarked, "The crisis is real, but the graft is unbelievable." In fact, executive compensation in the midst of the industry's crisis has shocked and awed even Republicans. Responding to reports of the doubling of Delta CEO Leo Mullin's compensation package, Sen. John McCain (who champions eliminating airline workers' right to strike) exclaimed, "You ought to be ashamed of yourself." Nonetheless, a new bailout is in the works for the airline industry. The bailout bill does include a cap on executive compensation, but at 2002 levels—a good example of closing the barn doors after the escape. It also requires the airline companies to reduce operating costs, a provision that will primarily bleed workers. The only bone the bill offers airline workers is a meager extension of their unemployment benefits.

Chain of Change

Wars have always had a deep impact on working people. In addition to the slaughter of war, wars have often undermined the strength of working class organization. Government repression tied to World War I all but destroyed the Industrial Workers of the World and the Socialist Party. Workplace regimentation in World War II played an important role in the long-term bureaucratization of unions, replacing militant shop floor activity with safer routinized grievance and arbitration procedures.

On the other hand, soldiers returning from war have also played an important role in reviving struggles at home. At the end of World War II and during the Vietnam War, opposition to the war surfaced among GIs, along with discussions of soldiers' rights to free speech and even to unions. Soldiers returning from

Vietnam played an important role in the antiwar movement as well as rebellions within a variety of unions, most notably the wave of auto-worker wildcat strikes from 1969 to 1972. African-American soldiers returning from both of these wars parlayed their wartime experiences into civil-rights activism.

There are some hopeful signs that workers will fight back against the current wave of assaults on their rights. Transportation Security Administration (TSA) employees are continuing to organize themselves with AFGE in spite of TSA director James Loy's directives to the contrary. AFGE succeeded in securing a one-year moratorium on the de-unionization of the Department of Homeland Security. Federal workers in Seattle and dozens of other localities have begun a campaign of public rallies to protest privatization.

Time will tell how working people in the military will respond to what they are enduring today. One thing is clear, though: The immediate impact of the war has been to strengthen the hands of corporations and weaken unions and other worker organizations while placing thousands of working people in harm's way. In the long term, whether grassroots activists can turn this tide will depend on how they understand and address the class dimensions of this and future wars.

Resources: Soldiers & Veterans: Citizen Soldier <www.citizen-soldier.org>; Military Families Speak Out <www.mfso.org>; Veterans for Common Sense <www.veteransforcommonsense.org>; National Gulf War Resource Center <www.ngwrc.org>; *Immigrant Rights:* National Network for Immigrant and Refugee Rights <www.nnirr.org>; *Labor:* US Labor Against War <www.uslaboragainstwar.org>; Dept. of Homeland Security Workers <www.dhsworkers.org>; Association of Flight Attendants <www.afanet.org>; Airline Mechanics Fraternal Association <www.amfanatl.org>; *See also:* David Cortright, *Soldiers in Revolt: The American Military Today* (Anchor Press/Doubleday, 1976); Kim Moody, *An Injury To All* (Routledge, 1997).

Chapter 9

OIL ADDICTION, CLIMATE CHANGE, AND CAPITALISM

INTRODUCTION

With scientists predicting that the earth's temperature may rise 10 degrees over the next century, the mainstream media have finally awakened to the peril of climate change. Yet they have largely cast the problem as an issue of individual consumer choice: too many people choose to drive SUVs, and no one's interested in hybrid or electric vehicles. The media have consistently failed to identify the deeper systemic problems involved: the economies of the United States and the other rich capitalist countries devour resources in breathtaking quantities, emit prodigious waste and pollution from the process of production, and manufacture voracious desires that require more of the same.

Mass media critics of the SUV—like the "Car Talk" guys—may be well intentioned, but they largely miss the point. Usually they call for consumers to make "better" choices. And even when they do support government regulation—for example, applying the same efficiency and emissions standards to SUVs as to regular cars—they still fall short. Proposals like this would leave intact a transportation system dominated by the private automobile, a primary contributor to climate change. As Alejandro Reuss points out, this transportation system is an environmental and public-health disaster, but it has been a keystone of U.S. capitalism throughout the postwar period, providing major subsidies to the most important companies. And, as Reuss emphasizes, it has been built on the destruction of public transportation and the privatization of public space ("Car Trouble").

Mainstream critics also tend to focus on narrow technological fixes, such as electric cars or fuel cells. The major auto companies have developed these technologies. But at the same time, as David Levy shows, the companies have extended their control over the regulatory process to ensure that it does not threaten their dominance or profitability. Voluntary displays of environmental "responsibility," Levy argues, have given the auto industry credibility to assume a dominant role in shaping government regulation which could otherwise bring more significant change ("Business and Climate Change: Privatizing Environmental Regulation").

While mainstream news sources no longer question the reality of climate change, it is still common to read that it's the fault of poor countries. In fact, the U.S. government has explicitly blamed rising global carbon dioxide emissions on China and other "developing countries," and used this claim as a pretext for rejecting international climate-change agreements. But as Ben Boothby shows, U.S. per capita emissions are by far the world's highest, and are increasing while China's much lower per-capita emissions are decreasing ("Who's to Blame for Climate Change?"). Looking beyond the responsibility of individual countries, John Bellamy Foster explains the role of an unsustainable economic system in the development of climate change. As he notes, capitalism depends on ever-increasing exploitation of natural resources, and today produces wastes at levels that can no longer be processed by the planet's natural systems. Responsibility for climate change, Foster argues, must be laid squarely at the doorstep of capitalism ("Not the Owners of the Earth").

BUSINESS AND CLIMATE CHANGE
PRIVATIZING ENVIRONMENTAL REGULATION
By David L. Levy
January/February 2001

Human-caused emissions of greenhouse gases have "contributed substantially to the observed warming over the past 50 years" and, if left unchecked, could cause the earth's average surface temperature to rise between 2.7 and 11 degrees Fahrenheit. So concluded an October 2000 report of the Intergovernmental Panel on Climate Change (IPCC), the international group of scientists charged with assessing the causes, extent, and impact of climate change. The IPCC's language is much stronger than in its previous report, issued five years ago, and the range of warming is nearly twice the previous estimate. Industries dependent on fossil fuels, however, did not react to the 2000 report with the stonewalling that once typified their public declarations on climate change.

Before the November 1997 Kyoto Protocol, an international agreement which established mandatory limits on the emission of greenhouse gases, large sectors of U.S. industry waged an intense and well-funded campaign against international regulation. Companies organized a strong industry association, the Global Climate Coalition (GCC), challenging the scientific basis for action and highlighting the economic costs of curtailing emissions. In the months leading up to the meeting of more than 150 country delegates in Kyoto, U.S. industry put $13 million into the Global Climate Information Project, a public relations campaign against any international agreement.

Even before Kyoto, however, the first signs of a major shift were visible in Europe. In May 1997, John Browne, the Group Chief Executive of oil giant British

Petroleum (BP), declared publicly, "The time to consider the policy dimensions of climate change is not when the link between greenhouse gases and climate change is conclusively proven, but when the possibility cannot be discounted and is taken seriously by the society of which we are part." By 1998, U.S. industry was also showing a change in stance. The GCC was weakened by a series of defections: BP left in late 1997, Shell in April 1998, and Ford in December 1999. In 1998, General Motors (GM) joined an initiative of the World Resources Institute called "Safe Climate, Sound Business," agreeing that precautionary action should be taken on climate change. That same year, 13 companies, including BP, Toyota, Boeing, Lockheed, and Enron, joined the newly formed Pew Center on Global Climate Change. The companies endorsed a series of newspaper advertisements stating that they "accept the views of most scientists that enough is known about the science and environmental impacts of climate change for us to take actions to address its consequences."

Smoke and Mirrors?

Many environmentalists doubt the sincerity of big business's sudden conversion. Given the history of industry hostility to emission controls, changed public statements can easily be dismissed as cynical posturing or "greenwashing." In May 1999, for example, William Clay Ford, Jr., the new chairman of Ford Motor Company, proclaimed that "more and more, the marketplace will demand vehicles that are truly clean." At the same time, Ford continued to produce ever larger trucks and sports utilities vehicles (SUVs), like the 12-mile-per-gallon Expedition, contributing to the continuing decline in U.S. fuel economy. Even Shell and BP, the apostles of the new movement, have not curtailed their oil exploration or refining activities at all. The $100 million a year Shell has pledged to invest in renewables is only about 7% of the company's total annual expenditure on petroleum exploration and production.

Incomplete though the conversion may be, investments of hundreds of millions of dollars cannot be discounted as mere public relations. Since its acquisition of Amoco, BP has become the world's largest producer of solar photovoltaic panels, with plans to reach $1 billion in sales by 2010. Shell has also announced that it will invest $500 million in photovoltaics over five years as part of a new International Renewable Energy Division. In 1998, European automakers (including European subsidiaries of U.S.-based companies) accepted a "voluntary" agreement to reduce carbon emissions by about 25% over the following decade. European car companies have introduced very small, light-weight cars, like Daimler-Chrysler's SMART car, and invested substantial amounts in a range of technologies from diesel to fuel cells. Even the most ardent opponents of mandatory emission controls have begun to invest in low-emission technologies. In December 1997, Ford invested about $400 million in a fuel-cell joint venture with Daimler-Chrysler and the Canadian company Ballard. Texaco was the first major U.S. oil company to break ranks and proclaim the need for precautionary action on climate, and in May 2000 it invested $67 million in Electronic Conversion Devices, a company which develops advanced batteries and solar technology.

This shift suggests something more than mere PR "greenwashing," though less than a conversion to sustainable practice. It is not surprising that large sectors of industry viewed action on climate change as a major stategic threat. Controls on the emission of carbon dioxide, the main greenhouse gas, would raise the price of fuels and hurt the revenues and profits of oil, coal, and car companies, as well as other energy-intensive industries. The companies seem to have concluded, however, that open defiance of the climate-change consensus could jeopardize their long-run interests even more—causing them to lose political legitimacy and therefore the power to shape the eventual regulatory outcome. This change of attitude illustrates the resilience of capitalism and the strategies by which business attempts to sustain hegemony—dominance based on consent, the projection of moral leadership, and an ability to present one's goals as the general interest. In the face of strong challenges from state institutions and civil society, companies are moving away from confrontation, and instead towards a strategy of accommodation, compromise, and cooptation.

Explaining the Turnaround

The change in Europe can be understood mostly as a response to political and social pressures. From a European perspective, the ratification of the Kyoto Protocol and the imposition of mandatory emission controls appear inevitable. European firms were concerned that, if they aggressively opposed emission controls, they might be jeopardizing their privileged access and influence with policymakers. In international negotiations, the European Union has called for bigger emission cuts than the United States, and European politicians were sensitive to charges that they talked tough but lacked the will to act. Therefore, they looked to industry for substantial, early emission reductions. The auto industry was already on the defensive for environmental reasons, even facing a total ban on cars in some cities. This complex of factors resulted in the European car industry's agreement to the "voluntary" emission reductions.

U.S. companies, meanwhile, have experienced growing pressure to respond to their competitors' moves in other countries. In the auto industry, Ford and GM saw Toyota launch the Prius, a hybrid electric-gasoline engine car, in Japan in 1998 and the United States in 2000. Honda leapfrogged Toyota, launching its own hybrid, Insight, in the U.S. market in December 1999. While U.S. companies publicly expressed skepticism about the market potential for small, expensive, fuel-efficient cars, they stepped up their own plans for low-emission technologies. Companies often prefer to make mistakes together rather than risk ceding a major advantage to competitors. After Daimler-Chrysler announced a target date of 2004 for introducing a commercial fuel cell vehicle, Ford, GM, BMW, and Honda followed with similar announcements. Ford's and GM's European subsidiaries had already agreed to substantial emission cuts, so these companies needed to develop the appropriate technologies anyway. When Ford announced in the spring of 2000 that it would improve the fuel economy of its SUVs by 25%, GM quickly followed suit.

Within the GCC, more companies were questioning the value of aggressively denying the climate problem. The public effort to challenge the legitimacy of the IPCC had little impact, and even threatened to backfire on industry. Environmental groups in Europe and the United States seized upon the lobbying and public relations efforts of the fossil fuel industry, issued a number of reports that documented industry support for climate skeptics, and attempted to frame the issue as big business using its money and power to distort the scientific debate. In the run-up to the Kyoto conference in December 1997, the GCC decided to shift strategy. Instead of challenging the science, industry's message shifted to the high cost and limited environmental effectiveness of an agreement that excludes developing countries from emission controls. After Kyoto, companies increasingly worried that they were losing political access. The Pew Center's Eileen Claussen was blunt in stating that "joining Pew gives companies credibility, and credibility means political access and influence."

In the years since Kyoto, companies have begun to reevaluate the threat posed to their economic interests by emission controls. In the oil industry, companies have come to realize that their primary markets for oil and gas will enjoy significant growth for at least 20 years. Rapid growth of car ownership in developing countries and the continued growth of vehicle-miles traveled in industrialized countries will offset the gradual introduction of low-emission car technologies. With global air travel growing at about 5% annually, aviation remains a strong market for the oil industry. Demand for natural gas, a relatively low-carbon fuel, is also booming worldwide, as small, efficient gas turbines replace large coal-fired electric power plants. In the auto industry, companies are realizing that they can stay in the business of making and selling cars, even if the engine undergoes radical change. Change is likely to be slow, in any event, because new technologies are expensive and could require massive investments in alternative fuel infrastructure.

The likelihood of stringent emission controls in the short term has also receded. Parties to the Kyoto Protocol only reached agreement in 1997 by deferring difficult decisions about implementation. It has therefore become easier for companies to win public sympathy and political credibility by expressing support for a weak and ineffective international treaty. As details have emerged, companies have realized that there will be plenty of room for fudging. The United States is planning to comply with its commitments on emissions by buying emissions credits from other countries. Russia and other East European countries, whose economies collapsed along with the Soviet Union, now emit far less carbon dioxide than in the 1990 baseline year, allowing them to sell billions of tons of carbon credits, labeled "hot air" by critics. The United States has resisted European efforts to restrict the percentage of a country's commitments that can be met by emissions trading. It has also pushed for credits rewarding hard-to-measure increases in "carbon uptake" (due to such factors as expanded forest lands).

There is still some danger that the whole process could collapse. It is becoming clear that even the modest emission-reduction targets established in Kyoto are unlikely to be met. The United States agreed to reduce emissions to 7% below 1990 levels by the "budget period" 2008–2012, but by 1999 its emissions were already 13.1% above 1990 levels. Although an agreement was reached in Kyoto, industry efforts have succeeded in blocking its ratification by the U.S. Senate. The Senate is unlikely to ratify the treaty without major revisions, which will be opposed by most other countries. Without the participation of the United States, which accounts for nearly one-quarter of global emissions, the Kyoto Protocol is meaningless. According to one anonymous industry source, the GCC did not collapse; it was more a case of "mission accomplished; now we can avoid the political cost of membership."

The Privatization of International Environmental Governance

Even as some environmentalists have welcomed industry's changed stance on climate change, some observers have expressed concern that increasing industry participation in shaping regulation amounts to the privatization of environmental governance. In fact, industry has been closely involved in international climate policy from the outset. The Business Council for Sustainable Development, a group of industrialists representing 48 of the world's largest multinational corporations, was particularly active at the UN Rio conference in 1992, and helped to ensure that the original Framework Convention on Climate Change contained no binding commitments.

Governments have encouraged industry involvement. In a 1996 speech announcing that the United States would no longer oppose binding international emission controls, U.S. State Department negotiator Tim Wirth proclaimed that "meeting this challenge requires that the genius of the private sector be brought to bear on the challenge of developing the technologies that are necessary to ensure our long term environmental and economic prosperity." The U.S. Environmental Protection Agency and Department of Energy have adopted the same stance. The Climate Wise program, jointly administered by the two agencies, bills itself as "a unique partnership that can help you turn energy efficiency and environmental performance into a corporate asset." At the international level, IPPC head Bob Watson attempted to head off criticism of its 2000 report by recruiting corporate experts as chapter authors and reviewers.

In the absence of an international mechanism to limit emissions, private bodies have been taking the initiative. The World Bank Prototype Carbon Fund (PCF) was established in 2000 as "public-private partnership" between a few national governments, including the Netherlands, Sweden, Japan, and Canada, and 26 companies, including Hydro Quebec, Daimler-Chrysler, Shell-Canada,

BP-Amoco, and numerous Japanese firms. The Fund's purpose is to raise $140 million for investments in renewables and efficiency in developing countries, projects that will earn carbon credits for the investing companies. The Environmental Defense Fund (EDF) brought together seven large companies, including Dupont, Alcan, Shell and BP, in the summer of 2000 to form the "Partnership for Climate Action," whose purpose is to enable emission trading among its members.

The Price of Accommodation
Compared to the history of corporate denial and hostility, these moves appear to be constructive and proactive. The cost of this accommodation and compromise with industry, however, is a loss of democratic process and accountability. Dan Becker of the Sierra Club has sharply criticized the EDF's emissions trading initiative, saying it offered only modest reductions in greenhouse gases while undercutting efforts to write strong regulations on emission controls as part of the 1997 Kyoto treaty. Peter Utting, in a UN report called "Business Responsibility for Sustainable Development," concluded that "the most significant concern with some forms of voluntary initiatives and partnerships is that they may serve to weaken key drivers of corporate responsibility, namely governmental and inter-governmental regulation, the role of trade unions and collective bargaining, as well as more critical forms of nongovernmental organization (NGO) activism and civil society protest."

The new business strategy on climate issues includes a strong dose of public relations, but it is not all hot air. Companies also have to demonstrate some tangible progress toward reducing emissions in order to blunt demands for more stringent regulation, and to protect their market positions in the event that mandatory emissions controls become a reality. While this strategy may sustain the political access and legitimacy of business, however, it is unlikely to result in the sustainable development that business now claims to champion. The IPCC report notes that greenhouse gases need to be slashed by more than 50% to stabilize the climate; the Kyoto Protocol called for a 5% cut in industrialized countries, and that target is fast becoming unreachable. There is still a long struggle ahead.

WHO'S TO BLAME FOR CLIMATE CHANGE?
By Ben Boothby
March/April 2003

It's now an indisputable fact that the global climate is changing. Scientists have warned for decades that "greenhouse gases," mainly carbon dioxide (CO_2), were building up in the atmosphere and trapping the sun's heat. Over the course of the

20th century, as fossil-fuel pollution expanded, the amount of CO_2 in the atmosphere rose by about 30%, increasing temperatures and causing extreme weather patterns worldwide. The greenhouse danger is now so undeniable that even George W. Bush's "blue ribbon" scientific panel on climate change admitted that global temperatures are on the rise.

If we hope to combat global warming, we need to drastically reduce the levels of CO_2 released into the atmosphere. Scientists consider even the targets set by the Kyoto Protocol (the international agreement to limit greenhouse gas emissions) inadequate compared to the urgency of the problem. But the Bush administration reneged on the United States' commitment even to these minimal standards, on the pretext that the agreement "exempts 80 percent of the world including major population centers, such as China and India."

Bush's scapegoats, however, are hardly responsible for the climate-change crisis. China accounted for just 7% of the world's CO_2 emissions over the course of the 20th century; India, for only 2%. The United States, in contrast, accounted for more than 30% of the total. (See Graph 1.) Moreover, emissions levels in the United States continue to surge, rising every year between 1991 and 2000, the latest year for which data is available. According to the Department of Energy, the country's fossil-fuel-related CO_2 emissions increased by more than 2.7 percent between 1999 and 2000. In contrast, China reduced its emissions by almost 2.2% in 2000, its third straight year of reductions.

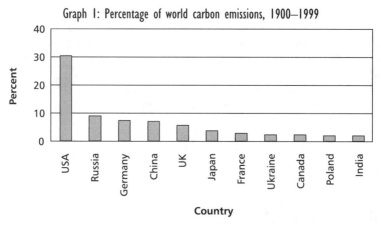

Graph 1: Percentage of world carbon emissions, 1900–1999

Source: World Resources Institute, "The U.S., Developing Countries, and Climate Protection: Leadership or Stalemate?" June 2001 <www.wri.org/wri/>.

The United States' ruling elite has never been as big about taking responsibility for its actions (e.g., slavery, support for dictatorships, etc.), as it has been about posturing as a world leader. So it comes as no surprise that the United States remains number one in CO_2 emissions (in both total and per capita terms) year after year. (See Graph 2.) If any country is in a position—technologically and economically—to "lead by example" towards a sustainable future, it is the United States. Yet the U.S. government has steadfastly refused to adopt common-sense measures like raising fuel efficiency standards, reducing automobile use, lessening dependence on coal and petroleum, or promoting alternative-energy technologies.

Graph 2: Per capita carbon emissions, 1999

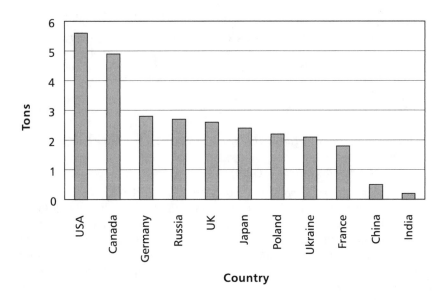

Source: World Resources Institute, "The U.S., Developing Countries, and Climate Protection: Leadership or Stalemate?" June 2001 <www.wri.org/wri/>.

Instead, less-developed countries with far fewer resources than the United States are leading in the reduction of greenhouse-gas emissions. "China's actions are nothing short of remarkable," notes a 2001 report by the World Resources Institute. "The world's most populous country reduced its emissions...by 19 percent from 1997 to 1999. This is simply unprecedented, especially considering that China's economy grew rapidly over the same period." Now that India, too, has ratified the Kyoto Protocol, it seems that Bush will just have to find himself some new scapegoats.

CAR TROUBLE: THE AUTOMOBILE AS AN ENVIRONMENTAL AND HEALTH DISASTER

By Alejandro Reuss

March/April 2003

(Scene: Los Angeles, the 1940s)

Eddie Valiant: A freeway? What the hell's a freeway?

Judge Doom: Eight lanes of shimmering cement running from here to Pasadena. Smooth, straight, fast. Traffic jams will be a thing of the past ... I see a place where people get off and on the freeway. On and off. Off and on. All day, all night. Soon where Toontown once stood will be a string of gas stations. Inexpensive motels. Restaurants that serve rapidly prepared food. Tire salons. Automobile dealerships. And wonderful, wonderful billboards reaching as far as the eye can see ... My god, it'll be beautiful.

Eddie Valiant: Come on. Nobody's gonna drive this lousy freeway when they can take the Red Car [trolley] for a nickel.

Judge Doom: Oh, they'll drive. They'll have to. You see, I bought the Red Car so I could dismantle it.

—Who Framed Roger Rabbit? (1988)

At the end of *Roger Rabbit*, a speeding train saves the day, destroying the solvent-spraying juggernaut that is set to level the fictitious Toontown for the freeway. In other words, the movie is a fairy tale about how the modern American city *did not* come into existence. In reality, Los Angeles came to represent the awful extreme of the U.S. car culture. Auto companies did buy up the city's Red Car trolley and dismantle it. The landscape became just the cluttered wasteland of highways, fast-food joints, filling stations, and billboards dreamed by the villainous Judge Doom.

The federal government rolled out an asphalt carpet for the automobile: It built the interstate highways that fueled "white flight" to the new suburban sprawl, and carried the new "middle class" on its summer vacations. Soon, freeways criss-crossed American cities, slicing through low-income neighborhoods and consigning commuters to the twice-daily ordeal of gridlock. Roads and highways (along with the military, for which the interstates were originally intended) were politically acceptable objects of public spending even in the postwar United States. And why not? They represented an enormous subsidy to the private industries at the heart of U.S. capitalism—oil, steel, and cars.

The car effectively privatized a wide swath of the public arena. In place of the city square, it created the four-way intersection. Instead of walking or riding a trolley, the motorists sealed themselves inside their individual steel cocoons. Cars offered convenience—for grocery shopping, trips to the mall, chauffeuring the kids to school and practice, etc.—to those who got them. Their real triumph, however, was to manufacture inconvenience for those who didn't. People who could not afford cars had such unenviable choices as navigating the brave new world of speeding traffic on foot or waiting for the bus. A genuine political commitment to public transportation might have lessened the class and race divide. Most public transportation funding, however, has gone to road and highway construction geared to the motorist, and much of what remains for mass transit has been devoted to commuter trains serving the suburban middle class. Low-income city residents have largely been abandoned to an infrequent and polluting diesel bus.

As it turned out, life inside the car was not all it was cracked up to be either—especially when traffic on the freeway slowed to a crawl. In gridlock, you can practically see the steam coming out of drivers' ears. As odious as much of the time spent in cars might be, however, Americans have learned, or been convinced, to "love the car." It has become a fetish object—a symbol of freedom and individualism, power and sex appeal. The commercials always seem to show a carefree motorist speeding through the countryside or climbing a secluded mountain to gaze on the landscape below. Fortunately, not too many SUV owners actually spend their time tearing up the wilderness. Unfortunately, they spend much of it spewing exhaust into the city air.

The SUV certainly ranks among the more absurd expressions of American overconsumption (General Motors' Yukon XL Denali, to cite an extreme example, is over 18 feet long and weighs about three tons). But it is too easy to condemn this overgrown behemoth and then hop self-satisfied back into a midsize sedan. Most of what is wrong with the SUV—the resources it swallows, the dangers it poses, and the blight it creates—is wrong with the automobile system as a whole. Automobiles pollute the oceans and the air, overheat cities and the earth, devour land and time, produce waste and noise, and cause injury and illness.

Here, in more detail, is an indictment of the car as an environmental and public-health menace:

The Bill of Particulars

Oil Pollution

Transportation accounts for over two-thirds of U.S. oil consumption, according to the Department of Energy. The problem of oil pollution, therefore, lands squarely at the doorstep of a transportation system based on internal combustion. Oil tanker spills are the most visible scourge of the world's oceans. According to the National Research Council study *Oil in the Sea*, tankers spew 400 million tons of oil into the world's oceans each year. Technologies to prevent or contain oil spills, however, cannot solve the problem of marine oil pollution, since the main cause is not spills, but the consumption of oil. Urban consumption, including runoff from roads and used motor oil just poured down the drain, accounts for more than half of the *ocean* pollution, over one billion tons of oil annually. That does not count, of course, oil that does not make it to the seas, that stains roadways, contaminates the land, or spoils fresh water supplies.

Air Pollution

Automotive emissions are a major source of ozone and carbon monoxide pollution. "[I]n numerous cities across the country," according to the Environmental Protection Agency (EPA), "the personal automobile is the single greatest polluter." Ozone, a major component of urban smog, is formed by unburned fuel reacting with other compounds in the atmosphere. It causes irritation of the eyes and lungs, aggravates respiratory problems, and can damage lung tissue. Researchers at the Centers for Disease Control in Atlanta took advantage of temporary traffic reduction during the 1996 Olympic Games to observe the effects of automotive emissions on asthma attacks. Their study, published in the *Journal of the American Medical Association*, showed a 28% reduction of peak ozone levels and an 11–44% drop in the number of children requiring acute asthma care (depending on the sample). Carbon monoxide, formed by incomplete burning of fuel, impairs the oxygen-carrying ability of the blood. According to the EPA, "In urban areas, the motor vehicle contribution to carbon monoxide pollution can exceed 90 percent." A 2002 study published in the journal *Circulation* showed a link between automotive exhaust and heart attacks, and Harvard Medical School researchers called exhaust an "insidious contributor to heart disease."

Climate Change

Automotive exhaust also contains carbon dioxide, a "greenhouse gas" and the principal culprit in climate change (or "global warming"). It is produced, in the words of the EPA, by the "perfect combustion" of hydrocarbons. Internal combustion engines generate this greenhouse gas no matter how efficient or well-tuned they may be. In the United States, the country with the world's highest per capita carbon dioxide emissions (See Ben Boothby, "Who's to Blame for Climate Change?" p. 185), transportation accounts for over 30% of total emissions, according to a 1998 report of the United Nations Framework Convention on Climate Change. More than half that amount, reports the EPA, is due to personal transportation. As average fuel efficiency gets worse (it declined by nearly 7% between 1987 and 1997) and U.S. motorists rack up more vehicle miles (they increased by a third over the same period), the automobile contributes more and more to global warming.

Heat Islands

The temperature in a major city on a summer day can be as much as 8?F higher than that of surrounding rural areas, according to the Berkeley National Laboratory's Heat Island Group. The automobile contributes to "heat islands" mainly through increased demand for roads and parking. The asphalt and concrete used for these surfaces are among the most heat-absorbent materials in the urban environment. Paving also contributes to the loss of trees, which provide shade and dissipate heat. In the 1930s, when orchards dotted Los Angeles, summer temperatures peaked at 97°F, according to the Heat Island Group. Since then L.A. has become one of the country's worst heat islands, with summer temperatures reaching over 105°F. This does not just make the city less pleasant in the summertime. Heat islands cause increased energy use for cooling and increased ozone formation. Researchers estimate a 2% increase in Los Angeles's total power use and a 3% increase in smog for every 1°F increase in the city's daily high temperature.

Land Use

Cars occupy a huge amount of space. Paved roads occupy over 13,000 square miles of land area across the United States—nearly 750 square meters per U.S. motor vehicle—and parking occupies another 3,000 square miles, according to a report by Todd Litman of the Victoria Transport Policy Institute. In urban areas, roads and parking take up 20-30% of the total surface area; in commercial districts, 50–60%. When moving, vehicles require a "buffer zone" that varies with size and speed. Litman calculates, for example, that a pedestrian walking at 3 miles per hour (m.p.h.) requires 20 square feet of space. A cyclist riding at 10 m.p.h. needs 50 square feet. At full occupancy, a bus traveling at 30 m.p.h. requires 75 square feet per passenger. Meanwhile, a car traveling at 30 m.p.h. demands 1,500 square feet. In short, much of the road space is not required by on-road transportation as such, but by the private car. The same goes for parking space. A parked car requires twenty times the space as a parked bicycle, and eighty times the space as a person.

Materials

In the words of the EPA, "Vehicles require a lot of energy and materials to make, consume a lot of energy when used, and present unique waste disposal challenges at end-of-life." The auto industry uses nearly two thirds of the rubber, over one third of the iron, and over one fourth of the aluminum produced in the United States. Over ten million cars, moreover, are junked in the United States each year. About three fourths of the average car's weight—including the vast majority of the steel—is recycled. The rest crowds garbage dumps and contributes to toxic pollution. About 270 million tires (about 3.4 million tons) are scrapped in the United States annually. While nearly half are burned for energy, about 500 million tires now swell U.S. junk piles, where they "act as breeding grounds for rats and mosquitoes," according to the EPA, and periodically erupt into toxic tire fires. The U.S. cars scrapped each year also contain upwards of 8 tons of mercury. Meanwhile, polyvinyl chloride from scrap cars produces dioxins and other toxic pollutants. The study *End-of-Life Vehicles: A Threat to the Environment* concludes that the cars scrapped in Europe each year (75–85% as many as in the United

States) produce 2 million tons of hazardous waste, about one tenth of the EU's total hazardous waste production.

Time

Car travel swallows more and more time as commutes grow longer and congestion more severe. The *2002 Urban Mobility Report* from the Texas Transportation Institute calculated, on the basis of data from 75 U.S. cities, that the average motorist wasted 62 hours per year sitting in rush-hour traffic. (That's just the difference between rush-hour travel time and the normal time required to make the same trip.) In Los Angeles, the figure reached 136 hours. All told, over one third of the average rush-hour trip in the very large cities surveyed was wasted on traffic congestion. How is that an environmental or health issue? According to report *Transport, Environment, and Health,* issued by the World Health Organization (WHO) Regional Office for Europe, studies have connected traffic congestion with increased stress and blood pressure, as well as "aggressive behavior and increased likelihood of involvement in a crash."

Activity

Lack of exercise contributes to coronary heart disease, hypertension, some cancers, osteoporosis, poor coordination and stamina, and low self-esteem. The WHO Regional Office for Europe argues that "walking and cycling as part of daily activities should become a major pillar" of public-health strategy, and that daily travel offers the most promise to "integrate physical activities into daily schedules." Car dependence, instead, extends the sedentary lifestyle even to mobility. Half of all car trips in Europe, according to the WHO Regional Office, are under 5 km, distances most people can cover by bicycle in less than 20 minutes and on foot in well under one hour. High levels of automotive traffic, moreover, may deter people from walking or cycling—due to the unpleasantness of auto exhaust, the fear of crossing fast-moving traffic, or the dangers of riding a bicycle surrounded by cars. Some people may substitute car trips, but those without access to cars (especially children and elderly people) may simply venture outside less frequently, contributing to social isolation (another health risk factor).

Noise

Noise pollution is no mere nuisance. Researchers are beginning to document the damage that noise, even at relatively low levels, can do to human health. A 2001 study by Gary Evans of Cornell University, for example, has shown that children chronically exposed to low-level traffic noise suffer elevated blood pressure, increased changes in heart rate when stressed, and higher overall levels of stress-related hormones. In a separate study, on children exposed to low-level noise from aircraft flight patterns, Evans also documented negative effects of noise pollution on children's attention spans and learning abilities.

Collisions

Finally, the car crash ranks among the leading causes of death and injury in the United States. The statistics for 2001, compiled by the National Highway Traffic Safety Administration, were typical: over 42,000 people killed, over 360,000 people suffering incapacitating injuries, and over 3 million people injured overall. Over the last 25 years, the number of people killed per vehicle mile has declined by over 50%—undoubtedly thanks to such factors as increased availability and use of safety belts and airbags, improved vehicle design, and improved trauma care. The absolute number of deaths, however, has decreased by less than 20% (using the benchmark of 51,000 in 1980), as total vehicle miles traveled have more than doubled. Overall, the U.S. death toll from car crashes over the last quarter century is over one million people. During just the last decade, the total number of people injured in U.S. car crashes has topped 32 million.

The Path of Redemption

The environmental and public-health problems associated with the automobile have often inspired well-meaning exhortations to car-pool, drive less, or drive smaller cars, as well as dreams of "cars of the future" requiring less material or burning cleaner fuels. On the whole, however, the problems are neither individual nor technological—but social. So no individual nor technological solution will do. A comprehensive solution requires turning the "machine space" built for and dominated by the car back into human space: In the place of sprawl, compact development with work, school, stores, and recreation nearby and reachable without a car. In the place of the private car, reliable, clean, and accessible public transportation (along with small, efficient, nonpolluting vehicles for those who need them). In the place of internal combustion, the cyclist and the pedestrian—no longer marginalized and endangered, but respected as integral parts of a new, sustainable transportation system.

Cuba and China are the world's leading countries in bicycle use. Even in the rich capitalist counties, however, there are islands of sanity where public and human-powered transportation exist at least on a par with the automobile. Groningen, the Netherlands' sixth-largest city, suggests the possibilities: low speed limits reduce the dangers of urban traffic to cyclists and pedestrians; cars are not permitted on some streets, while bicycles can travel on any public way (including bike-only lanes and paths); parking for cars is restricted to garages, while secure bicycle parking facilities are plentiful (especially near train stations); cars are excluded from all squares in the city center, while careful city planning ensures that places of work and commerce are accessible to public transportation, cyclists, and pedestrians. As a result, Groningen residents now make nearly half of all in-city trips by bicycle; less than one third by car. The Dutch city of Delft, and the German cities of Freiburg and Muenster, are similar harbingers of a possible sustainable future.

The sustainable-transportation movement has shown encouraging worldwide growth in recent years. Transportation activists in the United Kingdom have carried out direct-action "street takings," closing off roads and highways and prompting spontaneous street fairs, to show what a car-free future might look like. The "Critical Mass" movement, starting in San Francisco in 1992 but quickly spreading to other cities, has brought together cyclists for rolling protest "marches" against auto hegemony. Activists have promoted worldwide car-free days, in which residents of hundreds of cities have participated. Bogotá, Colombia, a city of 7 million, held its first annual car-free day in 2000, complete with fines for any motorists caught within the city limits. Its popularity among city residents has bolstered long-term plans to exclude cars from the city, on a permanent basis, during peak morning and afternoon travel hours. In 2002, Seattle became the first U.S. city to officially host a car-free day.

With greater struggle, a more thorough-going transportation reform might be possible even within the confines of capitalism. This would require, however, a colossal economic shift—away the production of private automobiles, gasoline, and roads, and toward the reconstruction of public transportation and public space in general. It's highly unlikely, considering the ruin of former auto production centers like Detroit and Flint, that the "free market" could manage such a shift without imposing a wrenching dislocation on individuals and communities dependent on auto production. Moreover, it's virtually unimaginable, considering the trends toward privatization and commodification rampant in contemporary capitalism, that it would carry out such a transformation spontaneously.

NOT THE OWNERS OF THE EARTH:
CAPITALISM AND ENVIRONMENTAL DESTRUCTION
An Interview with John Bellamy Foster

By Skip Barry
March/April 2003, excerpted May 2003

The success of the environmental movement in raising public consciousness can be seen and felt almost on a daily basis. From local recycling efforts to tighter automobile inspection standards, we are constantly reminded of environmental issues. Daily newspapers and nightly newscasts shower us with issues as varied as global warming, the plight of lobsters, and Arianna Huffington's recent attacks on SUVs. For many of us, this may all get a bit overwhelming.

Fortunately, John Bellamy Foster takes a step back and uncovers the connecting threads that tie together these diverse questions. Touching on history, economics, ecology, and philosophy, Foster delves seriously into the complexity and vast scale of today's environmental problems. He also reminds us that many of

today's reforms treat the symptoms rather than curing the disease—which is
capitalism itself.

Foster is coeditor of Monthly Review: An Independent Socialist Magazine
and a professor at the University of Oregon at Eugene. His books on society and
ecology (including The Vulnerable Planet: A Short Economic History of the
Environment, Marx's Ecology: Materialism and Nature, *and* Ecology Against
Capitalism*), as well as numerous articles on these issues, have provided those*
concerned about the environment with a critical analytical foundation for thinking
about and acting on today's environmental crisis. Here, he takes on the largest
and most pressing environmental and economic issues in a conversation with
Dollars & Sense*'s Skip Barry.*

**D&S: Since Earth Day in 1970 the environmental movement has been
successful in raising public awareness of the plight of the environment. To
what extent has it been successful in winning environmental protections and
more ecological forms of economic development?**

JBF: Environmentalists have scored a lot of important victories over the last
three decades. However, this has not prevented the environmental crisis as a whole
from getting much worse. One difficulty is that those environmental problems that
are easiest to fix within the present system (such as the elimination of lead in
gasoline) get addressed, while others that go against the grain of the system, like
reducing carbon dioxide emissions, continue on without amelioration. Another
difficulty is that the scale and complexity of environmental problems keep on
increasing along with the scale and complexity of the world economy—and indeed
new problems not previously imagined keep on arising. If you look back three
decades to the period following the first Earth Day and compare it to today you will
notice two things: First, most of the issues raised at that time, such as the role of
toxins in our environment, are still with us, and more often than not on a much
larger scale. Second, new problems have arisen that were scarcely on the radar
screen thirty years ago—or problems that we recognized then have been qualitatively
transformed and present themselves to us now in new forms.

We are still faced with the issue of pesticides raised by Rachel Carson in *Silent
Spring* (see Laura Orlando, "Industry Attacks on Dissent: From Rachel Carson to
Oprah," *D&S*, March/April 2002). Although a few of the worst pesticides, such as
DDT, were banned for use in the rich countries, we now produce in the United
States several times the quantity of pesticides that we did when Rachel Carson
raised the alarm and most such chemicals are effectively untested and unregulated
for their effects on humans.

But if the old environmental problems continue to haunt us, new ones have
arisen that are equally or more threatening. Global warming and depletion of the
ozone layer were not threats that one heard about commonly within the
environmental movement in the early 1970s. Species extinction was often raised
but the idea that we were entering a period of the "sixth extinction," in which the

extinction rate would rise to a minimum of 1000 times the background (or normal) rate—comparable to the five great mass extinctions in the history of the planet (the most recent being the destruction of the dinosaurs 65 million years ago)—that was not something that was or could have been foreseen on the first Earth Day.

The Worldwatch Institute talks about the "acceleration of history" where the environment is concerned. This acceleration is the product of the exponential growth of an unsustainable economic system, which now operates on a scale that rivals the basic biogeochemical processes of the planet. For example, carbon dioxide is not a pollutant. It is part of our own respiratory system. But when hundreds of millions of cars are driven trillions of miles per year, all pumping carbon dioxide into the atmosphere, the scale of human economic activity becomes of planetary significance, changing the balance within the biosphere. When one considers that a 3% annual rate of growth in world output means a doubling in the size of the economy every twenty five years, so that the size of the world economy would increase by sixteen times in a century, 250 times in two centuries, and 4,000 times in three centuries—it becomes clear that the main reason for what environmentalists call the "acceleration of history" is the exponential growth of the economy itself. China has the highest rate of economic growth in the world at present and this is fueling expectations about its future energy demands. The U.S. Department of Energy has estimated that China's demand for petroleum will increase by almost 1000% between 1997 and 2020.

D&S: The Bush Administration rejected an already watered down version of the Kyoto Protocol on global warming. Is the United States government the main barrier to adequately addressing environmental reform?

JBF: There is no doubt that the United States is the single most important political entity blocking environmental reform. The U.S. refusal to ratify the Kyoto Protocol was a major blow to the struggle against global warming. But this response was virtually inevitable given that the giant corporations were strongly opposed to the climate treaty. The Kyoto Protocol required the United States to reduce its greenhouse gas emissions to 7% below the 1990 level. But U.S. carbon dioxide emissions have actually *risen* by as much as 18% since 1990. The Clinton administration declared in 2000 that the United States would have to cut its carbon dioxide emissions by up to 30% if it were to meet its meet its targeted reductions under the Kyoto Protocol by 2010. This was viewed as potentially catastrophic by the vested interests (for example, the corporate lobbying group the Global Climate Coalition), since U.S. wealth and power is built around the auto-petroleum complex. The Clinton administration therefore made no attempt to ratify the Kyoto Protocol and did everything it could do to water down and escape the agreement. The Bush administration has simply been more honest in rejecting the climate treaty outright.

D&S: Does the environmental crisis call into question the sustainability of capitalist development?

JBF: The questioning of capitalism is omnipresent in the ecological critique. That is why I entitled my latest book *Ecology Against Capitalism*. Capitalism is all about the accumulation of capital. The commodification of nature in the service of accumulation involves the systematic disruption of spatial and temporal relations that are integral to a sustainable system. It frequently means not just the exploitation of nature but the robbing or pillage of the biosphere. I have tried over the years to find a way of conceptualizing the damaging effects that capitalism has on the environment. In *The Vulnerable Planet* I looked at how capital accumulation conflicts with Barry Commoner's four informal "laws" of ecology: (1) everything is connected to everything else, (2) everything must go somewhere, (3) nature (i.e. evolution) knows best, and (4) nothing comes from nothing. Capitalism, I argued, has its own built-in anti-ecological tendencies: (1) the only lasting connection between things is the cash nexus, (2) it doesn't matter where something goes (how it is externalized) as long as it doesn't reenter the circuit of capital, (3) the self-regulating market knows best, and (4) nature's bounty is a free gift to the property owner.

Recently I concluded that the most powerful way of understanding capitalism's destructive relation to the environment is in terms of what Marx called the "metabolic rift"—or the material estrangement of human beings from the natural conditions and processes that form the bases of their existence. (Marx's concept of metabolic rift is discussed in detail in my book *Marx's Ecology*.) Such a rift occurs when the circulation of commodities and exchange under capitalism ruptures the basic processes governing the circulation of matter and energy—the biogeochemical interactions on which ecosystems and the biosphere depend. For example, prior to growth of modern agribusiness livestock was raised on farms where it provided fertilizer for crops. This is of course part of an ecological cycle stretching back over the ages. Now, however, cattle are forced into giant feedlots and their manure, which cannot under these circumstances be used to fertilize the soil, collects in huge amounts and gives off methane gas, which has become a major factor in global warming.

D&S: Since lower-income people worldwide are disproportionately affected by adverse environmental conditions, it seems that the environmental movement must incorporate issues such as class, race, and the third world. To what extent have environmental movements done this? How do you think this can be achieved?

JBF: Within the environmental movement itself, which is really a collection of movements, the most vital element since the late 1980s has been the "environmental justice" movement—or that part of the movement that sees environmental degradation as inseparably connected to issues of class, race, gender, and international oppression. Leadership in this realm has come from those fighting environmental racism. But ecofeminists have also made crucial contributions. The anti-toxic movement as a whole has had a working class base. And more and more there is a globalization of the environmental struggle that recognizes the reality of ecological imperialism. It was this growth of the environmental justice movement, and the way that it has altered environmental struggles, that allowed environmentalists and labor activists to come together in Seattle in 1999 and in subsequent anti-globalizations struggles. I think that this is the tendency of the future. Capitalism in its relentless commodification and accumulation is breaking down all the barriers. Exploitation, once understood to be centered in factory labor, is now universalized. The earth itself has been brought within the factory, so to speak. In this context all struggles become one.

Chapter 10

POSITIVE DIRECTIONS

INTRODUCTION

For several years, economic news has been bad news. The United States has gone through a recession and "jobless recovery," Americans have felt the bite of social spending cuts and tax giveaways to the rich, and many have seen their retirement security disappear. Globally, neoliberal economic reforms have produced economic crises in developing countries and given corporations increasing freedom to exploit the world's workers and environment. And both at home and abroad, the "War on Terrorism" has given the U.S. government a pretext to attack the labor movement and shift resources to the military.

But for those interested in social justice and economic democracy, there have been hopeful developments, as well. Often, you just had to look outside the major papers to find them.

People

Amid the government's attacks on economic and civil rights, the U.S. labor movement scored one of its biggest victories in years: freeing the Charleston Five. Derek Wright describes the world-wide solidarity campaign that developed around these five longshore workers—members of an activist, majority-black union in South Carolina who had been placed under house arrest by a state government seeking to crush their union. ("Dockworkers Stand Up to Racism, Repression, and Corporate Globalization—and Win!").

Further south, the Landless Workers' Movement (Movimento dos Trabalhadores Rurais Sem Terra, or MST) has challenged persistent economic inequality in Brazil with direct action. The MST has seized unused land and built housing for 300,000 families, developed literacy programs, organized opposition to "free trade," and forced the government to devote resources to the poor ("They Can Walk With Their Heads Up").

Programs

All over the world, grassroots movements are developing programs to lessen poverty and inequality as well as the power disparities that produce them. Lena

Graber and John Miller look at the International Wages for Housework Campaign, which is organizing to force governments to count women's home-based work in official statistics—and remunerate it. Graber and Miller document the incredible amount of unpaid work that women do, noting that if this work were counted by governments, the GDP of industrialized economies would rise by 33% to 112%. They conclude that paying wages for essential home-based work makes economic sense, and would improve the social position of women worldwide ("Wages for Housework: The Movement and the Numbers").

In the United States, the living wage movement has won dozens of local ordinances raising the minimum wage for public-sector workers or those under public contracts. Chris Tilly proposes a number of strategies for expanding living wage victories, highlighting recent campaigns that have targeted private employers. He also argues for the strategic importance of the movement, noting that it can help build the labor movement and wider organizing for social justice ("Next Steps for the Living Wage Movement").

Trade unions in South Africa have integrated themselves into the country's social movements since the days when they helped dismantle apartheid. As Ravi Naidoo explains, South African unions today are making common cause with NGOs, religious groups, community organizations, and AIDS advocacy groups to take on issues from public budget priorities to health care to the country's unemployment crisis. He argues that South African "social-movement unionism" offers a model for unions worldwide. ("Social-Movement Unionism in South Africa").

Policies

Finally, Margaret Thatcher might still believe that "there is no alternative" to neoliberal economic policy, but plenty of communities and researchers have found otherwise. Thad Williamson, David Imbroscio, and Gar Alperovitz take on the myth that cities and towns must let capital move in and out at will, destabilizing jobs and local economies. They point to placed-based economic institutions throughout the United States that anchor jobs and capital—from community development corporations to worker-owned firms ("Capital Stability and Local Democracy"). Ellen Frank closes the chapter with a plan for eliminating poor countries' impossible debt burdens. Frank argues that debt forgiveness does not go far enough: that an international central bank, democratically structured and publicly controlled, is needed to ensure that intolerable debts don't mount again ("Disarming the Debt Trap").

DOCKWORKERS STAND UP TO RACISM, REPRESSION, AND CORPORATE GLOBALIZATION—AND WIN!

By Derek Wright

January/February 2002

For nearly two years, the most crucial fight in the U.S. labor movement has been the struggle to defend the "Charleston Five"—members of the International Longshoremen's Association (ILA) who faced felony charges after police attacked their picket line in January 2000. In November 2001, the Five were finally set free.

At a time when crackdowns on political dissent are sweeping the country, this was a triumph for freedom of speech and freedom of assembly. The victory came because of an international defense campaign, a massive outpouring of solidarity from labor and civil rights activists, and—perhaps most important—the threat of job actions by dockworkers around the world.

"I think the struggle in Charleston has brought to the table a multitude of issues—racism, having a voice at work, and civil rights in general," Leonard Riley, a member of ILA Local 1422's executive board, told reporters last summer. "These issues are very compelling when people all over the world look at them and see that they're the same ones that they face." (Local 1422 represents four of the five workers charged.)

The saga began in October 1999, when the Danish shipping firm Nordana Lines ended its 23-year relationship with the ILA and began using non-union labor on the Charleston, South Carolina, docks. According to Local 1422 President Kenneth Riley (Leonard's brother), union members responded with peaceful picketing, which briefly delayed work on two Nordana ships.

On January 20, 2000, as one of Nordana's ships was docking, 600 riot-clad local and state police officers were on hand. When about 130 workers began marching toward the dock to exercise their right to picket, police initiated a clash by pushing the picketers back and shouting racist slurs, Kenneth Riley says. When that happened, he and other officers of Local 1422 "created a buffer between the police and the pickets," according to the Campaign for Workers' Rights in South Carolina. At that point, the Campaign reported, one police officer "ran out of formation and clubbed Kenneth Riley in the head. A fight ensued." The police attacked the workers with rubber bullets, tear gas, smoke grenades, and nightsticks. About a dozen workers were arrested and charged with trespassing.

The crackdown was directed by state Attorney General Charlie Condon, an ambitious Republican who wants to be the next governor. Condon ordered the massive police presence under the auspices of South Carolina's anti-union "right to work" law, after the State Ports Authority requested protection for a non-union operation on the docks. After a local judge dismissed the trespassing charges,

Condon got a grand jury to indict five workers on federal charges of "rioting" and "conspiracy to riot." For nearly 20 months, the Charleston Five—Kenneth Jefferson, Elijah Ford, Jr., Peter Washington, Jr., Ricky Simmons, and Jason Edgerton—remained under house arrest. They were forbidden to leave their homes between 7 p.m. and 7 a.m. except to go to work or attend union meetings.

Another 27 workers faced a $1.5 million lawsuit filed by WSI, the company that ran the scab operation for Nordana. WSI sued to recover "lost profits" that it claimed the ILA picketers had caused.

The assault was aimed not only at labor rights but at civil rights too. ILA members in Charleston are overwhelmingly black, and Local 1422 played a key role in a 40,000-strong march on the statehouse in Charleston—held just three days before the police riot—to demand that the Confederate flag be taken down. Condon's vengeful actions suggest that he was hoping to ride a racist backlash into the governor's mansion.

At the same time, politicians were acting on behalf of giant multinational corporations—including Honda, Michelin, General Electric, and DuPont—that have poured investment into South Carolina in recent years. During the 1990s, the number of factories in the state has doubled. Companies have been attracted by wages that are 20% below the national average, and by low unionization rates. (South Carolina has the second-lowest percentage of unionized workers in the country, after North Carolina.)

In a low-wage state whose population is nearly 30% African-American, racist and anti-labor public officials were threatened by the fighting example of a virtually all-black union of well-paid workers. They figured that, if they could break a strong union like Local 1422, they could send a powerful message: that unions everywhere would be destroyed if they stepped out of line.

In the wake of the attack, organizers launched a worldwide effort to win justice for the Charleston Five. Locals and individual members of the International Longshore and Warehouse Union (ILWU), which represents West Coast dockworkers, raised hundreds of thousands of dollars for the defense campaign, and pledged to shut down the docks from San Diego to Seattle if the case went to trial. Other unions have raised money, organized defense committees, circulated petitions demanding justice, and helped to coordinate a speaking tour of ILA members to raise awareness of the case.

The struggle also had the support of the International Transport Workers Federation, which links dockworkers' unions around the world. Just days after the police riot, dockworkers in Spain and Australia refused to work Nordana's ships unless the company signed a union contract with Local 1422. That international solidarity helped pressure Nordana to sign.

In October 2001, Charlie Condon—faced with accusations of gross prosecutorial misconduct by defense attorneys—was forced to remove himself from the case. Soon after, the Five were freed from house arrest. Their trial was set to begin on November 14, and their supporters were planning an International Day of Action for that date. By early November, with the Day of Action looming, the prosecution agreed to drop all felony charges when the Five pleaded "no contest" (which is not an admission of guilt) to minor misdemeanor charges, and paid a token fine of $100 each.

The struggle for justice in Charleston is not over. The WSI lawsuit is still pending, although the case has been seriously weakened by the resolution of felony charges. In addition, the police who violently attacked unionists for exercising their basic right to picket have faced no repercussions or criminal charges. Finally, there is no compensation for the five men who lost 20 months of liberty as punishment for a crime they did not commit.

Still, in today's climate of racism and repression, the Charleston Five victory is nothing short of remarkable. If it inspires other workers to organize—especially in the South—that will be cause for celebration too. Most important, it shows that joining together to stand up for our beliefs is the best way to defend our rights to speak, assemble, and express dissent. Today, these rights are seriously threatened. The only way to keep them is to use them.

"THEY CAN WALK WITH THEIR HEADS UP"
An Interview with Joao Pedro Stedile, National Board Member, Movimento dos Trabalhadores Rurais Sem Terra
By Cynthia Peters and Justin Podur
May/June 2002

"In Brazil, where there is fertile land, wealth and a tropical climate," said Jean Ziegler, UN special rapporteur on the right to food, after a recent visit there, "hunger is not a destiny." Rather, it is "the product of a totally unjust order. Those who die of hunger in Brazil are assassinated."

Brazilian government officials were outraged by Ziegler's strong words, and pointed to their recent successes in improving health care and education, and in lifting millions out of extreme poverty. Still, the government does not dispute the fact that 40,000 Brazilians die every year of hunger and malnutrition-related diseases, and that more than 23 million of Brazil's 170 million people are malnourished.

How has Latin America's most resource-rich country ended up with such a large part of its population struggling to survive? Brazil's recent decades of dictatorship and still powerful military, its high concentration of wealth and landownership, and its struggle to develop under the weight of immense debt and IMF-enforced neoliberal economic policies have contributed to a fractured and impoverished society.

In the early 1960s, populist president Joao Goulart antagonized the U.S.-allied Brazilian military by instituting rent controls, seizing unused lands, nationalizing the petroleum industry, and restricting the repatriation of profits by foreign investors. Brazilian generals staged a coup in 1964, ushering in a 21-year military dictatorship that violently suppressed opposition political parties, independent labor unions, student movements, and landless workers' organizations. It also presided over the so-called Brazilian economic miracle—a dozen or so years of rapid growth financed by loans from foreign banks. This debt, incurred by the generals, helped enrich a few, but left to the general population a legacy of huge interest payments and punitive economic policies.

After a sustained economic crisis in the 1970s and early 1980s, brought on by skyrocketing oil prices and the generals' heavy borrowing, the military dictatorship signed an austerity agreement with the IMF in 1983. Being the world's largest debtor nation affected Brazil's poor in predictable ways. In order to generate cash to make interest payments on the debt, more and more land was put towards cash crops like coffee and soy, displacing hundreds of thousands of subsistence farmers. Many fled to the cities, where they settled in burgeoning shantytowns. Others were relocated to places such as the Amazonian Rondonia, where they cleared forests in an effort to farm the land. World Bank-sponsored programs, such as hydroelectric dams that flood vast tracts of rainforest and displace thousands of indigenous people, have contributed to the social and ecological disaster. Brazil suffers not just from its immense foreign debt, but also from the hidden costs of environmental destruction, many internally displaced people, and an impoverished rural population—what many Brazilians call the "social debt."

Even during the dictatorship, workers in Brazil's growing industrial sector organized powerful and combative unions. The unions and the fragments of the Brazilian left that had survived 15 years of dictatorship founded the left-wing Workers' Party (PT) in 1979. These developments helped spur the policy of *abertura*—or "opening"—which the Brazilian dictatorship implemented as a way to control the transition to civilian rule. The easing of repression, in turn, led to the growth of grassroots social change movements, such as the Landless Workers' Movement (Movimento dos Trabalhadores Rurais Sem Terra, or MST), and of opposition political parties such as the PT. Since the return to elections in 1988, the PT has won key state and local elections, and instituted important reforms. Perhaps its most groundbreaking reform is the participatory budget—a decision-making system that allows citizens a direct say over portions of their municipal budgets. The PT's best-known leader, the popular former auto worker Luis Inacio "Lula" da Silva, almost won the presidency in 1989 and is running again this year.

The MST, with support from the Catholic Church, began its struggle in 1985, taking over an unused plantation in the south of the country. The occupiers gained title to the land two years later. Since then, the MST has helped 300,000 families settle on previously idle land, while close to 100,000 other families are living on land they have occupied, waiting for government recognition. In May 2000, 30,000 MST members took over federal buildings across the country in a successful bid to persuade President Fernando Henrique Cardoso to address the country's extreme economic inequality. In response to pressure from the MST, Cardoso promised $1 billion in reforms. In addition to its successful resettlement program and considerable grassroots power, the MST boasts a sophisticated literacy program for adults and adolescents, as well as 1,000 primary schools, in which 2,000 teachers work with about 50,000 kids. According to Bill Hinchberger, writing for *The Nation* (March 2, 1998), "the MST represents Latin America's most dynamic popular movement south of Chiapas."

As such, it is not popular among certain segments of Brazilian society. The police and military, as well as landlords' private gunmen, still target activists. According to the Roman Catholic-run Pastoral Land Commission, over 1,100 people were killed in land disputes between 1985 and 1999. And only 47 cases have gone to trial, leading to just 18 convictions. In 2001, 16 MST activists were murdered, and few of the cases were properly investigated or brought to trial. "At least ten landowners are threatening me, saying that I will be next," José Brito, president of the Agricultural Workers Union of Rondon in the state of Para, has told the press. "Even thought I have registered complaints to the police station, I have never been called to give a deposition. Whoever fights for life here will have his own life threatened."

In addition to violent repression, the MST faces other challenges. According to Global Exchange, "landowners and some elected officials are trying to repeal the clause of the Brazilian constitution that says land should be used for social purposes—and can be redistributed if it is not. That provision has formed the legal foundation of the MST's occupations of unused lands." Furthermore, the World Bank's $2 billion "land bank" program, which offers loans to small farmers to purchase land, is transparently designed to undermine the grassroots-based MST. The MST must also contend with "free trade" agreements that knock down trade barriers, allowing cheap food to be imported from abroad, and undercutting domestic markets. The struggle ahead remains enormous. Today, 3% of Brazil's population still owns two-thirds of the country's arable land, much of which lies idle. Meanwhile, millions of peasants struggle to survive by working in temporary agricultural jobs.

At an MST cooperative in Herval, in the southern state of Rio Grande do Sul, which I visited in February 2002, I saw productive farms, well-built homes with electricity and running water, schools, and cultural activities. If the 40,000 who die from hunger each year in Brazil are the victims of "class warfare," as the UN's Ziegler argues, the MST is on the front line—fighting back, not with bullets, but with mass organizing and grassroots pressure to meet basic human needs.

While in Herval, Canadian activist and writer Justin Podur and I had the opportunity to talk with Joao Pedro Stedile, a member of the MST's national board.

—*Cynthia Peters*

D&S: What are the MST's main achievements?

JPS: Our most important success of all has been to build an organization and a social movement. We've won back the worth and dignity of the peasant. That has immeasurable value. It doesn't show up in statistics. But when a person stops being humiliated, stops being a slave, and they can walk with their head up, master of their own future, that's the most important thing we're building.

Beyond that, over the last 18 years, we've gotten land for 300,000 families, and though many of them remain poor, nobody in our settlements goes hungry. Everybody has work all year around. There are schools in all the settlements. All the children go to school. Everyone can build their own home. The houses may be humble, but nobody has to pay rent to anyone. At the very least, the people enjoy the basic rights of all people. That's what retaking the land means.

We're not satisfied with these modest achievements. Because in Brazil there are four million landless families. Our struggle is to broaden the movement, open up more battles, mobilize more people, because it's not just a matter of allowing a few people to solve their problems. This is important, of course. It offers an example. It's a form of mass education. But the fundamental thing is to change society, and solve the problems of all Brazilians, of all the poor.

D&S: You spoke of changing society. What are the next steps for the MST?

JPS: The challenges are huge. It's not going to be an easy struggle, nor a quick one. The road ahead will be rocky, not smooth. But there are both long-range struggles and more immediate ones.

In the long term, we're doing battle over what may decide the future of our country. I'm talking about the U.S. offensive to impose the Free Trade Area of the Americas (FTAA) on the Americas as a whole. The FTAA is more than a trade agreement. It is the U.S. government's plan to control our land, our wealth, our development, our technology, our currency, and our language. It would mean our submission to the interests of U.S. capital—to the less than 500 corporations at the top. And if that happens, we're back to being a colony, this time under the rule of the United States. So we have to fight to keep the FTAA from being imposed on Brazil. And not just on Brazil, but on the whole of Latin America. What we're going to do over the course of the coming months and years is help inform the people, organize them, raise their consciousness. In addition to fighting for land, health, and shelter, we have to stop the FTAA. That's going to mean demonstrations, mass meetings, lots and lots of different initiatives to inform and politicize people. Beyond that, every social movement has to continue its own specific work—we in the landless movement have to keep on occupying more and more landed estates. Our compatriots who have been displaced by dam construction will keep on fighting against the dams. The unemployed movements in the city will broaden their struggles for employment. The workers who are threatened will keep organizing, like for the general strike this March.

We're going to try and promote all these struggles in hopes of reawakening the people and reviving the mass movement here in Brazil. Because right now it's receding. With a revival of the mass movement, we can hope to change the government, and the reigning economic model.

D&S: What do you think of the Workers' Party's participatory budget process?

JPS: Well, there are some positive things about it, but also some criticisms to make.

D&S: What are the criticisms?

JPS: That, in the end, the people really only have a say over 5%—or, at the most, 10%—of the budget. Because the rest—including salaries, foreign debt payments, etc.—is fixed by law. All public budgets in Brazil have 13% of the total tied up by the IMF. They're required to deposit this in the bank to pay the debt. So, for example, in this state, which is governed by a people's government, by the left, education gets 11% of the budget, while the IMF gets 13%. That means the power of the people to change things through the participatory budget process is very limited.

D&S: So, what's the positive side?

JPS: It's that the participatory budget creates an opportunity for the people to voice their opinions. For the people to have a say about the overall problems of their society. It's like an exercise that points toward creating a general assembly of the society as a whole. Here in Rio Grande do Sul, we have a population of 12 million. You can't fit 12 million people into a single room. But the idea of the participatory budget process is that everyone can take part and have a say. So the main value of the process is not how much of the budget people have a say over, but as a democratic exercise that teaches people that they have a right to a say.

D&S: What would you say to activists and social movements in North America?

JPS: We're very interested in U.S. social movements. The landless movement enjoys the support of solidarity committees in many U.S. cities, which help us and help publicize our efforts. But what gratifies us the most is hearing about the people in the United States, even if they're not a majority yet, who are mobilizing as well, and fighting against their government. We understand that the people of the United States don't know the real impact of the actions of their government. We hope that, slowly, they will begin to realize that, as peoples, we're the same. It's like an old U.S. journalist put it. He was a "cousin" or an "ancestor" of you who have come here from the United States. And he really said it in your honor. Because he was a social activist, and he went to cover the Spanish Civil War, like you have come here to Porto Alegre. When he came back, he wrote a book, which was called *No Man is a Foreigner*—meaning "man" in the general sense. What does that mean? That all peoples are alike. It's governments and capital, which enriches itself from the labor of others, that are bad. So we have to build a great, international alliance, which is what this forum is for. And we hope and expect that U.S. activists, fighting in the dragon's own gut, will help us kill this monster.

Translated from Spanish by Alejandro Reuss.

WAGES FOR HOUSEWORK: THE MOVEMENT AND THE NUMBERS
By Lena Graber and John Miller
September/October 2002

The International Wages for Housework Campaign (WFH), a network of women in Third World and industrialized countries, began organizing in the early 1970s. WFH's demands are ambitious—"for the unwaged work that women do to be recognized as work in official government statistics, and for this work to be paid."

Housewives paid wages? By the government? That may seem outlandish to some, but consider the staggering amount of unpaid work carried out by women. In 1990, the International Labor Organization (ILO) estimated that women do two-thirds of the world's work for 5% of the income. In 1995, the UN Development Programme's (UNDP) Human Development Report announced that women's unpaid and underpaid labor was worth $11 trillion worldwide, and $1.4 trillion in the United States alone. Paying women the wages they "are owed" for unwaged work, as WFN puts it, would go a long way toward undoing these inequities and reducing women's economic dependence on men.

Publicizing information like this, WFH—whose International Women Count Network now includes more than 2,000 non-governmental organizations (NGOs) from the North and South—and other groups have been remarkably successful in persuading governments to count unwaged work. In 1995, the UN Fourth World Conference on Women, held in Beijing, developed a Platform for Action that called on governments to calculate the value of women's unpaid work and include it in conventional measures of national output, such as Gross Domestic Product (GDP).

So far, only Trinidad & Tobago and Spain have passed legislation mandating the new accounting, but other countries—including numerous European countries, Australia, Canada, Japan, and New Zealand in the industrialized world, and Bangladesh, the Dominican Republic, India, Nepal, Tanzania, and Venezuela in

Table 1: Women's Time Spent Per Day Performing Household Labor, By Activity, In Hours:Minutes

Country	Childcare Time	Cleaning Time	Food Prep Time	Shopping Time	Water/Fuel Collection	Total Housework Time[a]
Australia (1997[b])	2:27	1:17	1:29	0:58	n.a.	3:39
Japan (1999)	0:24	2:37	n.a.	0:33	n.a.	3:34
Norway (2000)	0:42	1:16	0:49	0:26	0:01	3:56
United Kingdom (2000)	1:26	1:35	1:08	0:33	n.a.	4:55
Nepal (1996)	1:28	2:00	5:30	0:13	1:10	11:58

Sources: Australia: <www.abs.gov.au/ausstats>; Japan: <www.unescap.org/stat>; Norway: <www.ssb.no/tidsbruk_en>; United Kingdom: <www.statistics.gov.uk/themes/social_finances/TimeUseSurvey>; Nepal: INSTRAW, *Valuation of Household Production and the Satellite Accounts* (Santo Domingo: 1996), 34-35; <www.cbs.nl/isi/iass>.

Note: Some activities, especially childcare, may overlap with other tasks.

[a] Totals may include activities other than those listed.

[b] Only some percentage of the population recorded doing these activities. Averages are for that portion of the population. Generally, figures represent a greater number of women than men involved.

the developing world—have undertaken extensive surveys to determine how much time is spent on unpaid household work.

The Value of Housework

Producing credible numbers for the value of women's work in the home is no easy task. Calculating how many hours women spend performing housework—from cleaning to childcare to cooking to shopping—is just the first step. The hours are considerable in both developing and industrialized economies. (See Table 1.)

What value to place on that work, and what would constitute fair remuneration—or wages for housework—is even more difficult to assess. Feminist economists dedicated to making the value of housework visible have taken different approaches to answering the question. One approach, favored by the UN's International Research and Training Institute for the Advancement of Women (INSTRAW), bases the market value of work done at home on the price of market goods and services that are similar to those produced in the home (such as meals served in restaurants or cleaning done by professional firms). These output-based evaluations estimate that counting unpaid household production would add 30-60% to the GDP of industrialized countries, and far more for developing countries. (See Table 2.)

Table 2: Value of unpaid household labor as % of GDP,
using output-based evaluation method

Country	% of GDP
Canada (1992)	47.4%
Finland (1990)	49.1%
Nepal (1991)	170.7%

Source: INSTRAW, *Valuation of Household Production and the Satellite Accounts* (Santo Domingo, 1996), 62, 229.

A second approach evaluates the inputs of household production—principally the labor that goes into cooking, cleaning, childcare, and other services performed in the home, overwhelmingly by women. Advocates of this approach use one of three methods. Some base their calculations on what economists call opportunity cost—the wages women might have earned if they had worked a similar number of hours in the market economy. Others ask what it would cost to hire someone to do the work—either a general laborer such as a domestic servant (the generalist-replacement method) or a specialist such as a chef (the specialist-replacement method)—and then assign those wages to household labor. Ann Chadeau, a researcher with the Organization for Economic Cooperation and Development, has found the specialist-replacement method to be "the most plausible and at the same time feasible approach" for valuing unpaid household labor.

These techniques produce quite different results, all of which are substantial in relation to GDP. With that in mind, let's look at how some countries calculated the monetary value of unpaid work.

Unpaid Work in Canada, Great Britain, and Japan

In Canada, a government survey documented the time men and women spent on unpaid work in 1992. Canadian women performed 65% of all unpaid work, shouldering an especially large share of household labor devoted to preparing meals, maintaining clothing, and caring for children. (Men's unpaid hours exceeded women's only for outdoor cleaning.)

The value of unpaid labor varied substantially, depending on the method used to estimate its appropriate wage. (See Table 3.) The opportunity-cost method, which uses the average market wage (weighted for the greater proportion of unpaid work done by women), assigned the highest value to unpaid labor, 54.2% of Canadian GDP. The two replacement methods produced lower estimates, because the wages they assigned fell below those of other jobs. The specialist-replacement method, which paired unpaid activities with the average wages of corresponding occupations—such as cooking with junior chefs, and childcare with kindergarten teachers—put the value of Canadian unpaid labor at 43% of GDP. The generalist-replacement method, by assigning the wages of household servants to unpaid labor, produced the lowest estimate of the value of unpaid work: 34% of Canadian GDP. INSTRAW's output-based measure, which matched hours of unpaid labor to a household's average expenditures on the same activities, calculated the value of Canada's unpaid work as 47.4% of GDP.

Table 3: Value of unpaid household labor in Canada as % of GDP, 1992

Evaluation Method	% of GDP
Opportunity Cost (before taxes)	54.2%
Specialist-Replacement	43.0%
Generalist-Replacement	34.0%
Output-Based	47.4%

Source: INSTRAW, Valuation of Household Production and the Satellite Accounts (Santo Domingo, 1996), 229.

In Great Britain, where unpaid labor hours are high for an industrialized country (see Table 1), the value of unpaid labor was far greater relative to GDP. The British Office for National Statistics found that, when valued using the opportunity cost method, unpaid work was 112% of Britain's GDP in 1995! With the specialist-replacement method, British unpaid labor was still 56% of GDP—greater than the output of the United Kingdom's entire manufacturing sector for the year.

In Japan—where unpaid labor hours are more limited (see Table 1), paid workers put in longer hours, and women perform over 80% of unpaid work—the value of unpaid labor is significantly smaller relative to GDP. The Japanese Economic Planning Agency calculated that counting unpaid work in 1996 would add between 15.2% (generalist-replacement method) and 23% (opportunity-cost method) to GDP. Even at those levels, the value of unpaid labor still equaled at least half of Japanese women's market wages.

Housework Not Bombs

While estimates vary by country and evaluation method, all of these calculations make clear that recognizing the value of unpaid household labor profoundly alters our perception of economic activity and women's contributions to production. "Had household production been included in the system of macro-economic accounts," notes Ann Chadeau, "governments may well have implemented quite different economic and social policies."

For example, according to the UNDP, "The inescapable implication [of recognizing women's unpaid labor] is that the fruits of society's total labor should be shared more equally." For the UNDP, this would mean radically altering property and inheritance rights; access to credit; entitlement to social security benefits, tax incentives, and child care; and terms of divorce settlements.

For WFH advocates, the implications are inescapable as well: women's unpaid labor should be paid—and "the money," WFH insists, "must come first of all from military spending."

Here in the United States, an unneeded and dangerous military buildup begun last year has already pushed up military spending from 3% to 4% of GDP. Devoting just the additional 1% of GDP gobbled up by the military budget to wages for housework—far from being outlandish—would be an important first step toward fairly remunerating women who perform much-needed and life-sustaining household work.

Resources: Ann Chadeau, "What is Households' Non-Market Production Worth?" *OECD Economic Studies* No. 18 (Spring 1992); Economic Planning Unit, Department of National Accounts, Japan, "Monetary Valuation of Unpaid Work in 1996" <unstats.un.org/unsd/methods/timeuse/tusresource_papers/japanunpaid. htm>; INSTRAW, *Measurement and Valuation of Unpaid Contribution: Accounting Through Time and Output* (Santo Domingo: 1995); INSTRAW,

Valuation of Household Production and the Satellite Accounts (Santo Domingo: 1996); Office of National Statistics, United Kingdom, "A Household Satellite Account for the UK," by Linda Murgatroyd and Henry Neuberger, *Economic Trends* (October 1997) <www.statistics.gov.uk/hhsa/hhsa/Index.html>; Hilkka Pietilä, "The Triangle of the Human Ecology: Household-Cultivation-Industrial Production," *Ecological Economics Journal* 20 (1997); UN Development Programme, Human Development Report (New York: Oxford University Press, 1995); Wages For Housework <ourworld.compuserve.com/homepages/crossroadswomenscentre/WFH.html>.

NEXT STEPS FOR THE LIVING-WAGE MOVEMENT
By Chris Tilly
September/October 2001

This past May, Harvard University students made national headlines by occupying a university building for three weeks to demand that Harvard and its contractors pay employees a living wage. While Harvard refused to grant the $10.25 wage that the students demanded, they did agree to form a study committee with ample student and union representation. In the days that followed, Harvard also ended a contract negotiation deadlock with food service workers by offering an unprecedented wage increase of over $1 per hour—a surprise move that many attributed to the feisty labor-student alliance built through the living-wage push.

Harvard's living-wage activists represent the tip of a much larger national iceberg, most of which has taken the form of attempts to pass local living-wage ordinances. Over 60 local governments have passed living-wage laws—almost all since a ground-breaking Baltimore ordinance passed in 1994—with more coming on board each month. Such ordinances typically require the local government, along with any businesses that supply it, to pay a wage well above the current federal minimum of $5.15. Living-wage coalitions originally set wage floors at the amount needed by a full-time, year-round worker to keep a family of four above the poverty line (currently about $8.40 per hour), but like the Harvard students, they are increasingly campaigning for higher figures based on area living costs. The community organization ACORN (Alliance of Community Organizations for Reform Now) has spearheaded many of the coalitions, and an up-to-date living-wage scorecard can be found on its web site <www.livingwage-campaign.org>. At the heart of the campaigns are low-wage workers like Celia Talavera, who joined Santa Monica's successful living-wage campaign last May. Referring to her job as a hotel housekeeper, she said, "I am fighting for a living wage because I want to work there for a long time."

The spread of living-wage laws reflects deep public concern about the unfairness of today's economy to those at the bottom of the paid workforce. A

Living Wages Overseas

A movement-building perspective helps us think about living wages in an international context. If people in rich countries try to decide the appropriate wage floor for people in poor countries, they run a serious risk of destructive paternalism. Consider the case of Haiti. A few years back, the National Labor Committee (the folks who blew the whistle on the sweatshops behind Kathie Lee Gifford's designer label) and others—me included—made much of the fact that Haiti's export assembly factories paid as little as 11 cents an hour. True enough, but it's also true that in the context of economic collapse, many in the Haitian countryside view this as a sufficiently handsome wage to crowd into shacks in Port-au-Prince for a chance to get one of these jobs. A U.S. trade law that barred goods produced by workers earning less than, say, $1 an hour would effectively shut Haitian goods out of this country, causing job loss in Haiti.

The alternative is to find ways to beef up Haitians' ability to place greater demands on employers, allowing Haitians to decide for themselves what is a living wage. That meant backing President Jean-Bertrand Aristide's adoption of a $2.50 per day minimum wage in 1991. It means supporting Batay Ouvriye (Workers' Struggle) when they help export-sector workers form unions. In general, it means taking a lead from workers, peasants, and pro-people governments in the global South, and conditioning trade privileges on respect for workers' right to organize rather than on any particular wage level. Consistently applying this principle means that goods produced by companies in the United States that flout labor laws—not just such companies in Haiti, Mexico, or China—should likewise be penalized.

recent *USA Today* poll rated "lack of livable wage jobs" as Americans' top worry, even ahead of such perennial favorites as "decline of moral values." This sentiment makes living-wage laws eminently winnable. But it is worth pausing to ask: What, exactly, has the living-wage movement won? And how can we adapt this strategy to win more?

Limited Victories

Opponents of living-wage laws argue that they will increase costs to local taxpayers, and drive business away from the locality. Living-wage boosters have two responses. First, fairness is worth the cost. And second, studies have shown that such ordinances have *not* escalated costs, nor repelled businesses. But why not? After all, economic theory suggests that companies compelled to pay higher costs will either seek to pass them on, or move on to greener pastures.

One reason is that living-wage ordinances typically affect very few workers. At passage, an average of only about 1,000 per locality actually have their wages boosted (in part because many of those covered already earn the mandated wage or more). This number is stunningly small, given that living-wage adopters include Los Angeles, New York, Chicago, and numerous other large cities and counties.

But smallness cannot be the entire explanation. Johns Hopkins University economist Erica Schoenberger and others followed specific contracts to the City of

Baltimore, looking at changes from before that city's living-wage law went into effect to two years after. They found that contract costs increased only about 1%, far less than inflation. One possibility, of course, is that the wage floor spurred contractors to find new ways to increase true efficiency—getting the same amount of work done with less labor and less effort. For instance, this can happen if higher wages allow employers to hold on to the same employees longer, shrinking employer expenditures on recruitment, hiring, and training. Or perhaps the businesses have simply accepted lower profit margins.

But there are three less pleasant possibilities as well. Contractors may have sped up their workers, extracting more work in return for the higher pay. They may have reduced the quality of goods or services they delivered. Or, they may simply have failed to comply with the law. The poor track record of many laws that declare labor rights without adequate enforcement mechanisms suggests that this last possibility may be quite real. Even the federal minimum wage is ignored by growing numbers of employers, says economist Howard Wial of the AFL-CIO's Working for America Institute.

Extend the Laws?

How should the living-wage movement respond to this evidence of limited impact? One possibility is to widen and sharpen living-wage laws' bite. Recent living-wage ordinances have set minimums as high as $12 per hour (in Santa Cruz, California). In Santa Monica, California, campaigners extended coverage to tourist-district businesses that had received city subsidies for redevelopment, and elsewhere coalitions aim to expand the law to include any business that receives substantial subsidies or tax abatements from the local government. Activists are also setting their sights on living-wage agreements with large private businesses—starting with those most vulnerable to political and public relations pressure, especially nonprofits such as Harvard. Even more ambitious are the advocates proposing state and federal living-wage laws; legislative proposals are pending in Hawaii, Vermont, and at the federal level. (See box, "Vermont's Livable Income Law")

Others are pursuing area-wide minimum wages set at levels closer to a living wage. Washington, D.C., has long had a minimum wage $1 above the federal minimum. Similar referenda were defeated in Houston and Denver, but New Orleans citizens will vote on a local minimum wage this coming February.

These initiatives are important, because there is certainly room for significant wage increases before we can expect negative effects on employment. When adjusted for inflation, hourly wages for the lowest-paid tenth of the workforce jumped by 9% between 1995 and 1999, in large part due to living-wage laws and federal minimum-wage increases. Yet the unemployment rate at the end of the 1990s fell to its lowest level in 30 years. More fine-grained studies of state and federal minimum-wage increases yield the same result: Such increases have caused little or no worker displacement over the last ten years. One reason is that

Vermont's Livable Income Law

While Vermont politics are famously progressive, its low wages (9% below the national average) and high living expenses (15% above national average) are anything but worker-friendly. Armed with these and other findings detailed in its *Vermont Job Gap Study*, the Burlington-based Peace and Justice Center set out to change those statistics with its Livable Wage Campaign.

The Vermont Livable Wage Campaign has achieved two significant legislative victories. Act 21, passed in 1999, raised the minimum wage by 50 cents, to $5.75 an hour (60 cents above the national minimum, though still a dollar less than in neighboring Massachusetts). The measure also provided funding for the state legislature to form a Study Committee on a Livable Income.

In 2000, the state's General Assembly agreed to some of the Study Committee's recommendations and passed Act 119, which took three more steps on the livable-wage issue:

- an increased minimum wage, now at $6.25 per hour
- a budget of $3.5 million (up 7%) for Vermont's Earned Income Tax Credit
- the publication of four annual reports by the state Joint Fiscal Office of Basic Needs Budgets / Livable Wage Figures.

Another bill, which would raise the minimum wage to $6.75, passed Vermont's Senate this year. This bill will be taken up in 2002 by the state House of Representatives, where it's passage is uncertain. After the 2000 elections, conservatives gained a majority, in a backlash against recent legislation permitting same-sex "civil unions."

The Livable Wage Campaign, however, continues on several fronts, including a multi-year strategy to increase wages for some of Vermont's worst-paid workers—child-care staff and public-school support staff at K-12 schools and state colleges.

—Beth Burgess

wages for the bottom tenth were beaten so far down over the 1980s and early 1990s—even after the recent wage surge, inflation-adjusted 1999 wages remained 10% below their 1979 level.

But if the movement succeeds in extending and increasing living wages, at some point economic theory is bound to be proven right: costs to taxpayers will climb, employment will decrease, or both. Even in the most positive scenario—that businesses find ways to increase productivity—remember that rising productivity typically means doing the same work with fewer workers. This was the experience of the Congress of Industrial Organizations (now part of the AFL-CIO), which unionized core manufacturing industries in the 1930s and 1940s. The CIO succeeded in hiking pay, and in the decades that followed, U.S. manufacturers avidly hunted for ways to boost productivity. The good news is that U.S. manufacturing became the most productive in the world for several decades. The bad news is that heightened efficiency shrank labor requirements dramatically. In fact, this is the main reason for declining U.S. manufacturing jobs, far overshadowing shifts in the global division of labor. Manufacturing is a slightly larger share of U.S. domestic output today than it was in 1960, but factory employment has dropped from 31% to 14% of the workforce.

If extending the living wage's impact will eventually either raise costs to taxpayers or diminish employment, it may be tempting to adopt the other major argument advocates use: fairness is worth the cost. And this answer makes a great deal of sense. Think for a moment about the federal *minimum* wage's effect. The average person who eats at McDonald's earns more than the average person who works at McDonald's, so if bumping up the minimum wage raises the cost of burgers, cash is shifting in more or less the right direction. By the same token, over the 1980s and 1990s, local and state privatization and tax cuts redistributed income from low-income workers to taxpayers who have higher incomes on average—so if living wages help to reverse this flow, that's a plus for equality.

What about job losses? Few would object to shutting down companies that rely on slavery or child labor. The same logic extends to exploitatively low wages. As with child labor laws, laws that bar low wages will put some workers out of a job. So it is important to view living-wage laws as part of a broader program that includes job creation, training, and income support for those unable to work. To achieve this broader program, we need a powerful movement. And the red-hot living-wage movement offers one of the strongest potential building blocks for such a broader movement.

Build the Movement?

That brings us to another response to the limited impact of living-wage laws to date: using the living wage as a movement-building tool. The living-wage issue encourages labor, community, and religious organizations to coalesce around genuine shared interests, creating an opportunity to open an even broader dialogue on wage fairness and inequality.

The goal should be to build movements that can address some of the weaknesses of current living-wage laws, including non-compliance and the potential for speed-up or job loss. Of course the U.S. institution that has been most effective in monitoring compliance with labor laws, curbing speed-up, and lobbying for job creation is the labor movement—and living-wage laws provide a golden opportunity for strengthening unions. Baltimore activists who won that city's 1994 living-wage ordinance, considered the spark of the current living-wage prairie fire, sought above all to slow down union-busting privatization. Living-wage laws close off low wages as a competitive strategy, dulling the edge of employer resistance to unions. Some coalitions have also won clauses requiring covered businesses to be neutral in union organizing campaigns or even to immediately recognize any union that signs up a majority of workers, foreclosing employers' usual anti-union tactics. A lower profile way to disarm anti-union employers is to ban retaliation against workers organizing for a living wage—which basically puts a local law against union-busting on the books to supplement weak federal laws.

In addition, living-wage advocates need to pay attention to winning laws that nurture the living-wage movement itself. For instance, some laws give living-wage coalition constituents the first crack at applying for jobs covered by the living wage, in some cases through coalition-controlled hiring halls. Patronage usually gets a bad name, but this kind of community control over hiring can help cement a living-wage movement's strength by giving it the ability to reward its members and supporters. Moreover, although advocates dream of short-cutting the process of passing hundreds of local laws by winning federal legislation, in reality the local mobilizations are the key to success with compliance. Any federal law is likely to remain a dead letter unless we have built those hundreds of robust place-based coalitions ready to monitor the law's implementation and use it as an organizing tool.

The biggest challenge in movement building is reaching beyond wages and jobs to the less obvious issues. For instance, how do we defend the quality of public services? Many nonprofits and community-based organization have been drawn into the game of privatizing social services. Sometimes these agencies enter unholy alliances with private businesses and city officials to oppose living-wage laws, because they fear it will threaten their job programs for disadvantaged workers. Organizations representing workers, communities, service providers, and clients must search for common ground based on high wages and adequate services. In Massachusetts, for example, unions and service providers have campaigned jointly for a state-funded living wage for human-service workers employed by hundreds of state contractors.

Another tough nut to crack is how to win adequate income for those who are unable to work for pay, or who end up working on a very part-time or part-year basis. Unfortunately, some of the same public attitudes that make it easy to build coalitions around living wages—equating work with virtue, for example—make it hard to defend welfare for people not working for wages. The principals from the living-wage movement—unions, churches, and ACORN itself—have also joined efforts to demand more adequate and less restrictive welfare benefits, but so far with much less success.

More Than Just a Living

The sixty local living-wage laws to date represent a tremendous victory for working people, but one that is, so far, narrow in scope. The challenge now is to extend the reach of the laws, while building and broadening the living-wage movement at the same time. Extending the laws' reach means bringing more cities on board, but even more importantly, boosting the numbers and types of workers covered within each city. To the extent that advocates succeed in passing stronger laws, they will engender fiercer resistance—both direct challenges to the legislation and more covert attempts to flout the laws or shift the costs. To successfully counter this resistance, movement-building efforts must go beyond the boundaries of the current living-wage movement. The end result will look less like a living-wage movement, more like a broad insurgent movement to redistribute income and other resources.

Resources: Robert Pollin and Stephanie Luce, *The Living Wage: Building a Fair Economy* (W.W. Norton, 1998); Lawrence Mishel, Jared Bernstein, and John Schmitt, *The State of Working America 2000–2001* (Cornell University Press 2001); David Card and Alan B. Krueger, *Myth and Measurement: The New Economics of the Minimum Wage* (Princeton University Press 1995).

SOCIAL-MOVEMENT UNIONISM IN SOUTH AFRICA: A STRATEGY FOR WORKING-CLASS SOLIDARITY
By Ravi Naidoo
September/October 2001

In recent decades, it has become fashionable to predict that labor movements will soon fade into irrelevance. *Farewell to the Working Class*—the title of a 1980 book by French social theorist Andre Gorz—captures this mood well. Within the left, this pessimism is most evident among observers of labor movements in the global North, which have in recent years seen sustained declines in their membership and the loss of their long-standing "social partner" arrangements.

According to Kim Moody's *Workers in a Lean World*, however, the number of industrial workers in the global South is on the rise—from 285 million in 1980 to 407 million in 1994. Indeed, Moody reports, the industrial working class in selected northern (OECD) countries actually grew slightly between 1973 and 1994. The ranks of the industrial working class, the traditional bedrock of unionism, are on the whole not declining. And in the more-industrialised southern countries, such as Brazil, South Korea, and South Africa, union membership is actually growing. For example, the Congress of South African Trade Unions (COSATU) has grown from 1.3 million members in 1994 to over 1.8 million today, an increase of 40% in six years. Overall levels of union membership in South Africa exceed 50% of formal-sector employment. There is certainly little evidence of trade-union decline.

The composition of the working class, however, is changing in both North and South. "Atypical" (temporary) formal employment, informal employment, and outright unemployment are, collectively, increasing faster than permanent, formal jobs. In South Africa, for example, part-time work has increased by 31% between 1998 and 2001; in the same period, full-time work has fallen by 8%. Much of the "new" working class therefore is essentially a "reserve army" of labor, consisting of those especially vulnerable workers and unemployed who employers can use to undermine the unionized workforce.

Rather than imply the "end of the working class," the reality on the ground presents the world's labor movements with new challenges: to bring into its ranks the growing "new" working class, until now generally excluded from union activities, and to find new ways of promoting working-class solidarity.

Connecting "Different" Struggles: The Case of South Africa

The old South African economy was built on apartheid, and the South African labor movement cut its teeth in the struggle against apartheid. Connecting "worker" and "community" struggles became its strength, and progressive trade unions associated the fight against social oppression with the fight against capitalism. Union strategy was founded on:

Building a political alliance for socio-economic transformation: A few years before the 1994 democratic elections, COSATU forged a "Tripartite Alliance" with the Communist Party and the African National Congress (ANC) to introduce democracy and transform the South African economy. This Alliance was based on a common Reconstruction and Development Programme (RDP), emphasizing growth through redistribution.

Forcing the government and capital to negotiate with labor: Through mass mobilization COSATU stopped the apartheid government from unilaterally restructuring the economy on the eve of democracy. The apartheid regime had sought to fully privatize key state institutions and deregulate important aspects of the economy, thus robbing future democratic governments of crucial economic power. In the face of this mass mobilization, there was an agreement that government's socio-economic policies had to be negotiated with labor and business groups. After democracy, this arrangement was formalized in the National Economic Development and Labour Council (NEDLAC), where proposed labor legislation and new economic policies had to be presented to representatives of labor and business before being sent to parliament.

Promoting militant labor struggles and joint worker-community mobilizations: Trade unions defied apartheid laws such as those outlawing black unions and pressured employers to do the same, or face mass mobilizations and strikes. Mass mobilizations included national stayaways, general strikes, and "community boycotts" of recalcitrant employers. COSATU has called general strikes and national mass mobilizations several times since the 1994 democratic elections—including actions focused on constitutional negotiations (particularly ensuring the inclusion of the right to strike), on negotiations of the new national labor laws, and on the massive wave of layoffs in recent years. These actions targeted both employers (public and private) and elements of the government.

A Post-Apartheid Balance Sheet

It is said that there are no final victories or defeats, only advances and setbacks. There have been a few key points of advance and setback for the South African labor movement since 1994.

Two key advances have been the introduction of the South African Constitution and the survival, against considerable odds, of NEDLAC, the socio-economic council.

The South African Constitution of 1996 dismantled the legal pillars of apartheid. The Constitution is among the world's most progressive, incorporating a strong bill of rights including socio-economic issues (such as the right to adequate health care) and imposing an obligation on the government to provide certain basic services. The progressiveness of the Constitution owes much to labor-driven social-movement pressure.

NEDLAC has not been popular with either advocates of neoliberalism or the far left. On one hand, neoliberals argue that globalization requires rapid and unpopular decisions that consultative processes cannot generate. This view holds that experts, shielded from political pressures, are most capable of formulating effective policy. On the other hand, many on the left often confuse national negotiations and social dialogues with government and employers with "social partnership" arrangements.

In reality, the South African labor movement approaches NEDLAC as one of many "sites of struggle," and not as an alternative to workplace and industrial struggles. NEDLAC has created an important space for the labor movement to contest the neoliberal program. In particular, the NEDLAC process has blocked neoliberal attempts to dismantle hard-fought labor laws. It has also offered opportunities for increased unity between labor and community sectors represented on the council. Nonetheless, the left is correct to maintain a healthy wariness. All national tripartite negotiations and consultation processes carry with them inherent risks of both defeat and co-optation.

There have, meanwhile, been two major areas of setback for the labor movement. The first has been the growth of income inequality and joblessness. South Africa's post-democracy class formation reflects a gradual transition from race-based inequality towards class-based inequality. The growth of a black elite has made the richest 20% of the population more racially diverse. The incomes of the poorest 40% of the population, however, have fallen by 20%, primarily due to the massive job losses brought about by industrial and workplace restructuring. The lack of progress in reducing unemployment, poverty, and inequality has been the most serious setback for labor.

The second setback concerns the incomplete and often contradictory implementation of the economic agenda set out in the RDP. While the government is constitutionally compelled to gradually improve people's living standards and access to services, under global market pressures it has liberalized the economy, introduced fiscal constraints, and tried to push social (and labor) concerns down the list of national priorities. This "global market" orientation is like a self-imposed structural adjustment program (SAP), based on the weak notion that "inefficient" state expenditure "crowds out" much-needed "efficient" private sector investment. While more and more people are now recognizing—after seven years of democracy—the fallacies in this argument, the standard arguments against an alternative approach still remain: redistributive policies will allegedly cause an exodus of the wealthy, undermine domestic and international investment, etc.

Social-Movement Unionism

There are promising signs, however, that the labor movement is beginning to build an effective response to these challenges. One key development is a strong and expanding social movement, going beyond traditional trade unions, against neoliberal globalization.

As part of its search for more powerful methods of struggle, COSATU set up the so-called September Commission in 1996 to consider strategy for labor into the 21st century. The commission recommended, essentially, that South African labor tackle its current problems by building on the country's history of social-movement unionism. Its report defined "social unionism" as "… concerned with broad social and political issues, as well as the immediate concerns of its members. It aims to be a social force for transformation. Its goal is democracy and socialism. Its influence on society is based on its organised power, its capacity to mobilise, its socio-economic programme and policies and its participation in political and social alliances."

Today social-movement unionism is beginning to deliver the goods. Social-movement union campaigns in South Africa include:

"The People's Budget": Despite a constitutional requirement that Parliament have the power to change the national budget, five years later there is still no law giving legislators this power. Further, the constitutional obligations on the state to deliver on socio-economic rights create a focus on the national budget. In response, COSATU, the National NGO Coalition, and several religious organizations began a "People's Budget" campaign in 2000—both to increase the budgetary commitment to social goods and quality jobs and to ensure that the budget process is more open and participatory. Many of these NGOs, now mobilizing around the strength of unions, are worker-advice offices addressing the needs of "atypical" and non-unionized workers. Partially as a result of this growing pressure, the government is expected to announce in the next few months a new social security system addressing the country's poverty and inequality.

"Crush poverty, create quality jobs": In May 2000, four million workers went on a one-day general strike as part of an ongoing campaign to put unemployment and the massive wave of layoffs on the national agenda. A few months earlier, COSATU organized a civil-society conference on the unemployment crisis, where a broad social coalition (similar to the one uniting around "The People's Budget") endorsed the campaign. The conference helped

galvanize a national debate about layoffs and job creation—and to mobilize a wide range of civil-society supporters for the labor-movement position.

"People before profits": Perhaps the best known recent social-movement victory came in April 2001 over thirty-nine of the world's largest pharmaceutical multinationals. These MNCs took the South African government to court to stop it from making less-expensive HIV/AIDS medicines available to poor people. COSATU and AIDS NGOs, as part of a wider social movement, created a massive local and international campaign against these MNCs under the banner of "putting people before profits." Eventually even CNN was carrying footage showing banners saying, "Capitalism is a sick system!" Under growing pressure key MNCs withdrew, scuttling the lawsuit.

Besides achieving their own specific advances, all the campaigns have helped strengthen the voice of labor in the national debate. These campaigns have also allowed other social formations to increase their own voice.

Though social-movement unionism campaigns are becoming a regular feature of today's South Africa, the definition of social-movement unionism remains a subject of debate. Crucially, however, social-movement unionism is an "orientation" rather than a fixed set of structures or goals. Historically, South African unions have placed themselves at the center of the country's social-change movements, but the nature of these movements has varied over time. The social-movement unionism of the 1980s was more socio-political (anti-apartheid focused), including even black business groups, whereas the social-movement unionism of today is more socio-economic (job and poverty focused), with support from the white working class.

Nonetheless, the popular demands put forward by social-movement unionism are linked by the common threads of class analysis and participatory governance. The trade unions can serve as "political schools" where workers become more conscious of how the economy's underlying patterns of ownership and control affect their everyday lives. Through a social-movement platform, unions effectively reach more people—increasing public awareness of what capitalism is doing to them.

Social-movement unionism creates space for the marginalized section of the working class currently reached only by NGOs and community-based organisations. Social-movement unionism can help the labor movement mobilize more of the so-called "atypical" and hard-to-unionize working class. This offers the strongest possible answer to the neoliberal jibe that unions merely represent a "labor elite."

While social-movement unionism has many strengths, it represents only a beginning in the struggle for alternatives to neoliberalism. Despite the recent advances, the South African labor movement is still hard pressed to hold its ground. Social-movement unionism could, however, lead to a broader and deeper challenge to capitalism over the long run. Indeed, rather than bidding farewell to the working class, we may be witnessing its resurgence.

Resources: *September Commission*, Sixth National COSATU Congress, 1997; Andre Gorz, *Farewell to the Working Class: An Essay on Post-Industrial Socialism*, Pluto Press, 1982; Kim Moody, *Workers in a Lean World: Unions in the International Economy*, Verso, 1997.

CAPITAL STABILITY AND LOCAL DEMOCRACY
By Thad Williamson, David Imbroscio, and Gar Alerovitz
November/December 2002

What's the worst-kept dirty secret about local politics in the United States? That in most American cities, business groups and private land interests have vastly disproportionate influence over the political process.

Why is this the case? Competition among localities for scarce jobs and investment. Local politicians need to show that they have done their part to bring "growth" and jobs to an area. This usually means making alliances with business groups and rolling out the red carpet and fine wine—and tax breaks—for any business that expresses an interest in relocating to the area. It also means avoiding regulations, taxes, and redistributive policies which scare businesses away.

In this environment, civic and political organizations representing working people, neighborhood interests, and social and environmental concerns face a continual uphill battle to defend, let alone advance, their interests. For instance, activist groups in Chicago, one of America's best-organized cities, would likely count it a substantial political triumph if they succeeded in securing $60 million in additional city and state assistance for low-income housing development in the city. (The $60 million would augment Chicago's current spending on affordable housing by about 20%.) A victory of that scale would probably require a concerted campaign lasting months or even years and thousands of hours of citizen effort.

If you're a big corporation, however, a few phone calls and visits with local officials can do the trick. In 2001, Chicago and Illinois officials offered Boeing a reported $63 million in inducements to persuade the aircraft giant to move its headquarters to town. Time after time, even liberal mayors elected with wide support from minorities and working-class people have found themselves making similar decisions.

Neoliberal, pro-market scholars accept this reality as just a fact of life; other scholars, including some on the left, think that deplorable as it is, little can be done to alter this fundamental structural feature of American politics.

We disagree with both positions. Even in the era of globalization, we think it is quite possible for citizens to shape their own local communities. Here's why (and how).

A Few Lucky Towns

Not all American cities lack vibrant progressive activism or large-scale citizen influence over local politics—think of places like Cambridge, Mass., or Madison, Wis. Such places have strong progressive cultures which have reproduced themselves over the decades. Less commonly noted is that both communities are largely exempt from the threat of economic decline due to corporate disinvestment and capital flight.

The presence of large, immobile universities in Cambridge and Madison underpin the cities' local economies. To be sure, business interests in these cities have a voice in local politics, but they do not have a credible threat to leave en masse if the community were to adopt policies which prioritize public well-being over the desires of private firms.

What if every community in America had the same advantages these favored places enjoy—namely, a stable job base more or less permanently anchored by immobile capital? Such a situation is necessary (though not sufficient) for a serious revitalization of local democracy—and the good news is, there are literally dozens of ways to begin moving toward that goal.

One way to stabilize a community's economy is through direct public investment, as in the case of towns anchored by state capitals or state universities. To take another example, many of the 3,000-plus community development corporations doing work in urban and rural communities have started their own businesses, taken equity stakes in other businesses, and/or acted as incubators for new, locally-rooted firms. Yet another possibility is local and state-level public enterprise, whereby the public undertakes business activities usually left to private firms. For instance, the small rural community of Glasgow, Kentucky owns its own cable television and telecommunications network, creating jobs and saving millions of dollars which used to go to the inefficient private cable company.

There are also ways to make economic activities now regarded as "private" more closely wedded to specific places. For instance, worker-owned firms are much more likely than conventional firms to be rooted in particular communities: workers in firms where most stock is owned by an Employee Stock Ownership Plan (ESOP) can block the sale of a company, and ESOP firms in general are less likely to go bankrupt than conventional firms.

Public-employee pension funds, which have often been perfectly willing to make risky investments overseas or in fancy derivatives, could also play a role by targeting their investments to local businesses or to firms in depressed areas. Dozens of states and several major cities already have some form of "economically targeted investment program," ranging from New York City's re-investment policy, which has led to thousands of low and medium-income housing units being built in the city, to politically-conservative Alabama's state-employee pension fund, which has aggressively sought to create jobs within the state.

These are just a few of the possible ways to anchor capital more securely in local communities. Already, in fact, the federal government operates dozens of programs, some well-known, some obscure, which honor the principle that local communities should not be permitted to wither and die when economic disinvestment occurs. Such programs, ranging from the Johnson-era Economic Development Administration and Appalachian Regional Commission to the Clinton-created Community Development Financial Institutions Fund, are generally woefully underfunded. But most have a long track record of on-the-ground activities and a wealth of experience upon which a more aggressive, adequately funded program might draw.

A Case for Action

A serious program to re-root capital in communities and thereby alter the structural equations governing local politics in America would require sustained public commitment and substantial funding over a period of many years. But the costs of such an initiative must be weighed against the costs of our current "economic development" policies, under which states and localities compete with one another to subsidize mobile corporations, and in effect pay for jobs that private firms would have created anyway. The costs of a new initiative must also be weighed against the sheer economic irrationality of allowing cities such as Detroit or Buffalo, with vast built-up infrastructure, to wither away at the same time that other places are booming (and building new sewers, roads, and power lines to accommodate America's internal migrants).

Most of all, the costs of a bold new agenda to secure the economic basis of American communities in an era of sprawl, job-chasing and globalization must be weighed against the costs of doing nothing—and continuing to let the processes of local democracy in America decay into nothing more than window dressing for business dominance over local politics.

This article is based on ideas detailed in the authors' book, Making a Place for Community: Local Democracy in a Global Era *(Routledge, 2002).*

DISARMING THE DEBT TRAP
By Ellen Frank
March/April 2001

Question: What if the International Monetary Fund (IMF), World Bank, and G-7 governments canceled the debts of the poorer countries right now, fully and with no strings attached? Answer: Within five years, most would be up to their necks in debt again. While a Jubilee 2000-style debt cancellation would provide short-term relief for heavily indebted countries, the bitter reality of the current global financing system is that poor countries are virtually doomed to be debtors.

When residents of Zambia or Zaire buy maize or medicine from the United States, they are required to pay in U.S. dollars. If they can't earn enough dollars through their own exports, they must borrow them—from the IMF, the World Bank, a Western government agency, or a commercial lender. But foreign currency loans are problematic for poor countries. If CitiCorp loans funds to a U.S. business, it fully expects that the business will realize a stream of earnings from which the loan can be repaid. When the IMF or World Bank makes foreign currency loans to poor countries—to finance deficits or development projects—no such foreign currency revenue stream is generated, and the debt becomes a burdensome obligation that can be met only by abandoning internal development goals in favor of export promotion.

Few poor countries can avoid the occasional trade deficit—of 93 low- and moderate-income countries, only 11 currently have trade surpluses—and most are heavily dependent on imports of food, oil, and manufactured goods. Even the most tightly managed economy is only an earthquake or crop failure away from a foreign currency debt. Once incurred, interest payments and other debt-servicing charges mount quickly. Because few countries can manage payments surpluses large enough to service the debt regularly, servicing charges are rolled over into new loans and the debt balloons. This is why, despite extraordinary efforts by many indebted less-developed countries (LDCs) to pump up exports and cut imports, the outstanding foreign currency debt of developing countries has more than tripled during the past two decades.

Many poorer nations, hoping to avoid borrowing, have attempted recently to attract foreign investor dollars with the bait of high interest rates or casino-style stock exchanges. But the global debt trap is not so easily eluded. A U.S. financial firm that purchases shares on the Thai stock exchange with baht wants, eventually, to distribute gains to shareholders in dollars. Big banks and mutual funds are wary, therefore, of becoming ensnared in minor currencies and, to compensate against potential losses when local currencies are converted back into dollars, they demand sky-high interest rates on LDC bonds. Thailand, Brazil, Indonesia and many other countries recently discovered that speculative financial investors are quick to turn heel and flee, driving interest rates up and exchange rates down, and leaving debtor countries even deeper in the hole.

If plans to revamp the international "financial architecture" are to help anyone but the already rich, they must address these issues. Developing countries need many things from the rest of the world—manufactured goods, skilled advisors, technical know-how—but loans are not among them. A global payments system based on the borrowing and lending of foreign currencies is, for small and poor nations, a life sentence to debtor's prison.

There are alternatives. First, there need to be far greater transfers of technology and productive resources from First World to Third World without expectation of payment. Second, when payment is expected, developing countries should be permitted to pay for foreign goods and services in their own currencies, rather than scrambling endlessly for the foreign currency they cannot print, do not control, and cannot earn in sufficient amounts through exporting. The U.S. routinely issues dollars to cover a trade deficit that will exceed $300 billion this year. Europe, too, finances external deficits with issues of euro-denominated bonds and bank deposits. But private financial firms will generally not hold assets denominated in LDC currencies; when they do hold them, they frequently demand interest rates several times higher than those paid by rich countries. The governments of the world could jointly agree to hold these minor currencies, even if private investors will not.

The world needs an international central bank, democratically structured and publicly controlled, that would allow countries to settle payments imbalances politically, without relying on loans of foreign currencies. The idea is not new. John Maynard Keynes had something similar in mind in the 1940s, when the IMF was established. Cambridge University economist Nicholas Kaldor toyed with the idea in the 1960s. Recently, Jane D'Arista of the Financial Markets Center and a number of other international financial specialists have revived this notion, calling for a global settlements bank that could act not as a lender of last resort to international banks (as the IMF does), but as a lender of first resort for payments imbalances between sovereign nations. Such a system would take the problems of debts, deficits and development out of the marketplace and place them in the international political arena, where questions of fairness and equity could be squarely and openly addressed.

The idea is beguilingly simple, eminently practicable, and easy to implement. It would benefit poor and rich countries alike, since the advanced nations could export far more to developing countries if those countries were able to settle international payments on more advantageous terms. A global settlements bank, however, would dramatically shift the balance of power in the world economy and will be fiercely opposed by those who profit from the international debt trap. If developing countries were not so desperate for dollars, multinational corporations would find them less eager to sell their resources and citizens for a fistful of greenbacks. That nations rich in people and resources, like South Africa, can be deemed bankrupt and forced into debt peonage for lack of foreign exchange is not merely a shame. It is absurd, an unacceptable artifact of a global finance system that enriches the already rich.

CONTRIBUTORS

Gar Alperovitz is Lionel Bauman Professor of Political Economy at the University of Maryland and President of the National Center for Economic and Security Alternatives.

Sarah Anderson is the Director of the Global Economy Program of the Institute for Policy Studies in Washington, D.C., and the co-author (with John Cavanagh and Thea Lee) of *Field Guide to the Global Economy*.

David Bacon is a journalist and photographer covering labor, immigration, and the impact of the global economy on workers.

Dean Baker is co-director of the Center for Economic and Policy Research.

Skip Barry is a former member of the *Dollars & Sense* collective and develops affordable housing in Boston.

Phineas Baxandall is a lecturer at the Committee for Degrees in Social Studies at Harvard University and a *Dollars & Sense* associate.

Ben Boothby is a *Dollars & Sense* collective member.

Heather Boushey is an economist at the Economic Policy Institute in Washington, D.C., where she conducts research on labor markets. She is co-author of *The State of Working America*.

Beth Brockland is a Communications & Research Associate at the National Campaign for Jobs and Income Support.

Beth Burgess is a member of the *Dollars & Sense* collective.

Lisa Climan is a former *Dollars & Sense* intern.

Chuck Collins, a member of the *Dollars & Sense* collective, is the Program Director at United for a Fair Economy and co-author, with William H. Gates, Sr., of *Wealth and Our Commonwealth: Why America Should Tax Accumulated Fortunes* (Beacon Press, January 2003).

Thatcher Collins is a former *Dollars & Sense* collective member.

James M. Cypher teaches economics at California State University, Fresno.

Dan Feder is a former *Dollars & Sense* intern.

Ellen Frank is a member of the *Dollars & Sense* collective, and teaches economics at Emmanuel College.

Tami J. Friedman is a Senior Associate at the Center on Wisconsin Strategy, University of Wisconsin-Madison, and a former *Dollars & Sense* co-editor.

Amy Gluckman is a *Dollars & Sense* co-editor.

Lena Graber is a former *Dollars & Sense* intern.

Rosie Hunter is a researcher with United for a Fair Economy in Boston.

David Imbroscio is Associate Professor of Political Science at the University of Louisville.

David L. Levy, a *Dollars & Sense* associate, teaches management at the University of Massachusetts, Boston.

Arthur MacEwan, a *Dollars & Sense* associate, is professor of economics at the University of Massachusetts, Boston. His most recent book is *Neoliberalism or Democracy? Economic Strategy, Markets, and Alternatives for the 21st Century* (Zed Books, 1999).

John Miller is a member of the *Dollars & Sense* collective, and teaches economics at Wheaton College.

Ravi Naidoo is the Director of the National Labour and Economic Development Institute (NALEDI), an autonomous think-tank established by the Congress of South African Trade Unions (COSATU).

Amy Offner is a *Dollars & Sense* co-editor.

Dara O'Rourke is an assistant professor of Urban Studies and Planning at the Massachusetts Institute of Technology (MIT)

Nomi Prins is a former investment banker turned journalist, and author of a forthcoming book on corporate corruption, *Money for Nothing* (The New Press).

Alejandro Reuss is a member of the *Dollars & Sense* collective and a board member of Bikes Not Bombs <www.bikesnotbombs.org>.

James Ridgeway is the Washington correspondent for the *Village Voice*.

Abby Scher, a former co-editor of *Dollars & Sense*, is director of the Independent Press Association-New York.

Chris Tilly, a member of the *Dollars & Sense* collective, teaches at the University of Massachusetts, Lowell.

Richard J. Walton teaches at Rhode Island College, and has visited Iraq as part of an International Action Center delegation.

Rodney Ward is a longtime labor and peace activist, laid-off flight attendant, and staff member at *Dollars & Sense*.

Thad Williamson is a doctoral student in political theory at Harvard and a *Dollars & Sense* collective member.

Derek Wright is a member of United Faculty and Academic Staff (American Federation of Teachers Local 223) and the International Socialist Organization in Madison, Wisconsin.